Human Resource Management in the Project-Oriented Organization

I first learned about the Project-oriented Organization and the theories and methods of Martina Huemann in 2000. She is one of the pioneers and was in charge of research projects in this area for the IPMA at that time. This book represents her research achievements in this field over the last 15 years and is a great contribution to the PM profession.

Anbang Qi, Nankai University, China and Chairman of the Research Management
Board of the International Project Management Association (IPMA)

In order to be successful as a project oriented organisation, the HR management has a lot more responsibilities than in the past – the whole strategy of HR needs to change. This book gives a very comprehensive and ready-to-use overview of what is needed in this area.

Mag. Brigitte Schaden, President of Projekt Management Austria

The book illustrates the complexities and difficulties of HRM applied to projects. It explains, in an easy-to-read way, the roles and the human-characteristic requirements to fit, as well as organizational and PM concepts required to fully understand what a HRM system for PM should be. Moreover, the book presents a model for such a HRM system. It constitutes an excellent reference for both scholars and practitioners, and is an invaluable support tool in teaching PM.

Juan Carlos Nogueira, Universidad ORT Uruguay

I find this book by Dr Huemann an important contribution to the field because of its original approach to the human factor in project management. Being involved in projects and in contact with project practitioners for more than 25 years, I realized that experienced project managers ask themselves 'Who?' before 'What?', 'When?' and 'How?' when starting a project. Dr Huemann addresses this question analyzing crucial matters such as temporary organizations, project based organizations, the roles of the project manager and other stakeholders, and human resource management in projects. This work has also a very deep analysis of current literature on the subject, with rich quotations and reference. I will recommend this book to HR professionals and project practitioners when they ask me about projects and the 'Who?' question.

José Daniel Esterkin, Director and co-founder of IAAP;
PMI Argentina Chapter President; and PMI Academic Advisory Group member

Martina Huemann successfully manages to prove how important it is to relate project management and human resource management in organizations. She offers an applicable model of a 'project-oriented HRM system' for managing project personnel in the project-oriented organization. With this model and her elaborations on this topic, this book is a 'must' for practitioners and researchers in the project management community.

Dagmar Zuchi, enable2change

This book not only offers comprehensive scientific background information and a working model 'towards a viable project-oriented HRM system', but also supports the development of project-oriented organizations. I strongly recommend it for line managers with project business, for their HRM and, for example, for PMO or project excellence leaders who are interested in rethinking the status quo and are striving for continuous improvement.

Erwin Weitlaner, Principal Consultant, Siemens AG

To Karl and Magdalena Huemann – my beloved parents.
They taught me that any issue has multiple perspectives
and showed me how to combine dedication with fun.
Thank you for empowering me to become who I am.

Human Resource Management in the Project-Oriented Organization

Towards a Viable System for Project Personnel

MARTINA HUEMANN

WU Vienna University of Economics and Business Administration, Austria

Routledge
Taylor & Francis Group

LONDON AND NEW YORK

First published 2015 by Gower Publishing

2 Park Square, Milton Park, Abingdon, Oxfordshire OX14 4RN
52 Vanderbilt Avenue, New York, NY 10017

Routledge is an imprint of the Taylor & Francis Group, an informa business

First issued in paperback 2020

Gower Applied Business Research
Our programme provides leaders, practitioners, scholars and researchers with thought provoking, cutting edge books that combine conceptual insights, interdisciplinary rigour and practical relevance in key areas of business and management.

British Library Cataloguing in Publication Data
A catalogue record for this book is available from the British Library.

Library of Congress Cataloging-in-Publication Data
Huemann, Martina, 1969-
  Human resource management in the project-oriented organization : towards a viable system for project personnel / by Martina Huemann.
     pages cm
  Includes bibliographical references and index.
  ISBN 978-1-4724-5204-7 (hardback) 1. Project management. 2. Personnel management.
  I. Title.

  HD69.P75H8396 2015
  658.3--dc23

                                                                    2015012436

ISBN 978-1-4724-5204-7 (hbk)
ISBN 978-0-367-66867-9 (pbk)

Contents

List of Figures

List of Tables

Preface

Wege entstehen dadurch, dass wir sie gehen.
New paths are created when we go.

I consider myself as a knowledge creator. In the notion of Radical Cnstructivism, that means we can only actively create knowledge in our brains and not passively receive it from outside; this is also true for the reader of this book. While reading this book, you will create knowledge yourself based on your background, context and your own experience with human resource management in project-oriented organizations. You may generate viable theoretical, conceptual or practical thinking for your contexts inspired by this book. In a broader sense, I consider myself a knowledge co-creator engaging research and practice to create viable solutions that further develop theory as well being suitable to practice.

To understand this book and the way it is written, I would like to share with you some background and how and why this book came into existence. I live in the lovely city of Vienna, where I was born. Although internationally oriented, I have spent most of my academic career at WU Vienna, starting as research and teaching assistant in 1994. At this large European business school, I am today a Professor, Head of the Project Management Group and Academic Director of the Professional MBA: Project Management. Over the last 20 years, I have been working as researcher, educator, trainer and consultant in the field of management, particularly in managing projects and project-oriented companies, organizational design and human resource management. As co-founder and manager of enable2change – a network of independent experts that helps to translate strategy into action – I am interested in change and development processes. I would like to know how and why change processes come into existence and how to design and enable them. The interaction and co-operation with other researchers, consultants and practitioners, nationally and internationally, in an attempt to continuously challenge perceptions, including my own, are important to me in research as well as in consultancy. My aim is to bridge theory and practice, strategy and operations and co-create knowledge to widen horizons.

The book documents a multi-year research journey into human resource management in the specific context of project-oriented organizations. The book was written in my mid-career with the aim being to open up a new research field with relevance to theory and practice. It is a scientific monograph with the main purpose to qualify for a *venia docendi* in business administration to receive a professorship with WU Vienna.

There are some small adaptions between this book and the scientific monograph submitted at WU Vienna. The main difference is that the chapter that describes the research paradigm, process and methods was moved to the appendix. However, I would like to encourage you to have a look at it in order to understand the systemic–constructivist paradigm upon which the research is based.

I would like to invite you to become a knowledge co-creator!

Acknowledgements

As the research and the writing of this book accompanied me for many years, there is also a long list of people and institutions to mention in the acknowledgements.

Most important to mention is my teacher Professor (emeritus) Dkfm Roland Gareis, with whom I had worked together for many years and who influenced my thinking and my academic career significantly. Thank you for your long-term co-operation and for being part of the habilitation committee at WU Vienna. My gratitude goes to the members of the habilitation committee Professor (emeritus) Dr Fritz Scheuch, Professor DI Dr Edeltraud Hannappi-Egger, Professor Dr Johannes August Schülein, Professor Bodo Schlegelmilch, PhD, Professor Dr Wolfgang Elsik and Professor Dr Barbara Stöttinger. I'd also like to thank the assessors Professor Dr Hans Georg Gemünden, TU Berlin Germany, Professor Monique Aubry, PhD, UQAM Canada and Professor Dr Ralf Müller BI Oslo, Norway.

The data of some of the research presented here was collected together with my colleagues and dear friends Professor Dr Rodney Turner SKEMA Business School, France and Professor Dr Anne Keegan Amsterdam University, the Netherlands. The co-operation with them sharpened my perception and arguments, for which I am very thankful to them.

The research presented in this book was financed by different additional sources. In a very early phase, the research was supported by a grant from Project Management Institute, USA and by the Dr Maria Schaumayer Habiliationsstipendium and both of these allowed me a close co-operation with SKEMA Business School France and to extend my leave from WU Vienna. The research was also partly supported financially, but especially in kind by the companies who served as case study partners. Thank you to all the HR Managers, Project Management Office Managers, Project Managers, Line Managers and Project Team Members who shared their knowledge with me. Representatively, I would like to thank Mag Bernd Lauer who was then my contact in Telekom Austria and Mr Erwin Weitlaner from Siemens Germany.

My gratitude goes to my colleagues and friends who encouraged me to continue the long research journey:

- My colleagues at the Project Management Group, Department of Strategy and Innovation at WU Vienna, especially Dr Claudia Ringhofer;
- Dr Dagmar Zuchi, co-founder and manager of enable2change and friend for many years;
- My board member colleagues from Project Management Austria, especially its chair Mag Brigitte Schaden;
- My colleagues from the Research Management Board of the International Project Management Association, which I served between 2005 and 2012;
- My colleagues from the Academic Management Group of Project Management Institute especially its chair Dr Carla Messikomer, and my colleagues Dr Harvey Maylor and Dr Svetlana Cicmil.

Thank you for cheering me up and sharing the laughs that gave me the endurance to finish this monograph.

Finally, yet most importantly, my family, especially my partner Bernhard and my sons Daniel and Florian who have given me the freedom to pursue an academic career that is not a nine to five job.

Martina Huemann
Vienna

Introduction

1.1 The Purpose of this Book

Human Resource Management (HRM) is central to any organization. HRM practices ensure the organization's potential to perform, but more comprehensively, a viable HRM system that supports and is supported by company strategy, structures and culture ensures sustainable development of any organization, in particular the project-oriented organization.

The project-oriented organization,[1] with its organizational strategy *Management by Projects*, its combination of permanent and temporary structures and its specific project-oriented culture (Gareis 1990; 2005), is a specific context for the HRM system. The project-oriented organization requires the adoption of the HRM system to create a viable design that acknowledges projects and project-orientation. This is evident in recent and not so recent studies. However, HRM practitioners often have little understanding of projects or project management, and thus do not understand and initiate organizational consequences that project-orientation brings for the HRM system (Turner et al. 2008a). To support project-orientation, often HR departments concentrate on organizing project management training for project managers, instead of asking themselves how projects as temporary organizations may affect strategies, goals, processes, organization, infrastructure and the HRM system values, in order to truly ensure alignment with the needs of the project-oriented organizations, the projects and the expectations of the project personnel. Nevertheless, there are some HRM systems in project-oriented organizations that have changed to be able to support project-orientation. They have developed towards a project-orientation HRM system in order to increase the potential that projects can bring to the organization.

1.2 The Relevance of Projects and Project-Oriented Organizations

The management of projects is of considerable economic importance. A careful estimate indicates that projects initiate about one-third of the global gross domestic product (Turner et al. 2010). Thus projects support the creation of considerable economic and social value. Projects are increasingly widely applied in organizations (Cleland/Gareis 2006; Whittington et al. 1999). In addition to traditional contract projects, internal projects such as marketing, product development and organizational development have gained importance in all kinds of industries and in public administration (Morris 1997).

---

1   The term project-oriented organization was explicitly chosen to allow all organizations, whether from the private or public sector, to feel included.

The word project means *idea* or *plan*. While projects have had a much longer history, the birth of modern project management can be dated to around 1940.[2] As an offshoot of operation management, scheduling methods like the gantt chart, originally invented for routine processes, were adapted for project management (Geraldi/Lechler 2012). The first projects to do this were technology and science projects.[3]

During the 1960s and through to the 1980s, the application of projects as an efficient working form and their management concepts were transferred to different industries. A number of companies began to establish projects that cut across functional lines in order to accomplish project objectives. The first industries to implement project management were construction and engineering, as their projects were often technically complex and relatively similar to the military sector, one of the first industries to apply project management.

In his analysis of classic literature about project management, Söderlund (2012) outlines what Sayles and Chandler (1971) refer to as a temporary organization, and that project management as an organizational concept goes far beyond the application of tools. However, in general and over a long period of time, project management has been perceived rather narrowly and has been reduced to tools such as PERT diagrams and gantt charts which have been considered as synonyms for project management (Maylor 2001; Schelle 1989) as these have been easy to communicate in textbooks (Söderlund 2012).

Gradually, projects spread to different industries and different types of projects were applied. While originally reserved for the defence and space industries, investment projects began to appear in engineering and construction, and in the 1980s and 1990s information technology and hi tech businesses began practicing project management, mainly when contracting assignments and product development. Over the last 20 years, projects have become popular in all kinds of organizations and increasingly in the public sector. Various external and internal projects such as marketing, organizational development and personnel development have taken place. Today, projects can be found in private and public organizations for both development and production. Projects are especially prevalent in growth industries such as information technology, management consulting, technology consulting, knowledge and technology-based companies, entertainment, culture, media and advertising, but also in the mature industries such as the automotive industry and the electronic equipment industry (Morris 1997; Söderlund 2011).

Table 1.1 illustrates the expansion of project management over the years and the spread of projects into different industries and into the public sector. This spread of projects and project management is closely linked to the rise of global project management associations, which have contributed to the establishment of a project management profession.[4] The relevant topics shown for the different periods indicate that in research the unit of analysis has expanded from the project to the project portfolio, the project-oriented organization, and society.

---

2   Many authors believe that viewing projects as temporary endeavours has existed before the twentieth century. Examples include the building of the pyramids or the conquests of other nations. Also the essays of Daniel Defoe called *Upon Projects* in 1697 refer to projects. He rather uses the term in the sense of plan or endeavour to bring change to society.

3   While the US is widely considered as the originator of modern project management, there is evidence that the Soviet Union also had similar PM methods to manage their space projects.

4   The European-based International Project Management Association (IPMA) was founded in 1965. It is an umbrella organization of project management associations in more than 50 member countries, and with more than 200,000 IPMA project management certified professionals worldwide in 2014. The US-based Project Management Institute (PMI) was founded in 1967 and has about 640,000 Project Management Professional credential holders in 2014. The existence of project management associations and project management certifications may be considered to be evidence of the widespread nature of project management and project-oriented working.

Table 1.1   Overview on project management periods

Period	Topics	Objective	Project types	Industries
1940–1950	Quantitative techniques, such as Critical Path Methods (CPM) and Program Evaluation and Review Technique (PERT)	A project is a system to be optimized	Technology and infrastructure	Military, air force, defence, science
1960–1970	Project organization structures (matrix organization) Project leadership, Project team	Application of standard project organizations	Technology and infrastructure	Construction, engineering
1980–1990	Expert systems for project planning, control, risk analysis; Project success	Sophistication of methods and techniques, optimization and modelling	Contract projects and product development	Information technology, tele-communication
1990–2000	Management by Projects Project as a temporary organization	Projects bring competitive advantage for organizations	Contract projects, and all kinds of internal projects, e.g., organizational development	All industries and public sector
2000–2010	Project-oriented organization, industry and society Programme management Project portfolio management Embeddedness of the project in a broader context	Projects and programmes bring competitive advantage for organizations, industries, societies	Contract projects, and all kinds of internal projects and programmes e.g., organizational development	All industries increasing importance in public sector
2010–current	Projects, programmes and Project-oriented organizations as a specific context for management and governance Projects and programmes to organize change; Relation to sustainable development	Projects and programmes as an established mode of organizing for organizations, industries, and societies	All kinds of internal and external projects, Size from small to mega. Importance of programmes increasing	All industries increasing importance in public sector

Source: Adapted from Morris 1997; Söderlund 2011, extended by Huemann.

Related to the increasing importance of projects and the notion that projects can bring competitive advantage (Wheelwright/Clark 1992), the management of projects becomes a capability increasingly required in more or less any contemporary organization (Thomas/Mullaly 2008). The project-oriented organization as a form of the contemporary organization (Martinsuo et al. 2006; Ruigrok 1999; Whittington et al. 1999) is different to a classically managed organization, as managing projects requires specific organizational strategy, structures and culture (Gareis 1990). In society as well as in organizations, the role of the project manager is increasingly being recognized as an occupation and profession in its own right (Morris et al. 2006).[5]

With this increased recognition of the importance of projects and the impact of project managers, there have been developments in both practice and theory. The developments of practice have been heavily user-driven, notably by the two leading project management associations (International Project Management Association, Project Management Institute), which currently retain their influence over practice. This influence comes through their highly normative and universalist project management standards, which form the base for project management certification of project managers. Project management research has become more theoretically-based over time, but has remained mostly practice-oriented with the aim of contributing to contemporary management practice (Söderlund/Maylor 2012). In contrast to the normative practices being advocated by the professional associations, scholars have started developing more context-related theories (e.g., Hodgson/Cicmil 2006). In addition, multiple streams of project management research have built on different theories and perceptions, with the result that project management has grown into a young academic field of some diversity and complexity (Söderlund 2011; Turner et al. 2010).

As an applied field, project management research has long concentrated on the sophistication and optimization of tools and techniques to ensure that projects are delivered on time, in scope and within set costs. Optimization tools such as the Critical Path Methods (CPM) and Program Evaluation and Review Technique (PERT) reflect the genesis of project management (Turner et al. 2010). Having its roots in engineering and operation research, project management has long been lacking an organization theory approach. However, project management is more than Gantt Charts (Maylor 2001) and has considerably broadened its horizon (Söderlund 2004) during the last ten years. The broadening of the field includes two developments, namely the conceptualization of projects as temporary organizations and an increasing interest in the organization being able to conduct projects – the project-oriented organization.

Today, a critical mass of researchers uses the conceptualization of projects as temporary organizations (for a detailed literature review see Bakker 2010; Lundin/Söderholm 1995), which adds a different view to the traditional perception of projects. The traditional view of the project as a complex technical system (for example Cleland/King 1983) is characterized by rationality and the management of time, cost and scope. The perception of a project as a temporary organization adds to the relevance of the project organization, project culture, personnel and the project contexts when managing a project (Engwall 2003; Sahlin-Andersson/Söderholm 2002). Whilst project HRM has long been considered as part of project management, prevailing project management standards reflect a limited and rather traditional HRM paradigm, considering HRM mainly as a planning and scheduling issue of the project (PMI 2013). By contrast, conceptualizing projects as temporary organizations opens up a much broader perspective of HRM for projects and project-oriented organizations, which will be discussed in this book.

The project-oriented organization has become an object of consideration in research. Organizations that conduct projects are called 'projectified', 'project intensive', 'project-led',

---

5   In 2002, the Project Management Institute (PMI) estimates that about 16 million people worldwide consider project management as their profession (Gedansky 2002). Relevance and numbers are increasing, in 2013, PMI suggests, that between 2010 and 2020, 15.7 million new project management roles will be created globally.

'multi-project', or 'project-based'. While labels and conceptual underpinning vary, the basic assumption is shared, that projects can be considered as a means of organizational differentiation to allow the increasing complexity of the environment to be dealt with (Morris 1997). In contemporary organizations a paradigm shift with projects as a specific and significant characteristic is observable (Clegg 1990; Whittington et al. 1999). Nevertheless, not every project-based organization is project-oriented – by that I mean adequately equipped to perform projects. I explicitly use the term project-oriented organization for an organization that applies *Management by Projects* as a strategic option for organizing business processes by projects, when adequate (Gareis 1990; 2005). This implies that the organization chooses between temporary projects and permanent organization to perform business processes, and is capable of doing so. It also implies that the organization is sufficiently equipped to perform projects.

Other temporary organizations can also be programmes. I acknowledge that programmes as temporary organizations are of relevance for the project-oriented organization, and there are specifics of programmes and programme management (see for example Pellegrinelli 1997). While programme and the programme management personnel are not specifically addressed in this research, many of the discussions in this book are equally relevant for HRM on programmes and for programme personnel.

1.3 Is a Fresh Perspective on HRM Required?

It is common practice to argue that Human Resource Management (HRM) is of strategic importance in all organizations (Boxall 2011), contributing to the financial success of the organization (Guest 1987; Huselid 1995; Pfeffer 1998). Boxall and Purcell (2011) position HRM as one of the vital parts of any organization – if it fails, then the company fails.

In Strategic Human Resource Management (SHRM) there is the claim that HRM practices should support strategy and eventually contribute to shaping strategy (Ulrich 1997). However, scholars describe HRM research as unbalanced. This is because Micro HRM concentrates on very distinct HRM practices or sub functions, and is often silo-based (Wright/Boswell 2002). In contrast, strategic HRM is critiqued for remaining on an abstract level and lacking operational relevance (Legge 2005).

While a central scholarly focus of SHRM has been on performance measuring issues and the effects of single HR practices or bundles of HR practices, the field has developed further and today takes a more holistic perception of a viable HRM system adequate for its purpose and context. A viable HRM system is aligned to its organizational context, which includes strategy, structure and culture of the organization, as well as its institutional context (Wood 1999).

The HRM literature acknowledges the contextual nature of HRM (Paauwe 2004), the diversity of HRM practices deriving from the contemporary organization (Poole/Jenkins 1997), the differences of HRM in comparative HRM research (Brewster 2012), as well as the need to bring in principles of sustainable development into Human Resource Management to ensure the expectations of the organization, individuals and society (Zaugg 2009).

However, research into what projects – as temporary organizations in addition to the permanent structures in an organization – mean for the HRM system is rare. While there is evidence that project HRM is considered as a core knowledge element in project management standards (e.g., PMI 2013) and project excellence models (IPMA 1997), project HRM is relatively immature (Belout 1998; 2004). Little awareness exists that HRM is taking place beyond the line on the project (Bredin/Söderlund 2011; Keegan et al. 2012). On the other hand, the theme is not new, as HRM implications, due to project-orientation of the organization, have been indicated by recent and not so recent studies. Engwall et al. (2003: 130) note the necessary changes in HRM when an organization applies projects:

As organizations move into project-based structures, human resource management, hiring of staff, and competence development all seem to be affected. This is, however, a virtually unexplored area of empirical research. Furthermore, issues concerning working life must be readdressed in this new corporate context design. From the perspective of the individual employee, factors like motivation, commitment, empowerment, job satisfaction, time pressure, and medical stress seem to be reconceptualized in the projectified context. Working life issues also include accounts of project work as a new career path and as ways of linking project organizations to individual goals.

On the one hand, the list of HRM challenges in project-oriented organizations indicated in literature is quite long and includes the authority and responsibility of project managers (Fabi/Pettersen 1992; Gaddis 1959), the careers of project managers (Jones/DeFillippi Hölzle 2010; 1996; Keegan/Turner 2003; Larsen 2002), salaries and promotion of project managers (Allen/Katz 1995), employee well-being, stress (Aitken/Crawford 2007; Gällstedt 2003; Zika-Viktorsson et al. 2006), resource planning and allocation of personnel (Engwall/Jerbrant 2003; Eskerod 1998), and *no home syndrome* of the project manager (Keegan/Turner 2003), as well as the HR quadriad, a configurational framework to describe the interplay between line managers, project managers, project workers and HR specialists in the project-based organization (Bredin/Söderlund 2011). On the other hand, there are little considerations regarding the potential that project-orientation may provide to the HRM system, although there is evidence that there are HRM related benefits to be gained from the introduction of projects and project management into an organization (Thomas/Mullaly 2008).

There are no offers of viable solutions as to what a HRM system could look like in order to support project-orientation − particularly, there are no viable solutions that consider the organizational context as well as the expectations of the project personnel to support sustainable development of the project-oriented organization. Thus, this study addresses the following research question:

Which HRM system is viable to the project-oriented organization in order to raise the HR related potential that project-orientation can bring?

1.4 What is the Fresh Perspective?

In this research, I include and build upon a series of related studies in which I was involved (Huemann et al. 2007; 2004; Keegan et al. 2012; Turner et al. 2008a; 2008b) and consider relevant studies of other researchers (Bredin/Söderlund 2011; Loosemore et al. 2003) to develop a more comprehensive understanding of a viable HRM system for managing project personnel in the project-oriented organization.

Theoretically, this research combines HRM and PM, by putting HRM in the context of the project-oriented organization. Some scholars claim that there is a lack of engagement between these two fields (Clark/Colling 2005). This research is based on HRM and PM literatures as well as on five comprehensive case studies of project-oriented organizations, of which one was turned into a longitudinal case study. This allowed for observing changes in the HRM system, as the organization became more project-oriented. In addition to the case studies, more than 40 interviews with project managers, project team members, portfolio managers, line managers and HR managers were conducted to ensure viability of the models and the propositions developed.

Whilst conversations in the HRM literature have been criticized as being either at an abstract strategic level or at a highly detailed level of practice, research linking HRM practices and strategy is scarce (Legge 2005). To target this gap, I am interested in the HRM system. I go beyond HRM as a functional department and analyse where in the project-oriented organization HRM decisions are carried out by different roles. Whilst the HRM literature discusses the devolution of HRM responsibilities to line managers and the challenges that come with it (Francis/Keegan 2006), I argue that HRM does not stop at the line manager. In the project-oriented organization, HRM is carried out beyond the line manager in the temporary part of the organization: the projects (Bredin/Söderlund 2011; Keegan et al. 2012). I demonstrate that project-orientation accelerates the devolution of HRM from the HR department to the line managers and beyond. Project-orientation ultimately influences the HRM system and may lead to a more networked understanding of the HRM system, challenged by the interplay of many different roles such as the HR department, the Project Management Office (PMO), the Project Portfolio Group (PPG), the line managers, the project owners and project managers.

I seek a better understanding of changes in the HRM system in the context of the project-oriented organization, to create and sustain human resource advantage. Boxall (1998) defined the construct of human resource advantage as consisting of two components, the human capital advantage and the organizational processes advantage, which are interlinked. In the case of the project-oriented organization, human capital advantages refer to the quality of the personnel that the organization employs for their projects, which I will refer to as project personnel. By project personnel, I mean those personnel that frequently engage in projects. Relevant roles that the personnel take on include project manager, project team member, the project team as a collective and the project owner. The quality of these personnel groups, including knowledge, skill, commitment and motivation, is essential for the project-oriented organization. The organizational process advantages refer to the adequate internal structures of the HRM system to manage these personnel.

The research study on HRM in the project-oriented organization offers a fresh perspective, which is based on:

- A systemic-constructivist research paradigm as a theoretical stance;
- The understanding of the project-oriented organization as a construction;
- The understanding of projects as temporary organizations and social systems, which constitute secondary temporary organizations, sub systems in a project-oriented organization;
- The perspective of HRM as a sub system that requires alignment to its context to be viable;
- The explicit consideration of HRM related potentials that project-orientation may bring;
- Sustainable development as an important contemporary context for any organization.

In the following sections, I introduce the fresh perspective, and the specific approach taken, and disclose the basic constructs which underpin it.

1.4.1 THE THEORETICAL STANCE

The research study is based on a systemic–constructivist research paradigm, based on radical constructivism (Von Glasersfeld 1995) and Social System Theory (Luhmann 1995), and uses a qualitative research approach. Social system theory enables me to conceptualize an approach to HRM with multiple perspectives (Mayrhofer 2004) to analyse the HRM related interplay between personnel, temporary project and the HRM structure in the permanent organization within the project-oriented organization. Radical constructivism allows me to challenge existing practice and propose the model of a project-oriented HRM system as a viable research solution that fits practice.

1.4.2 THE HRM SYSTEM AS A SOCIAL SUB SYSTEM IN ITS SPECIFIC CONTEXT

If the HRM system is to provide long-term viability to the organization, it needs to support the specific requirements of the project-oriented organization. It is common in HRM to exclusively focus on HRM practices. Taking a distinct perspective, I focus on the HRM system viable for managing project personnel in the project-oriented organization. I assume that in a diversified and networked organization such as the project-oriented organization, the HRM tasks are rather widespread. The HRM system goes far beyond the HR department, and thus includes all communications/decisions relevant to HRM. In other words, the HRM system includes all HRM decisions, regardless of who carries them out and where they take place. HRM is carried out in the permanent parts of a project-oriented organization as well as in the temporary projects, which might even go beyond the boundaries of a single project-oriented organization.

1.4.3 THE PROJECT-ORIENTED ORGANIZATION AS A CONSTRUCTION

A project-oriented organization pursues the strategy *Management by Projects*, applies temporary and specific permanent structures, and develops a project-oriented culture (Gareis 1990; 2005). But as it is a construction, the project-oriented organization as such does not exist in practice. In practice, a variety of organizations exist which require a greater or smaller number of projects or programmes to carry out their business processes. Further, these organizations have more or less potential, and thus are more or less adequately equipped to carry out projects and programmes. The project-oriented organization describes an organization that is equipped to perform projects. Thus, it makes a quality statement about the internal structures of an organization, whether the organization is capable of performing projects and programmes professionally. In practice, the organizations range from project-based organizations, which have a high demand for projects, but may not be sufficiently equipped to carry out these projects for those project-oriented organizations which have made the strategic choice to perform projects when adequate and also have the internal structures to do so. However, any organization conducting projects can be perceived through the lens of project-orientation.

1.4.4 PROJECTS AS TEMPORARY ORGANIZATIONS AND SOCIAL SYSTEMS

From the perspective of social systems theory (Luhmann 1995), the project can be considered as a social system that is differentiated from and embedded in a wider context. In particular a project can be perceived of as a sub system of a project-oriented organization, created by the permanent organization, with the intention to end it when it has fulfilled its purpose. According to Asbby's law that states '*only variety can absorb variety*', projects can be considered as a means of organizational differentiation to absorb the complexity of the environment. In addition, a project is a distinct form of a social system, and a temporary organization (Lundin/Söderholm 1995). If a project is an organization, then it requires HRM. This takes more than the traditional view of assigning human resources to projects and optimizing resource planning based on scheduling. Thus, managing project personnel on a project is more than just using and consuming human resources to perform the task and accomplish the project objectives.

1.4.5 CONSIDERATION OF POTENTIALS

The HRM-related challenges that project-orientation bring are well known (Bredin/Söderlund 2011; Huemann et al. 2007; Turner et al. 2008a). On the other hand, project-orientation also brings HRM-related potential, which can be raised with a viable HRM system that fits the project-oriented organization. This potential has not been discussed much until now, but includes the consideration of projects as learning opportunities, projects as an attractive working form and source of motivation for project personnel, and finally the consideration of organizing HR processes that will make projects run smoothly. Currently, organizations do not take advantage of all the potential HRM opportunities.

1.4.6 STRUCTURE OF THE BOOK

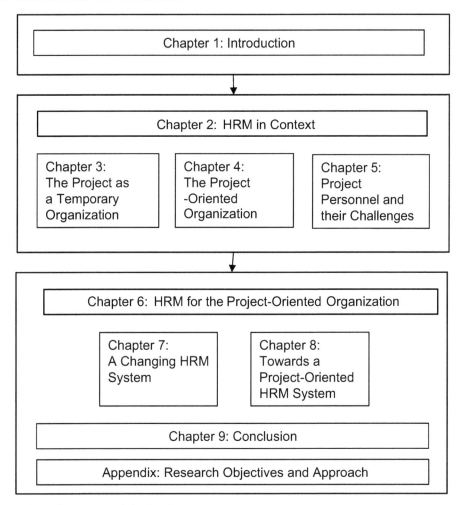

Figure 1.1   Structure of the book

Chapter 1: Introduction

The current chapter has laid out the main aims, basic assumptions and arguments of the book.

Chapter 2: HRM in Context

In this chapter, I turn more specifically to HRM and trace its development from a universalist understanding of best practices to a more contextualized contingency understanding, that the HRM system should be viable in its context of adding value to the company. Secondly, the chapter outlines the development towards a more comprehensive understanding of the goals of HRM. The HRM debate indicates a shift from performance as organizational effectiveness for shareholder interest to a more comprehensive contemporary understanding of HRM goals, including economic and social goals for sustainable development.

Chapter 3: The Project as a Temporary Organization

The chapter introduces different theoretical lenses with which to perceive projects. It discusses the traditional perception of a project as a complex task, and the evolution of its conceptualization into a temporary organization, social system and construction. To make the project clearer as a construct, I differentiate the project from related constructs, such as investment, process and programme, and discuss different project types. I finally summarize my understanding of projects as temporary organizations and social systems, which serves as the theoretical lens for understanding projects in this book.

Chapter 4: The Project-Oriented Organization

The chapter discusses the organization that is capable of conducting projects: the project-oriented organization. The chapter draws on early management theories to clarify the origins and then provides an overview on the different approaches to the organization, which performs projects as a central means of organizing business processes. I describe the project-oriented organization with its specific strategy, structures and culture. To deal with the high diversity due to the temporary character of projects, project-oriented organizations apply specific permanent structures such as a Project Portfolio Group (PPG), a Project Management Office (PMO) and Expert Pools. I finally suggest a definition for the project-oriented organization, and derive its specific features to describe the context to which HRM will be related.

Chapter 5: Project Personnel and their Challenges

This chapter specifies project personnel and their roles on projects. It outlines the challenges that project personnel face when working on projects or working for project-oriented organizations. The chapter concludes with issues of employee well-being, which the project-oriented organization needs to deal with if they want to raise the potential benefits that project-orientation can bring.

Chapter 6: HRM for the Project-Oriented Organization

In this chapter, I relate the HRM system to the specific context, the project-oriented organization. I develop the working model: the HRM system in the project-oriented organization, and describe it with propositions. This model will be further developed in the remainder of this book.

Chapter 7: A Changing HRM System

This chapter offers findings from a longitudinal case study of a telecommunication company that has developed into a project-oriented organization. The objective of this chapter is to illustrate the fundamental changes that are required in the HRM system when developing into a project-oriented organization. The chapter illustrates and discusses changes in the HRM system. The findings especially indicate the acceleration of the devolution of HRM responsibilities beyond line, when becoming more project-oriented. The case study further points to the fundamental changes of HRM from an administrative function to a proactive, project-oriented HRM organization explicitly supporting project-oriented management.

Chapter 8: Towards a Project-Oriented HRM System

The objective of this chapter is to describe more comprehensively the HRM system in mature project-oriented organizations. In this way, the HRM system and its context are better illustrated.

Chapter 9: Conclusion

This chapter summarizes the findings of the study and introduces the *Model: Project-oriented HRM system*. The model is described using propositions. Limitations and a research agenda for further research are provided.

Appendix: Research Objectives and Approach

This chapter describes the research approach taken. The chapter starts by explicitly stating the underpinning research paradigms, which are Radical Constructivism and Social Systems Theory combined with Qualitative Social Research. After explaining the theoretical stance, I state the consequences for the research process and describe the research methods.

HRM in Context

2.1 Introduction

In this chapter, I firstly trace the development from a universalist approach of HRM to an increasingly contextualized understanding of HRM. Secondly, the chapter outlines the developments of a more comprehensive understanding of the goals of HRM. The HRM debate indicates a shift from performance as organizational effectiveness for shareholder value interest to a more comprehensive contemporary understanding of HRM goals, including economic as well as social goals to support and create sustainable development of the organization.

2.2 Putting HRM in Context

As Brewster and Mayrhofer (2012) note classic HRM identifies HRM as employee influence, human resource flow, reward systems and work systems (Beer et al. 1984) or selection, performance, appraisal, rewards and development (Fombrun et al. 1984), but little agreement on the term HRM can be found. Different perspectives on HRM are offered, which also reflect the development and diversification of this vibrant field. However, three major sub-fields within HRM are distinguished (Boxall et al. 2010; 2011; Brewster/Mayrhofer 2012; Lengnick-Hall et al. 2009) as shown in Table 2.1.

Table 2.1   Overview HRM sub fields

HRM sub fields	Micro HRM	Strategic HRM	International HRM
Themes	• HRM processes and sub functions of HRM for example • Recruiting • Developing • Appraising • Work system • Career system	• Universalist approach: Best practice school • Contingency approach: Best fit school • Configurational approach • Resource-based view • Knowledge-based view	• Individual working abroad • HRM in multi-national companies • Comparative HRM

One of the first strategic HRM models developed was the Michigan Model (Fombrun et al. 1984), which suggests that organizational effectiveness depends on achieving a tight fit between HRM strategy and the business strategy of the company. According to their Human Resource Cycle, performance is dependent on selection, appraisal, reward and development of personnel. The HRM processes required in any organization are:

* Selection, which includes matching available human resources to jobs;
* Appraisal and performance management;
* Rewards, which include rewarding short as well as long-term achievements for driving organizational performance;
* Development of personnel.

The Michigan Model is often criticized as reminiscent of scientific management in treating human resources as any other non-human resource in the organization (Sparrow/Hiltrop 1994). It focuses on a limited set of HRM processes, and is based on linear assumptions and relations, for example on a fairly stable organizational strategy based on shareholder interests, and ignores further context. It neither considers other relevant environments/stakeholders such as employee groups, unions, government, communities and so on, nor does it consider the organizational design of the company, or any other context.

Around the same time, Beer et al. (1984) developed the Harvard Model which acknowledges the broader context such as stakeholder interests and other factors. By that, the model starts with a situational perspective, and puts the HRM policy choices in a particular context described by situational factors and the interests of different stakeholder groups. The HRM system is shaped on this social and content-related context, which leads to proximate HRM outcomes such as commitment, competences, congruence and cost effectiveness, and more distant long-term consequences such as individual well-being, organizational effectiveness and societal well-being. Although a classic model, it has retained its relevance for contemporary organizations, especially as it also considers long-term consequences beyond financial outcomes.

What becomes evident in the field of HRM is that there has been a development from universalist approaches and models to more context-oriented approaches to describe a HRM system viable to a particular organization (Paauwe 2004). In the following, I will provide a brief overview on different HRM approaches, which will make the developments in Strategic Human Resource management visible.

2.2.1 UNIVERSALIST APPROACH

The universalist approach, also known as the best practice school, is interested in defining (bundles of) best HRM practices that will ultimately lead to better performance of the company. The description of the recommended HRM practices and the construction of the HRM outcomes and company outcomes vary considerably between the models. What is shared is the common understanding that the specific organizational context is to be ignored. But there is the assumption that there are (bundles of) universalist HRM practices that lead to better performance.

Guest (1987) described relevant HRM practices such as selection, training, appraising, rewards, job design, involvement, status and security that will ultimately lead to better financial performance for the organization. Figure 2.1 describes the linkage of HRM and performance.

Huselid (1995) published a seminal paper in the *Academy of Management Journal*, and demonstrated a correlation between the degree of sophistication of HRM and the market value per employee in US companies. Thus, he was able to provide empirical evidence that a sophisticated HRM system leads to better financial performance of the organization.

HRM strategy	HRM practices	HRM outcomes	Behaviour outcomes	Performance outcomes	Financial outcomes
	Selection		Effort / Motivation	High: Productivity Quality Innovation	Profits
Differentiation (innovation)	Training	Commitment			
Focus (quality)	Appraisal		Cooperation		
	Rewards	Quality		Low: Absence Labour turnover	ROI
Cost (cost-reduction)	Job design		Involvement		
	Involvement	Flexibility	Organizational citizenship	Conflict Customer complaints	
	Status and Security				

Figure 2.1   Linking HRM and performance
Source: Guest 1997: 270.

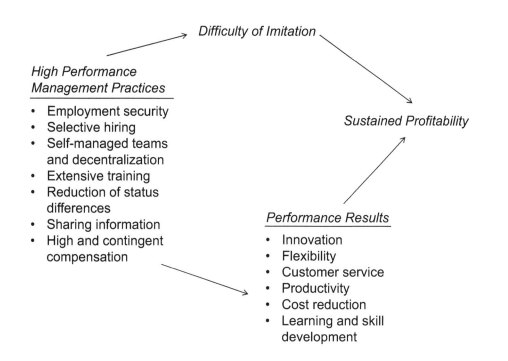

Figure 2.2   People-centred management
Source: Pfeffer 1998: 301.

Meanwhile there seems to be agreement in the HR literature that it is not the single practices that lead to better performance, but rather coherent bundles of HR practices, also referred to as a high performance work system that leads to better performing personnel and ultimately to better financial performance (Huselid 1995) or sustained profitability (Pfeffer 1998).

As an example of a high performance management system, Figure 2.2 shows the people-centred management approach by Pfeffer (1998). He describes seven bundles of HRM practices which are firstly, difficult to imitate, and secondly, will lead to performance improvements in innovation, flexibility, customer service, productivity, cost reduction, learning and skill development. The high performance management practices are employment security, selective hiring, self-managed teams and decentralization, comparatively high compensation, extensive training, reduction of status differences and extensive sharing of information through the organization.

Not only are the bundles of relevant HRM practices different in the different models, but the way that the desired outcomes are described also varies in different studies (as summarized by Jiang et al. 2012), from positive HRM performance outcomes as higher commitment (Gong 2009) and lower turnover (Batt 2002), to organizational outcomes such as higher productivity (Macduffie 1995), better service performance (Chuang/Liao 2010), better financial performance (Huselid 1995), or sustained profitability (Pfeffer 1998).

Despite HRM literature offering robust evidence of a positive relation between HRM and performance (Combs et al. 2006), several questions remain unanswered. As argued by Jiang et al. (2012), firstly, the mechanism that links HRM systems (or more precisely bundles of HRM practices) with rather proximate HRM outcomes and with more distant organizational outcomes remains fragmented. Legge (2005) stated that the deeper nature of the strategic alignment of HRM still remains conceptual and rather unclear. She is critical of the fact that these alignments are often perceived from a classical rationalist perspective, neglecting systemic approaches, the interest of different groups of stakeholders and the diversity of business strategies pursued by diversified companies. Pauwee (2004) raised the issue that a HRM system needs to be viable for a certain context to raise value for the organization, despite the fact that the context of the HRM system is not considered through a universalist approach, nor are the relations between the bundles of HRM practices taken into account.

Most of the large-scale studies that try to capture an accurate picture of the positive effect of HRM systems for performance are based on statistical calculations, which require simplification. This leads to the question of whether such linearity in the assumptions and correlations between bundles of practices and certain HRM performance outcomes creates a promising way forward. This challenge can be argued from at least two perspectives. The relations between the elements might be too complicated/complex and mutual to grasp them all, as the HRM system can be approached on multiple levels and there are links to a multitude of related outcomes (e.g., Guest 1997). The other argument in line with the theoretical stance of this study is that from a systemic point of view, organizations are not mechanistic machines with input and output relations, but they are self-referential, follow their own dynamics and remain unpredictable (Kasper 1990; Luhmann 2006).

However, the aim of book is not to solve performance measurement issues, which become even more complex when context is considered (but there is a stream of literature in SHRM dedicated to the sophistication of measurement – for an overview of research streams in SHRM see the studies by Paauwe (2009). What this study can contribute is a better understanding of the HRM system in a particular context: the project-oriented organization.

2.2.2 ALIGNING FOR BEST FIT

In contrast to the universalist approach, the contingency approach, also labelled best fit school, argues that in order to create value for the organization, the HRM system needs to fit its context.

Table 2.2   Role behaviours and required HR practices

Strategy: Innovation	
Desired role behaviour	**Required HR practices**
• High degree of creativity • Long-term focus • Relatively high level of co-operative and independent behaviour • Moderate concern for quality • Equal degree of concern for process and change • Greater degree of risk taking • High tolerance of ambiguity and unpredictability	• Job design that stimulates close interaction and co-ordination among groups and individuals • Performance appraisals that are more likely to reflect longer-term and group achievements • Jobs that allow employees to develop skills that can be used in other positions in the firm • Compensation systems that emphasize internal equity rather than external market equity • Pay rate that tends to be low, but employees to be stock holders and have more freedom of choice for pay package • Broad career paths to reinforce development of a broad range of skills

Source: Schuler/Jackson 1987.

The starting point for different organizational context is different company strategies. For example, the well-known model of Schuler and Jackson (1987), based on Porter's generic strategies, propose that the desired role behaviours of employees need to be supported by fitting HRM policies and practices. Table 2.2 provides the example of an organization that pursues an innovation strategy[1] and lists the desired role behaviours of employees (Schuler/Jackson 1987: 209) and the HRM practices that should create these desired behaviours (Schuler/Jackson 1987: 213).

To add value to the organization and to achieve competitive advantage, the HRM system needs alignment both with company strategy, or so-called vertical strategic integration (Butler et al. 1991; Lengnick-Hall/Lengnick-Hall 1988; Schuler/Jackson 1987), as well as among the HRM components, so-called horizontal integration (Wright/McMahan 1992).

2.2.3 CONFIGURATIONAL APPROACH

As a further development of the contingency approach, in recent years scholars made the attempt to more describe the HRM system comprehensively with components such as HR principles, HR policies, HR programmes, HR practices and HR climate (Arthur/Boyles 2007). Table 2.3 gives an overview about HR system components and representative studies.

These different components can be combined and blended into different configurations to fit the particular organization (Lengnick-Hall et al. 2009). Based on the assumption that the personnel of an organization are diverse, and different groups of personnel have different degree of uniqueness (firm specificity of skills) and different value for the organization (strategic importance of skill), Lepak and Snell (1999) conclude that these groups of personnel will be treated differently in the organization (see also Pfeffer 1988).

---

1   I have selected the innovation strategy as an example, as the project-oriented organization is considered to be an innovative organization as discussed in Chapter 5.

Table 2.3   Examples of studies of HR system components

HR system component	Representative studies
HR principles: stated values, beliefs, and norms regarding what drives employee performance and how organizational resources and rewards should be allocated	Denison (1990) McGregor (1960) Miles (1975) O'Reilly and Pfeffer (2000)
HR policies: organizational goals or objectives for managing human resources	Lepak and Snell (1999) Osterman (1988) Ouchi (1980) Walton (1985) Arthur (1994)
HR programmes: the set of formal HR activities used in the organization HR programmes by lower-level managers and employees	Delery and Doty (1996) Guthrie (2001) Huselid (1995)
HR practices: the implementation and experience of an organization's HR	Marsden, Kalleberg and Cook (1996) Wright, Dunford et al. (2001a) Wright, Gardner et al. (2001b) Wright, McMahan et al. (2001c)
HR climate: shared employee perceptions and interpretations of the meaning of HR principles, policies and programmes in their organization	Bowen and Ostroff (2004) Collins and Smith (2006) Gelade and Ivery (2003) Riordan, Vandenberg and Richardson (2005)

Source: Arthur/Boyles 2007: 79.

Among the first authors who used the term HR architecture were Becker and Gerhart (1996). In their view, HRM architecture refers to the design of the HRM system linking HRM philosophy, HRM policy and HRM practice (Kepes 2006). Lepak and Snell (1999) building on Osterman (1987) define HR architecture as a frame of how an organization manages the different types of personnel to accomplish its goals. They argue for a differentiated HRM architecture, as an organization may shape different configurations of the HRM components for different employee groups. The strategic core personnel of an organization may be managed differently than peripheral employees (Delery 2001; Rousseau/Wade-Benzoni 1994).

Table 2.4   Forms of HRM fit

	Criterion-specific	Criterion-free
Internal	Fit as an ideal set of practices	Fit as gestalt; Fit as bundles
External	Fit as strategic interaction	Fit as contingency

Source: Adapted from Guest 1997.

2.2.4 THE CONCEPTS OF FIT

Guest (1997) describes the vertical fit between corporate strategy in more detail and identifies four different perspectives on the linkage between corporate strategy and HRM. Table 2.4 illustrates the four different types of fit according to internal or external focus, and if the linkage is criterion-specific or criterion-free. Below the single fits are described in more detail.

Fit as strategic interaction

This kind of fit represents the vertical linkage between corporate strategy and HRM. According to Guest (1997: 270) superior performance can be reached with the appropriate response and the right match of strategy and HRM. For testing the fit, the typologies of Porter or Miles and Snow can be used while relating them to HRM practices. Schuler and Jackson (1987) serve as an example. Through the relation of the strategy typologies and HRM practices, a positive effect on measures of performance should be gained.

Fit as contingency

This kind of fit is based on the traditional contingency approach. Guest (1997) argues that, according to this fit, organizations that are more responsive to external factors in their HRM policies and practices will reach superior performance. External factors could be the product market combination and related corporate and business strategy, and also the labour market, legislation and the specifics of that branch of industry.

Fit as an ideal set of best practices

This fit considers a set of universally applicable so-called best practices. The performance of the company is better the closer the HRM strategy matches with the ideal set.

Fit as gestalt or bundles

The first 'fit as gestalt' is an appropriate combination of practices to bring about effective HRM. The sum of those practices is greater than single parts. This kind of fit is either a synergistic combination of practices or the specific organizational architecture that binds those practices together. The second 'fit as bundles' is closely related to 'fit as gestalt'. Those bundles are distinctive patterns or configurations of practices. They bring about superior performance.

Kepes and Delery (2007) defined the internal fit further and proposed four types of internal fit based upon a multi-level conceptualization of HR systems:

- Within-HRM system vertical fit, which is the degree of fit between different HRM activities on different levels of abstraction (e.g., fit between compensation policies, practices and processes);
- Inter-HRM activity area fit, which is the fit between different HRM activity areas (e.g., between selection and compensation);

- Intra-HRM activity area fit, which is the alignment between specific HRM activities within a certain set of HRM activities (e.g., HRM practices within the selection area);
- Between-HRM system fit, which is the fit between one HRM system and another within the same organization (e.g., between knowledge-based workers and job-based workers).

Wood (1999) summarizes the need for aligning the HRM system in any organization and differentiates four required fits. In addition to the vertical strategic fit: HRM is aligned with the organizations' strategic choices and the horizontal internal fit: HRM processes and sub-functions are mutually consistent and supportive. He further proposes the organizational and the environmental/societal fit.

Organizational fit: HRM processes are consistent with and support operational processes of the organization: 'The issue here is whether managers can, or should, mould their HR strategies to fit in with other critical features of their particular business, including its wider strategy and its structural features' (Boxall 2011: 79). There is the idea that the size of an organization makes a major difference as to the kind of HR practices that the management adopts, and the level of formalization involved in HRM is strongly supported (Boxall 2011).

Environmental fit comprises social fit and industry fit. Societal fit means that the HRM strategy is aligned with the environment of the organization, for example, legal system, national or industry context (Wood 1999). It is concerned with the question of whether organizations adapt to the characteristics of the societies in which they are located, and additionally, if they are wise to do so. This kind of fit relates to a range of economic and social factors. Furthermore, it goes beyond law regulations in the countries in which the organization operates, but societal fit is concerned with the way national features affect HRM (Boxall 2011). Industry fit concerns the question of whether firms adapt to their industry contexts. In strategic management, the industry, according to Porter, plays an important and critical role of analysis. 'Firms tend to imitate what is seen to work in their industry, and this includes approaches to managing people' (Boxall 2011: 76). The characters of an industry influences HRM.

As development and change is not an exception, but rather routine in contemporary organizations (Gareis/Huemann 2010), more flexibility is required in the organization and in the HRM system, leading to a more fluid understanding of the fit. Adding to the concept of fit a resource-based view of the firm to SHRM, de Pablos (2005) argues that to create a sustainable competitive advantage, organizational flexibility (both resource and co-ordination) and fit (both internal and external) must be achieved simultaneously to create a firm that renews itself and can respond quickly to environmental demands. From this perspective, the notion of HR contingencies has evolved from making specific choices to accommodating development.

2.3 The Contextually-Based Human Resource Theory by Paauwe

Of particular note is the contextually-based Human Resource Theory (CBHRT) by Jaap Paauwe (2004). He incorporates elements of the contingency and configurational approaches to HRM, and combines these with institutionalism, resource-based theory, action theory and path dependency theory (Barney 1995). Paauwe highlights the intrinsic tension in shaping HRM policies that arises between economic rationality, which is concerned with added value (PMT dimension) and relational rationality, the latter of which is concerned with moral values (SCL dimension). In addition to the dimensions PMT and SCL, the Organizational/Administrative/Cultural heritage need to be explained, which is concerned with the unique configuration or 'gestalt' of the organization. Those three forces influence the dominant coalition, which is his expression for the HRM system. Those single parts of the framework are explained in more detail below.

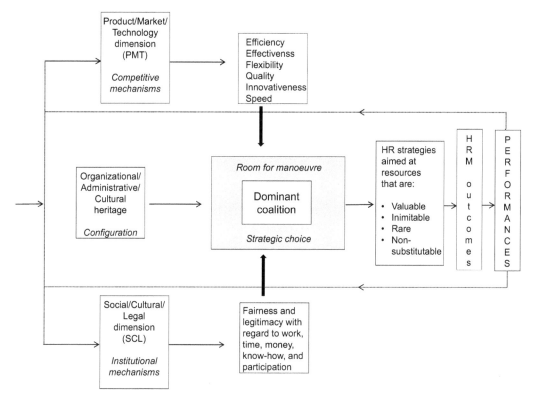

Figure 2.3   Contextually-based human resource theory
Source: Adapted from Paauwe 2004: 91.

- **Product/Market/Technology dimension (PMT):** HRM is determined to a certain degree by demands arising from relevant product market combinations and the appropriate technology. Demands can be expressed in terms of criteria such as efficiency, effectiveness, flexibility, quality and innovativeness, and those dimensions represent economic rationality of national and international competitiveness. Rationality ('Zweckrationalität') is based on criteria of efficiency and effectiveness.

- **Social/Cultural/Legal dimension (SCL):** The free market is embedded in a socio-political, cultural and legal context. The outcomes of the market forces are channelled and corrected by prevailing values and norms and their institutionalization. Furthermore, societal values and legitimacy also have an impact on the shaping of HRM policies and practices. Fairness can be explained as a fair balance in the exchange between organization and individual, and legitimacy can be described as the acceptance of organizations in the wider society in which they operate. Relational rationality represents the establishment of sustainable, trustworthy relationships with internal and external stakeholders.

- **Organizational/Administrative/Cultural heritage:** The shape and structure of HRM policies and practices are furthermore influenced through historical, grown configuration of a firm. These configurations could be seen as the outcomes of past choices of strategy in interaction with structuring issues. Those originally posed structuring issues could be influenced by the kind of organizational culture.

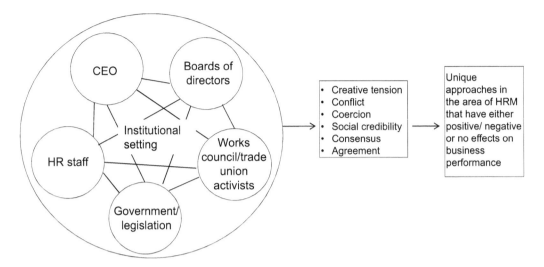

Figure 2.4   Interaction process and outcomes by the dominant coalition
Source: Paauwe 2004: 92.

- **Dominant coalition:** The dominant coalition (Figure 2.3) describes the process of an actors' network, constituting of CEO, board of directors, work council/trade activist, government/ legislation and HR staff which together shape the HRM strategies, policies and practices. Of course, these actors represent different interests. If there is a lack of shared ideology, tensions and conflict could arise.

The grey area in the CBHRT in Figure 2.5 shows the degree of room for manoeuvre for the dominant coalition in making its own strategy choices. Conditions determining the room for manoeuvre are labour-capital ratio, financial health of the company (solvability), rate of unionization and market strategy. The room for manoeuvre is small when manufacturers are numerous, keen competition exists and financial resilience is low. However, conversely, if organizations have a market monopoly, the room for manoeuvring is considerable. At this point, Paauwe brings in the institutional context, which influences the possible decisions within the HRM system.

In contrast to other HRM models (for example Guest 1997, shown earlier in this chapter) that concentrate on the link between the HRM system and performance, Pauwee (2004) adds a deeper understanding of the shaping of HRM strategies, polices and practices. By adding the process of shaping and negotiating the HRM strategies, he makes the notion of fit more dynamic and allows the HRM system to oscillate within the room for manoeuvre under consideration of the context.

The discussion of the SHRM approaches in this chapter has indicated that the field of SHRM has developed a more comprehensive understanding from single HR practices, to bundles of HR practices and more comprehensively, components of differentiated HRM systems that can be blended to a particular HRM architecture of an organization. In conjunction with these developments goes the increasing importance of different dimensions of the context as units of analysis to understand the HRM system in a particular organization.

2.4 Context of the HRM System

Society, country, industry and the organization are considered as a suitable context for the HRM system (Boxall 2011). Different contextual factors that influence HRM are described (for example, Beer et al. 1984). In the following, I will use a systemic distinction of the context into social, content related and time-related dimensions, which will later be applied in the working model in Chapter 5.

2.4.1 SOCIAL CONTEXT

Social context is represented by social environments in the language of system theory or, in the language of stakeholder theory, stakeholders. Relevant social environments/stakeholders are persons, groups of persons or organizations that are related, have an influence or can be influenced by the social system. Figure 2.5 shows the stakeholders of a company.

For the HRM system in particular these are HR managers/experts, CEO, top management, middle management, employees and particular employee groups, potential employees, competitive employers, education/training institutions, government, work councils, unions and so on (Beer et al. 1984; Paauwe 2004).

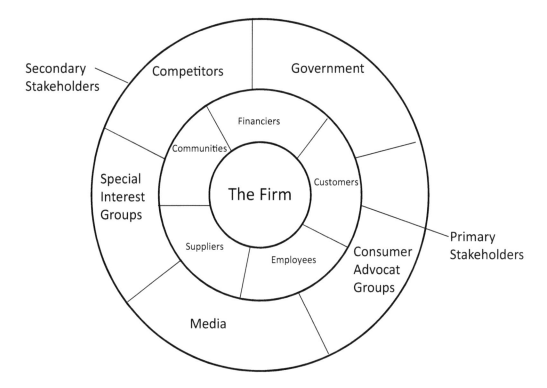

Figure 2.5   Stakeholders of a company
Source: Freeman et al. 2010: 24.

2.4.2 CONTENT RELATED CONTEXT

Situational factors which fall under the content-related context dimension are ones such as country or industry specific factors, technology, laws and societal values – or for this research, more important organizational internal features such as size of organization, its strategies, its structures and culture (Wood 1999). Whereas the focus in SHRM is the company strategy and the contribution the HRM system can make to fulfilling this, by adapting the HRM system accordingly (for example Schuler/Jackson 1987).

2.4.3 TIME RELATED CONTEXT

Paauwe (2004) describes the history related context as the Organizational/Administrative/ Cultural heritage. According to path dependency theory (Barney 1995), the history influences the decision taken today. In addition, the decisions today are influenced by future expectations (Gareis/Stummer 2008; Luhmann 2006).

2.5 Strategies and Goals of the HRM System

2.5.1 HR STRATEGY

HR strategy is a pattern of strategic choices in HRM (Boxall 2011). HR strategy content is concerned with the actual strategies that the organization adopts, while HR strategy process refers to the process by which the strategy is developed. The HR strategy implementation is concerned with the way in which the strategy is employed in practice in the organization. The implementation will influence employees' actual experiences (Truss 2012). According to HRM strategy, choices are third-order strategies because they follow from first-order decisions, as in for example the long-term direction of the firm and second-order decisions are those that occur at the divisional or business unit level.

2.5.2 SUSTAINABLE DEVELOPMENT AND HUMAN RESOURCE MANAGEMENT

During the last decade, many firms have committed themselves to the concept of sustainable development.[2] The essence of sustainable development is managing the balancing economic, ecological and social orientation, as well as broadening of the temporal scale to consider not only short, medium, but also long-term perspectives, and as a normative concept it reflects certain values and ethical considerations (see e.g., Adams 2006; Davidson 2000; Martens 2006; Meadowcroft 2007; Robinson 2004).

Sustainable development is of relevance to HRM for at least two reasons. Firstly, the HR departments are involved in introducing the concept of sustainable development into the organization (Müller-Camen 2011)[3] and, secondly, 'the shaping of the employment relationship takes place in an area of continuous tension between added value and moral value' (Paauwe 2004: 3).

---

2   For sustainable development in organizations several terms are used, but they derive from a different background. The most prominent concepts are Corporate Social Responsibility, Corporate Social Performance, Corporate Sustainability, Social Responsibility, Social Entrepreneurship, Business Ethics, Corporate Philanthropy, Corporate Citizenship, Corporate Social Responsiveness and Corporate Governance (Gareis et al. 2013).

3   Special issue, Green Human Resource Management, *German Journal of Research in Human Resource Management* 2011, 25: 2.

Figure 2.6   Tension between strategic and moral values
Source: Paauwe 2004: 4.

2.5.3 BALANCING ECONOMIC AND SOCIAL-ORIENTATION

Paauwe (2004) further explains that there are two sides represented in the word Strategic Human Resource Management. In a narrow definition, *Strategic* refers to the added value for shareholders, while *Human* refers to the core sphere of managing people, the social aspect and the moral values. Figure 2.6 illustrates those two sides.

It is not only the economic viability of the HRM system that is of importance for creating long-term competitive advantage for an organization, but it is also the social viability of the HRM system (Boxall 2011), including employee well-being. In the long run, it requires a balance to be found between economic and social orientation of the HRM system in an organization to achieve long-term viability (Paauwe 2004).

2.5.4 BALANCING INDIVIDUAL, ORGANIZATIONAL AND SOCIAL GOALS

The stakeholders' interests in the HRM system are manifold (Zaugg 2009). Based on a modern stakeholder theory approach of managing for stakeholders (Freeman et al. 2010), different interests can be internalized into the HRM goals. Table 2.5 provides individual goals, organizational goals and social goals that are fulfilled in a HRM system which applies a strategy that supports sustainable development.

The objectives of a HRM system are to design and keep the relationships between personnel and the organization. The HRM system requires that individual, organizational and social goals are balanced.

Table 2.5   Individual, organizational and social goals

Individual goals	Organizational goals	Social goals
• Job satisfaction • Work–life balance • Retention and expansion of the own competitiveness in the labour market • Personal and professional development • Health and security • Self-responsibility and participation • Culture of trust • Fulfilling and diversified tasks • Appropriate compensation • Encouragement through superiors and HRM managers • Self-organization • Social relationships • Approval from superiors • Pleasant work climate • Employment security	• Productivity • Customer orientation • Time saving • Business success • Innovation • Commitment of employees • Development of organizational capability for change and flexibility (organizational competence) • Setup of organizational knowledge (knowledge competence) • Approval of organizational learning • Setup, development and retaining of future oriented potentials of personnel (competence of personnel) • Self-organization and co-operation • Self-responsibility of employees (reduction of control) • Minimization of work conflicts (good climate with employee representatives) • Reduction of absence of work	• Job security • Prevention of illness caused through work place • Protection of competitiveness on the labour market for employees • Security on the job • Legality • Competitiveness of economy • Reintegration of unemployed persons • Economic growth • Social freedom (industrial peace) • Overtaking of social responsibility through organizations and individuals

Source: Zaugg 2009: 68.

2.6 HRM Processes and Infrastructure of the HRM System

2.6.1 HRM PROCESSES

Often, HRM practices are broadly clustered into categories such as employee involvement, training and development, rewards (Poole/Jenkins 1997) and include 'activities concerned with recruiting and selecting, designing work for, training and developing, appraising, rewarding, directing, motivating and controlling workers' (Wilton 2011: 3); 'HRM can be considered as the set of the processes involved in managing people in organizations' (Armstrong 2007: 3). Schein (1978) in his HR planning and developing model links organizational and individual perspectives and explicitly refers to recruiting and selection, training and development, work opportunities and feedback, promotion, supervision and coaching, career counselling, organizational rewards as (matching) processes between individual and organizational needs and expectations. Commonly accepted HRM processes are recruiting, developing, appraising, awarding and releasing.

2.6.2 HRM INFRASTRUCTURE

'A human resource information system (HRIS) is a system used to acquire, store, manipulate, analyze, retrieve, and distribute pertinent information about an organization's human resources' (Tannenbaum 1990). Broderick and Bourdreau (1992) define human resource information systems as 'the composite of data bases, computer applications, and hardware and software that are used to collect/record, store, manage, deliver, present, and manipulate data for Human Resources (HR)' (Kossek et al. 1994: 135). Finally, organizational capital refers to 'institutionalized knowledge and codified experience stored in databases, routines, patents, manuals, structures, and the like' (Youndt et al. 2004: 338).

2.7 Roles and Organization of the HRM System

2.7.1 HRM ROLES

Scholars have mapped out the roles that need to be performed by the HRM system. These include the model of HR power and intervention (Legge 1978), building site analogy (Tyson and Fell 1986) and the strategic/tactical model (Storey 1992). The business partner model (Ulrich 1997) was further developed by Ulrich and Brockbank (2005). They describe the role of the HR managers/ experts as strategic partner, functional expert, employee advocate, human capital developer and HR leader, as summarized in Table 2.6.

It is now commonly accepted that expectations towards HRM are changing, as organizations are striving to make the HR leaner and more 'strategic' (Francis/Keegan 2006; see also Mohrman/ Lawler 1997; Whittaker/Marchington 2003). Generally, HRM takes on a more strategic role in organizations and reduces the time spent on administrative and regulatory HR activities (Mohrman/Lawler 1997). The idea that HR managers take on strategic roles is not new of course (see, for example, Legge 1978), but has recently gained widespread support in the HR literature and is increasingly coupled with recommendations for widespread changes in how HRM is designed in general. Recent studies suggest that devolving HRM tasks to line managers is both increasingly common and not without problems (Francis/Keegan 2006; Hope-Hailey et al. 2005).

Table 2.6   HR functional roles

Strategic partner	Partnering with line managers, help them to reach goals, provide advice, contribute to and manage change
Functional expert	Applying the body of HRM professional knowledge
Employee advocate	Champion for employees, caring for employees, communicating with them, representing their concerns to senior management
Human capital developer	Developing the workforce for the future, matching individual goals with organizational goals
HR leader	Leading HRM, developing the HR function, implementing HR initiatives

Source: Ulrich/Brockbank 2005.

2.7.2 DEVOLUTION OF HR RESPONSIBILITIES

Ulrich (1997) explicitly expresses that HRM is also the responsibility of line managers and seeks to clarify responsibility shared between HR department, line managers and other parties such as, for example, consultants. HRM is not only the responsibility of the HR department or the HR manager, but as Guest (1987) argued, the line managers play an important role in the HRM processes. The division of HR responsibilities between line managers and HR managers is an important aspect (Brewster et al. 1997; Schuler 1990) when considering the organizational design of the HRM organization.

The devolution of HR responsibilities to the line managers has long been analysed in HRM and general management literatures (Child/Partridge 1982; McConville 2006; Poole/Jenkins 1997). Some scholars go so far as to define the devolution of HRM responsibilities beyond the HR department, to the line as a constituting factor of modern HRM (Kirkpatrick 1992; Legge 2005; Ulrich/Brockbank 2005). Other scholars indicate that line managers have long been involved in HRM (Poole/Jenkins 1997).

Line managers are definitely considered as key players in the delivery and implementation of employment policies (McGovern et al. 1997). Hutchinson and Purcell (2003) point out the important role line managers play in HRM acting as a vital link between the policies developed by the HR department and the employees. They stress that the line managers therefore have a central influence on employees' performance. But diversity prevails in how line manager involvement in HRM takes place, especially when international studies are considered (CIPD 2007; Larsen/Brewster 2003; Mayrhofer et al. 2011; Morley et al. 2006).

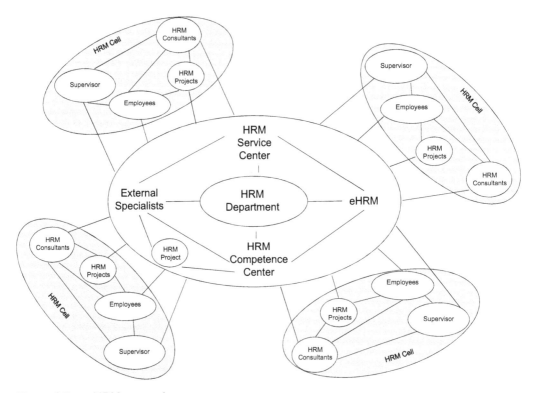

Figure 2.7   HRM network
Source: Adapted from Zaugg 2009: 349.

2.7.3 HRM ORGANIZATION

Brandl et al. (2012) differentiate three ways of organizing the HRM organization, into classic, neo-classic and modern.

Classic organizational design of the HRM system: The HRM tasks are precisely formulated and centralized in the HR department. The major role of the HR department is to set rules for HRM delivery and to administrate the HRM processes. The role of the line manager is to follow the HR rules set out by the HR department. While the HR department has specialized knowledge, line managers require no specialist knowledge in HRM. Empirical studies suggest that this organizational design of the HRM function is very common in practice.

Neo-classic organizational design of the HRM system: HRM tasks are considered more holistically. The HR department's relation to top management is important to support strategy and develop HRM solutions suitable for the organization. The devolution of HRM to line managers is necessary, as line managers as direct supervisors understand the needs of the employees. This creates a mutual supportive relationship between line managers and the HR department, where HRM specialists support line managers in their delivery of HRM.

Modern organizational design of the HRM system: The HRM organization is decentralized, flexible and non-linear. HRM tasks are varied and HRM is a task of all managers, employees take HRM responsibility for themselves. HRM topics are integrated in strategy. These HRM organizations can be found in highly complex and dynamic environments, and the organization is networked and has flat hierarchies. HRM specialists should steer the organization between contradicting forces like short-term and long-term orientation, as well as organizational and individual needs.

2.8 Consequences

This chapter has laid out the development of the field of SHRM, from the universalist approach of best practices for all organizations, to a more contextual understanding of HRM. HRM needs to consider its context to achieve long-term viability.

It is relevant for the remainder of the book that there should be a general description of the HRM system as derived from the literature presented. This is summarized in Table 2.7.

Table 2.7   Definition of HRM system

DEFINITION: HRM SYSTEM

I understand the HRM system as being structures that emerged from HR related decisions/communications for designing and maintaining the relationships to personnel and other relevant stakeholders in order to support performance and create sustainable development for the company and its stakeholders. The HRM system's internal structures include HRM strategies, goals, roles, organization, processes and infrastructure. The HRM system is dependent on its context. Context dimensions are the social, the content related, and the time related context.

Table 2.8   Summary: HRM context and structures

HRM system	
Context of the HRM system	
Social context/stakeholders	For the HRM system particular social stakeholders are for example HR managers/experts, CEO, top management, middle management, employees and particular employee groups, potential employees, competitive employers, education/training institutions, government, work councils, unions, etc.
Content-related context	These are specific contextual factors for example size, structure, culture strategy of organization, specific of industries or markets, demand for sustainable development, relation to other functions/sub systems of the company.
Time-related context	History (historical heritage) and future expectations, for example, regarding developments in the market.
Internal structures of the HRM system	
HRM strategy	HR strategy is a pattern of strategic choices.
HRM goals/objectives	Objective of the HRM system is to support performance, and in the long run, sustain the existence of the organization and ensure its sustainable development by providing a viable HRM system and by ensuring adequately qualified personnel as members of the organization.
HRM roles	HRM roles are carried out by HR managers/experts in co-operation with top management and line managers/expert pool managers.
HRM organization	Patterns of interplay between the HRM roles ranging from administrative function to networked HRM organization.
HRM processes	HRM processes include recruiting, developing, appraising, rewarding, releasing. The HRM practices include how these processes are delivered, for example, which methods are applied.
HRM infrastructure	HRM related infrastructure such as databases, for example, resource-planning database, competency/knowledge management database.

3

The Project as a Temporary Organization

3.1 Introduction

This chapter introduces different theoretical lenses to observe projects. It discusses the traditional perception of a project as a complex task, and the evolution of its conceptualization into a temporary organization, social system and construction. It differentiates the project from related constructs such as investment, process and programme, and discusses different project types. I close the chapter with the consequences for the research, and summarize my understanding of projects as temporary organizations and social systems, which serves as this book's theoretical lens for understanding projects.

3.2 Theoretical Lenses to Analyse Projects

Different theoretical lenses draw distinctions in the way that projects can be analysed. Each one stresses a certain perspective and thus must neglect other possible perspectives. Over the years, several perspectives on projects have developed (Söderlund 2011; Turner et al. 2010). While projects can be defined in different ways (Hodgson/Cicmil 2006), all project definitions emphasize their temporary character and (relative) uniqueness. Turner and Müller (2003: 1) state that a project has specific features such as:

- Uniqueness: no project before or after will be the same;
- Novel processes: no project before or after will use exactly the same approach;
- Transient: the project has a beginning and an end.

Generally, task related and organizationally related project definitions are differentiated (Andersen 2008). Pollack (2007) refers to this as the hard and the soft paradigm in project management. Gareis (2005) differentiates projects as tasks, as temporary organizations and as social systems. In the following sections, I discuss project definitions based on the following differentiations:

- Project as a complex task;
- Project as a temporary organization;
- Project as a social system.

3.2.1 PROJECT AS COMPLEX TASK

Traditionally, projects are defined as unique, complex tasks, whereby complexity is defined as technical complexity and the relation between its parts. Andersen (2008) states that this is still the prevailing project definition in project management standards (see Table 3.1 below). The project as a task represents a rather traditional and mechanistic paradigm. Many of the classical project definitions stress the role of a project as a production function, just as the earliest definitions of the firm in classical economics (Turner/Müller 2003). A project as a task is characterized by rationality (Borum/Christiansen 1993), represents a Taylorian way of thinking (Turner et al. 2010) and is based on the prevailing perspective before 1950, the so-called 'economic man' (Homo Economicus), who is completely self-seeking, completely rational and completely informed (Andersen 2008: 7).

Typical definitions of a project as a series of tasks are presented in Table 3.1. The definition by Cleland and King (1983)[1] is a classical one. They developed a first theory of project management, which is based on the following premises (Turner et al. 2010):

- The project delivers against objectives of time, cost and scope (functionality), set outside the project;
- Project management methods such as critical path analysis and work break down structure are essential for projects;
- Projects move through a life cycle;
- Project management comprises managing and controlling;
- The project organization is a temporary matrix and resources are drawn from the company.

Thus, the relevant objects of consideration to manage in projects are schedule, cost and scope, represented in the so-called iron triangle (Cleland/King 1983). The iron triangle, also known as the triple constraint, is presented in Figure 3.1, and is considered the basis for traditional project management.

Table 3.1   Definitions of projects as complex tasks

Author	Definition
IPMA (2006: 13)	'A project is a time and cost constrained operation to realize a set of defined deliverables (the scope to fulfill the project's objectives) up to quality standards and requirements'.
PMI (2008: 5)	'Temporary endeavor undertaken to create a unique product, service or result'.
Cleland and King (1983: 70)	'A complex effort to achieve a specific objective within a schedule and budget target, which typically cuts across organizational lines, is unique and is usually not repetitive within the organization'.
Meredith and Mantel (2006: 9)	'A project is a specific, finite task to be accomplished'.
Kerzner (2009: 2)	'A project can be considered to be any series of activities and tasks that: • Have a specific objective to be completed within certain specifications • Have defined start and end dates • Have funding limits (if applicable) • Consume human and nonhuman resources (i.e., money. People, equipment) • Are multifunctional (i.e., cut across several functional lines)'.

---

1   First published 1968.

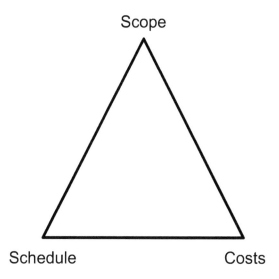

Figure 3.1   Iron triangle

Other objects of consideration relevant for managing projects, such as the project organization and the project personnel are neglected. The project organization is reduced to a specific form of organization, which is the matrix (Cleland/King 1983). Personnel are reduced to human resources required and consumed for the performance of the tasks on the project. The project is seen as protected and in isolation, and the project context is ignored (Engwall 2003).

3.2.2 PROJECT AS A TEMPORARY ORGANIZATION

The perception of projects as temporary organizations is a relatively new one, although Janowicz-Panjaitan et al. (2009) indicate that research on temporary organizations can be traced back to the 1960s, but in organizational theory, temporary organizations received little attention in these early years. A temporary organization is defined as:

> (...) a set of diversely skilled people working together on a complex task over a limited period of time. (Godman, R.A. 1976: 494)

The term 'temporary organization' may be perceived as a broader term than projects, as it not only refers to projects, but encounters different temporary forms of organizations, which include for example: joint ventures, consortia, presidential commissions, court juries, election campaigns, rescue operations and disaster relief operations (Janowicz-Panjaitan et al. 2009). A project may be defined as a temporary organization, but not every temporary organization is a project.

Some project definitions have already referred to the project as an organizational unit, but rather in the notion of a production unit.

> A project is an organization unit dedicated to the attainment of a goal – generally the successful completion of a developmental product on time, within budget, and in conformance with predetermined performance specification. (Gaddis 1959: 89)

Thus, early on, the project is perceived as an organization that focuses on a task and is dissolved after the task is accomplished (for a similar view see Sayles/Chandler 1971). In other words, the project is considered as a temporary organization that is dedicated to a specific goal and at the beginning of its existence is founded with the intention of a limited duration.

In 1995, Rolf Lundin edited a seminal special issue of the *Scandinavian Journal of Management* with the theme 'Temporary organizations and project management',[2] and positioned the project as a temporary organization. This special issue set the ground for defining projects differently, not as tasks but as temporary organizations. Inspired by Godman and Godman (1976), Lundin and Söderholm (1995) offer a theory of the project as a temporary organization. They base it on action theory and institution theory. They differentiate temporary organizations from other kinds of organizational settings such as permanent organizations. For the differentiation of temporary and permanent organizations they use the concepts of time, task, team and transition (Lundin/ Söderholm 1995: 438–439):

- **Time:** Time is crucial. There are time limits for the temporary organization, which have implications for action. The existance of an end date may be the best way of spreading a sense of urgency. In a permanent organizational setting, the focus is on survival rather than time.
- **Task:** A temporary organization is dependent on one or a very limited number of defined tasks (or focuses of attention). The task definitions provide the raison d'être for the temporary organization. The task may be regarded as unique, but could have a more standardized character. Different resources are also needed to define a temporary organization. In one sense, both task and time are constituted by resource allocations, for example, economic and material resources.
- **Team:** The team forms around the task at hand and the time available, thus focusing on individuals both as resources and as bearers of such things as conceptions and attitudes.
- **Transition:** Temporary organizations are created in order to fulfil a special purpose. This purpose also contains an element of change. The temporary organization is the means for achieving it.

To better understand the temporary organization, it can be compared with the permanent organization, as shown in Table 3.2. Packendorff (1995: 215) defines the temporary organization more specifically:

- (...) a deliberately created structure aimed at evoking a unique process or completing a unique product;
- Has a predetermined date or time-related conditional state when the organization is supposed to cease to exist;
- Has clearly stated performance goals;
- Is so complex in terms of roles and number of roles that it requires managerial skills and methods.

---

2   The perception of projects as temporary organizations is often related to the Scandinavian School of Project Studies (Sahlin-Andersson/Söderholm 2002). In 1994 the International Research Network on Organizing by Projects (IRNOP) was established to spread the perception of projects as temporary organizations. The network performs a bi-annual conference with a growing community. As a further indication of the increasing importance of the perception of projects as temporary organizations, a special interest group on project organizing was established in 2009, with a standing track within the annual meeting of the European Academy of Management (EURAM).

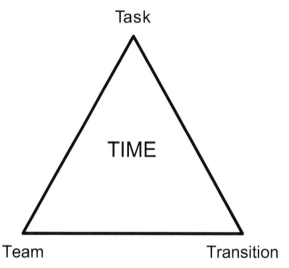

Figure 3.2   Basic concepts in the theory of temporary organizations
Source: Lundin/Söderholm 1995: 451.

Packendorff (1995) suggests that a temporary organization such as a project must have a certain complexity and scope that needs to be managed, otherwise it is not a project. Uncertainty is inherent to projects, as projects are dynamic and complex (Cicmil et al. 2009). Thus, projects are subject to uncertainty, create a need for integration and are performed as subject to urgency (Turner/Müller 2003). The PRINCE2 project management standard (OGC 2009) offers a definition that emphasizes the organizational character of the project and points out that the project creates benefits for the permanent organization, as it follows an agreed Business Case.

Table 3.2   Comparing the temporary project with the permanent organization

	Project	Permanent organization
Goal structure	Only one main task	A broad set of goals
Time dimension	Delimited time	Unlimited times, eternal, continuous
Boundaries	Given by the task	Legal boundaries
Uniqueness	Unique: Experimenting, piloting in order to create competitive advantage for the company's future	Repetitiveness of daily business
Uncertainty	Risk management as project management function	Predictable daily business
Actors	Team members chosen especially for the task Cross functional/corporate/ inter corporate co-operation as challenge	Members with different but permanent functions
Control	By way of a plan and subsequent revisions	By annual statements and/or evaluation

Source: Adapted from Heitger/Sutter 1990; Lundin/Steinthórsson 2003: 245.

Table 3.3   Definitions of a project as a temporary organization

Author	Definition
Turner and Müller (2003: 7)	'A project is a temporary organization to which resources are assigned to undertake a unique, novel and transient endeavor managing the inherent uncertainty and need for integration in order to deliver beneficial objectives of change'.
Turner et al. (2010: 14)	'A project is a temporary organization to which resources are assigned to deliver beneficial change'.
OGC (2009: 3)	'A project is a temporary organization that is created for the purpose of delivering one more business products according to an agreed Business Case'.
Andersen (2008: 10)	'A project is a temporary organization, established by its base organization to carry out an assignment on its behalf'.
Gareis (2005: 41)	'A project is a temporary organization for the performance of a relatively unique, short- to medium-term strategically business process of medium or large scope'.

Table 3.4   Differences between the project as a task and the project as an organization

	Project as task	Project as organization
Theoretical foundation	The economic man Engineering, complex system theory	Agency theory Organizational theories
Main focus	Execute the defined task	Value creation
Project success	Keep to iron triangle, time, cost and scope (quality)	Accomplish the mission and achieve the goals
The nature of the goals	Fixed, determined at the start, revolutionary delivery	Moving targets, evolutionary development
Planning	Done at start, activity oriented	Global plan at start, rolling-wave planning, milestone oriented
Time schedule	Delivery as quickly as possible	Entrainment; deliveries that fit the receiving organization's processes
Kind of organization	Action oriented	Action and politically oriented
Leadership style	Transactional leadership	Transformational leadership
Controlling	Controlling time, cost, quality and earned value analysis	Socialization, embracing a holistic view on delivering the project as expected

Source: Adapted from Andersen 2008: 49.

Gareis (2005) explicitly states that projects are temporary organizations, in addition to permanent structures of an organization (e.g., profit centre, department). Similarly, Andersen (2008) draws a distinction between project and the permanent organization and then sets them in relation. Andersen (2008), based on Agency Theory, stresses the assignment so that the project is considered as an agency of the project-oriented organization. Gareis (2005) defines a project as a temporary organization to perform a business process with certain characteristics. These process characteristics comprise relatively unique, short to mid-term strategic business processes of medium or large scope. According to the organizational strategy Managing by Projects, not all task work should be organized as a project (Gareis/ Stummer 2008).

Table 3.3 shows definitions of a project as a temporary organization. What these definitions have in common is that the project is considered more comprehensively and in its specific context. These definitions emphasise the importance of the project organization and value creation, rather than the fulfilment of a predefined task. Andersen (2008) compares the project as task and the project as organization (see Table 3.4).

The perception of projects as temporary organizations has started to become the prevailing definition amongst scholars. The importance of the context for understanding the project has become of increasing relevance in project management. The traditional triple constraint perspective of the project as a task is considered as almost irrelevant to project success, but the benefits that stakeholders receive from a project are the measure for project success (Shenhar/Dvir 2007). The relevance of the relation of a project to its contexts is a perception that becomes even clearer when the project is perceived as a social system.

3.2.3 PROJECT AS SOCIAL SYSTEM

There has been a long tradition in project management to perceive projects as systems, which is strongly related with the task definition of a project, as I discussed earlier. It also strongly relates to the engineering field, where projects and project management were introduced during the 1960s (Morris 1997). A system is defined as:

> (...) an organized or complex whole; an assemblage or combination of things or parts forming a complex or unitary whole. (Cleland/King 1983: 17)

> (...) a set of interrelated components that accepts inputs and produces outputs in a purposeful manner. (Meredith/Mantel 2006: 120)

In this mechanistic way, projects are perceived as machines, in the notion of von Foerster's (1985) trivial machines, for which a particular input produces the expected output in a linear way. See Figure 3.3.

Cleland and King (1983) outline a theory of project management based on an understanding of the project as a technical system. In essence, Cleland and King's theory suggests that a project is a complex system to be optimized. In contrast to perceiving projects as complex technical systems, it is a relatively new approach to perceive projects as social systems based on the Social Systems Theory by Niklas Luhmann (1995). Table 3.5 shows the different paradigms in managing technical systems in comparison to social systems.

As outlined in the appendix, Luhmann (1995) differentiates different types of systems, such as machines, organisms, social systems and psychic systems. Based on complexity, social systems are further differentiated into interactions, organizations and societies. Interaction represents the less complex and society the most complex social system. Gareis (2005) adds the differentiation of the organization into project or programme as temporary organizations, and companies as permanent organizations, see Figure 3.4.

Figure 3.3   Trivial machine: Input–system–output

Table 3.5   Management of technical systems versus social systems

Technical system	Social system
Predictable	Not predictable
Not depending on the contexts	Depending on the contexts
Possible to influence directly	Not possible to influence directly
Results of influence are clear	Results of influence are unclear
Application of standards	Allowance of contradictions

Source: Adapted from Kasper 1990: 210.

In contrast to technical systems, projects can be perceived as social systems that are socially constructed. A project is a temporary organization and thus can be perceived as a social system (Gareis 2005: 40). A project as a social system clearly differentiates itself from its environments and has relations to these environments. A project requires boundaries (Sahlin-Andersson/Söderholm 2002). What is part of a project or not part is a social construction (Gareis 2005). Gareis and Stummer (2008) differentiate the internal project structures, the environment of the project and the relationships of the project to the contexts.

The internal project structures comprise: objectives, objects of consideration, strategies, scope, schedule, resources, costs, income, risks, personnel, organization, culture and infrastructure (Gareis et al. 2013). The project context comprises (Gareis et al. 2013):

- Pre-project and post-project phases;
- Relationships to project stakeholders;
- Relationships to other projects and to company strategies;
- Investment initiated by the project.

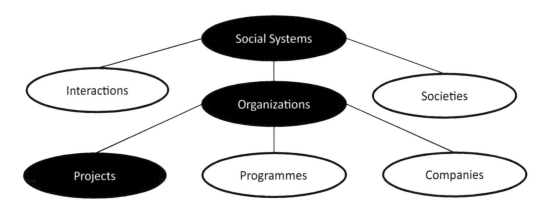

Figure 3.4   The project as a social system
Source: Gareis 2005: 40.

Projects need to be considered in their contexts. Bakker (2010) points to the importance of the organizational and social context to explain project behaviour. A project is embedded in its contexts and needs to make sense of its contexts to deliver the purpose, or why it was created (Engwall 2003; Sahlin-Andersson/Söderholm 2002). Following on from this, the characteristics of a project as a social system are described (Heitger/Sutter 1990: 138):

- The project has to relate itself to many different project stakeholders;
- Normally, there is a high diversity and lack of clarity of expectations of the project stakeholders towards the project;
- Predictability of 'what happens, if' is rather low, or in other words, uncertainty and risk are rather high;
- Concrete definition of project success is difficult and determined from the specific point of view from the particular project stakeholder.

Engwall (2003) draws similar conclusions. He states: 'no project is an island', but suggests that any project is dependent on events and expectations outside the project. In contrast to the traditional view of projects in isolation, he extends the perspective of the context using a time dimension as well as the organizational context. Projects are considered as history dependent and organizationally embedded, as shown in Figure 3.5. The construction of project boundaries comprises different perspectives, which also relate to each other.

The project as a temporary organization may also be perceived as a social system. The systemic perception provides an additional lens that stresses the importance of the project contexts to understand the project. As outlined before, the project as a social system needs to differentiate itself from its surroundings, but at the same time is dependent on its contexts and needs to design relationships to the social environments (stakeholders) as part of their social context (Luhmann 1995). In taking a systemic-constructivist perspective to construct project boundaries, we may again differentiate a time-, a social- and a content-related context dimension (Gareis 2005; Huemann 2002).

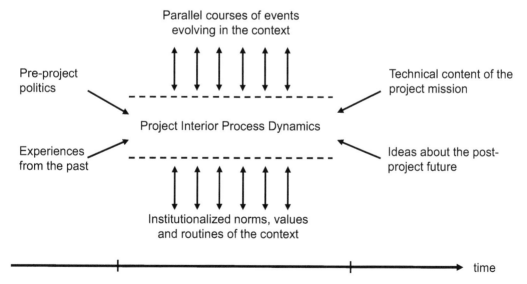

Figure 3.5   No project is an island
Source: Engwall 2003: 805.

A project has a planned start and end date. The time-related project context therefore comprises the pre-project and the post-project phase. Before the project, there is the pre-project phase, during which some decisions are already made, which may influence the project very strongly – for instance, the selection of central suppliers to work with. After the project is closed down, there is the post-project phase. There are particular expectations in the pre as well as the post project phase that influence the project. As projects are temporary, time is of central importance, indicating a start and a planned end of a project. As time for organizations is especially limited and not open ended or eternal, the time dimension influences the behaviour on the project (Lindkvist 1998), as deadlines and milestones tend to increase the pace and sense of urgency.

The content-related perspective comprises the boundaries of the contents: the task, or more precisely the business process that is fulfilled by the project. There are objectives to be fulfilled within the project, as well as other objectives like so called non-objectives, which can be excluded from the project. The content-related context comprises the contribution to the investor organization's strategy, the contribution to the business case, and the relation to other projects.

The social context comprises relevant social environments, more commonly labeled as project stakeholders, as shown in Figure 3.6. Social environments can be differentiated into project external and project internal social environments. Project external environments are for instance clients, users, suppliers, project partners, competitors, and so on. Internal project environments comprise the project personnel such as the project manager, the project team members and the project owner. It is important to differentiate who becomes a member of the project organization and in which role, and who remains in the social environment. By differentiating the project from its social context, it also becomes clear that designing relations to relevant environments (project stakeholders) becomes important.

The project manager, project team members and project owner are considered as part of the internal social environment of a project. The relationships between the project and these players need to be explicitly managed and this is closely related to project HRM, described later in this book.

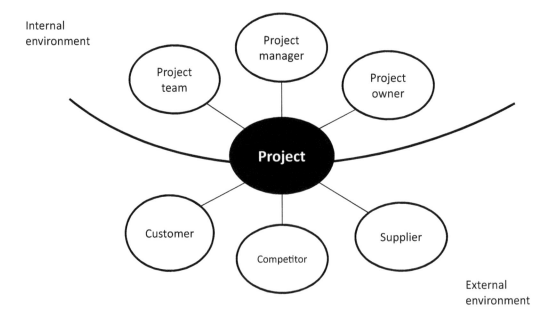

Figure 3.6   Social environments/stakeholders of a project

The project boundaries might change in the course of the project. Similarly, Sahlin-Andersson and Söderholm (2002: 243) state that project boundaries do not appear automatically when a project is formed, they need to be created. As projects are dynamic, these project boundaries are not set in stone once and for all, but can change during the course of the project. Thus, the project boundaries need to be actively managed during the course of the project. A project is a construction to be differentiated from its context, but determined and closely related to its contexts, as *no project is an island* (Engwall 2003).

3.3 Differentiating from and Relating Projects to other Constructs

Although there is an emerging consensus on perceiving projects as temporary organizations in the project management research community, still no shared understanding on the term project exists. To provide a clearer perception on this term, I offer a differentiation from other related constructs, such as investment, process and programme.

3.3.1 PROJECT AND INVESTMENT

Investments are long-term employment of capital in assets, for example in buildings and machinery, but also in customer relationships, products, organization or in personnel. Thus, investments can be customer relationship related, product, and/or market related, infrastructure related, organizational related and personnel related. An investment can be initiated by a project, which is then followed by the utilization of the investment object created by the project; finally the investment life cycle ends with de-investment after the end of the utilization of the object (Gareis 2005; Gareis et al. 2013). Figure 3.7 illustrates this relationship.

Project definitions often refer to beneficial change as the purpose for the project (e.g., Turner/Müller 2003). The change perspective relates the project to the investment life cycle, which is initialized by the project. Lundin and Söderholm (1995) suggest that projects are means for organizing change. But the relation between project and change is widely confused. The last sentence in the quote below is misleading, as the project is dissolved at the project end.

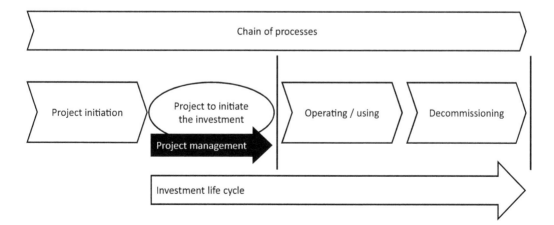

Figure 3.7   Investment and project
Source: Gareis et al. 2013: 31.

This purpose also contains an element of change. Some change is needed, and the temporary organization is the means for achieving it. There is an expectation that there should be a qualitative difference in the temporary organization 'before' and 'after'. (Lundin/Söderholm 1995: 439)

Nevertheless, change may relate to the project itself or to a different social system for which the change is organized by the project (Gareis/Huemann 2010). Projects are complex and dynamic, thus change is inherent and is managed within the project through project controlling. On the other hand, change may relate to a different social system. When the project is considered as a case of a new product development, the temporary project will be dissolved when the project objectives are fulfilled. But the company for which the new product was developed needs to adapt itself, for instance, to sell the product to new future markets. So in this case, the project dissolves, but the social system which has to change is the company for which the project was performed.

Projects can segment the investment life cycle. An example of how an investment life cycle is segmented is a conception project followed by a project to implement the concept, or a bid project followed by a contract project, if the bid has been won. Thus, the segmentation of an investment typically leads to a chain of projects. But not all parts of the investment life cycle are required to be performed in projects. Figure 3.8 shows the typical projects within a product investment, an infrastructure investment and a customer relationship investment (Gareis 2005).

Table 3.6   A basic project management life cycle

Stage	Name	Process	Outputs
Germination	Concept	• Identify opportunity for performance • Diagnose problem	• Initial options • Benefits map • Commit resources to feasibility • Estimates ±50%
Incubation	Feasibility	• Develop proposals • Gather information • Conduct feasibility	• Functional design • Commit resources to design • Estimates ±20%
Growth	Design	• Develop design • Estimate costs and returns • Assess viability • Obtain funding	• Systems design • Money and resources for implementation • Estimates ±10%
Maturity	Execution	• Do detail design • Baseline estimates • Do work • Control progress	• Effective completion • Facility ready for commissioning • Estimates ±5%
Metamorphosis	Close-out	• Finish work • Commission facility • Obtain benefit • Disband team • Review achievement	• Facility delivering benefit • Satisfied team • Data for future projects

Source: Turner et al. 2010: 206.

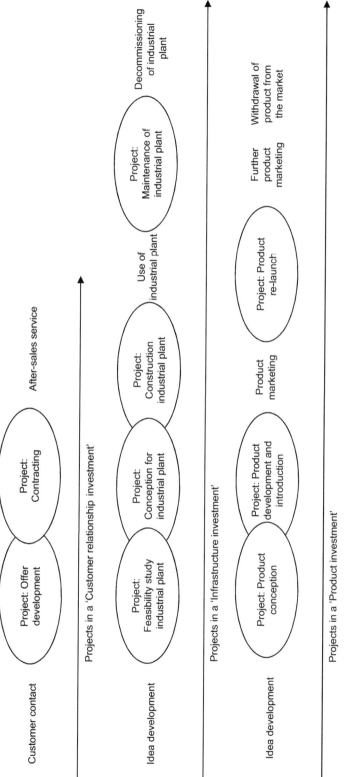

Figure 3.8 **Segmentation of investments by projects**

Source: Gareis 2005: 50.

A related perspective is provided by project (management) life cycle models, such as in Table 3.6 (Turner et al. 2010). Project life cycle models differentiate between phases or stages, but also consider the whole or a huge part of the investment as a project. In extreme cases the missing differentiation between projects and investment then leads to the notion of 20–30-year 'projects', especially when the maintenance of the object is also included. While in literature and in practice the project and the investment are often not adequately differentiated, I do make this distinction.

3.3.2 PROJECT AND PROCESS

A business process is a defined organizational work flow, conducted by several roles and/or organizational units. A process consists of a cluster of tasks, has input-output relations, has a distinct start and end event, and defined objectives and results. Scholars suggest that many companies are challenged to link project and business processes (Gann/Salter 2000). Gareis and Stummer (2008) investigate the relation between processes and projects and define different types of processes based on process characteristics. They argue that the process is the basis for how an organization is selected to perform the process. Gareis (2005) differentiates between process types and relates these to how organizations prepare to perform the process, as shown in Figure 3.9.

    Repetitive processes of small to medium scope, with a rather short duration and one or a few contributing organizational units, are performed by the permanent organization. Typical examples are the recruiting of an employee, the opening of an account, the payment of an invoice, and so on, or relatively unique processes of medium to large scope, where some contributing organizational units are performed by a project. Typical projects are the organization of an event, upgrade of an IT solution, development of a new product, preparation of bid, performance of a feasibility study or the production of a movie (Gareis 2005).

Process characteristic	Attribute		
Frequency	often	once	once
Scope	small-medium	medium-large	large
Importance	low	medium-high	high
Duration	short	short-medium	medium-long
Resources	few	some	many
Costs	low-medium	medium-high	high
Number of organizations	few	several-many	many

Type of organization	Permanent organization	Project	Program

Figure 3.9   Adequate organizations for different process types
Source: Gareis 2005: 22.

Table 3.7 **Programme definitions**

Author	Definition
OGC (2007: 6)	'Programs, (…) initiate, monitor and align the projects and related activities that are needed to create new products or service capabilities, or to effect changes in business operations'.
PMI (2008: 1)	'A program is a group of related projects managed in a co-ordinated way to obtain benefits and control not available from managing them individually'.
IPMA (2006: 13)	'A program is set up to achieve a strategic goal. A program consists of a set of related projects and required organizational changes to reach a strategic goal and to achieve the defined business benefits'.
Gareis (2005: 357)	'A program is a social construct. It is used as a temporary organization to fulfill a unique and business process of large scope'.

3.3.3 PROJECT AND PROGRAMME

As indicated in Figure 3.9, projects may also be differentiated from programmes. Both projects as well as programmes are temporary organizations, but programmes are based on processes with larger scope, involve more organizational units and are consequently more socially complex. Programmes usually have a longer duration, a higher budget and higher risk in comparison to projects. Programmes are strategically more important. Typical programmes are the development of a new product family, implementing an enterprise resource planning system in an organization, a merger or the reorganization of a holding. As a programme is a relatively new concept, there is still a lack in understanding and theoretical underpinning. In literature, programmes are mostly defined as consisting of several projects and related tasks aimed at reaching a common goal. Table 3.7 provides an overview of programme definitions found in literature.

3.4 Project Types

3.4.1 THE PURPOSE OF DIFFERENTIATING PROJECT TYPES

Organizations have several reasons for differentiating projects into different project types (Gareis 2005; Turner et al. 2010):

- Strategic alignment: to assign priority for projects within their investment portfolio, track the efficacy of their investment in projects, create strategic visibility;
- Promote the project management approach: to decide that the process is done as a project, differentiate projects from operations, provide a common language for project management within the organization;
- Create project capabilities: to develop project type specific standards, assign appropriate project personnel;
- Give orientation to the project organization.

To differentiate projects into different types allows specific challenges and potentials to be analysed. Literature on project types has mostly focused on tailoring project management practice to suit the specific project type (Shenhar/Dvir 2007).

3.4.2 GENERAL MODELS

For instance, Shenhar and Dvir (2007) suggest a categorization based on the familiarity of the technology, and differentiate four project types:

1. Low technology: well-known mature technology.
2. Medium technology: adaptations of familiar technology.
3. High technology: first use of new technology.
4. Super-high technology: radical new developments.

A well-known project typology (Andersen 2008; Turner 2009) is presented in Figure 3.10. The differentiation is based on how well known the goals of the project are, and how well known the process/method to achieve the goals are. So four project types are defined:

*   **Type 1 projects:** Both goals as well as methods/process for achieving the project goals are well defined. A typical example is an engineering project, the project team can move quickly into the planning of the project. These are known as earth projects, built on a solid foundation.
*   **Type 2 projects:** Goals are well defined, but the methods/process for how to achieve them are not. A typical project can be found in product development, when the functionalities of the product are defined but, like goals, the process/methods for how to achieve them are not. These are labelled water projects.

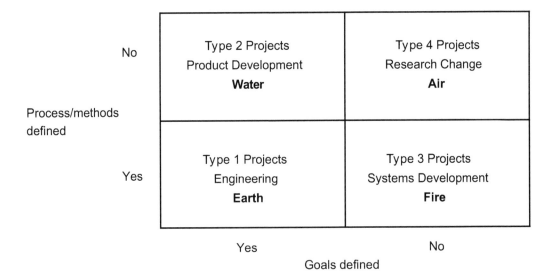

Figure 3.10   Goals and process matrix
Source: Adapted from Andersen 2008; Turner 2009.

- **Type 3 projects:** The project goals are poorly defined, but the methods/process are well defined. A typical example is an information system development project. These projects are labelled fire projects.
- **Type 4 projects:** Both goals as well as methods/process to achieve the project goals are not well defined. Typical examples are research or change projects. These are labelled air projects.

3.4.3 DIFFERENTIATION CRITERIA

An empirical study identified that project-oriented organizations categorize their projects in different ways. Attributes used include (Crawford 2005):

- Application area/product of project;
- Stage of life cycle;
- Stand-alone or grouped;
- Strategic importance;
- Strategic driver;
- Geography;
- Project scope;
- Project timing;
- Uncertainty, ambiguity, familiarity;
- Risk;
- Complexity;
- Customer/supplier relations;
- Ownership/funding;
- Contractual issues.

Commonly used differentiation criteria are industry, location, ownership, duration and relation to business process (Andersen 2008; Crawford 2005; Turner et al. 2010). Table 3.8 offers a categorization of project types.

Table 3.8   Project types

Criterion for differentiation	Project type
Industry	Construction, engineering, IT, pharmaceutical, non-profit organizations
Investment type	Customer relations (contracts), products and markets, infrastructure, personnel, organization
Investment phase	Study, conception, realization, re-launch, or maintenance
Location	National, international
Degree of repetition	Unique, repetitive
Customer	Internal customer, external customer
Duration	Short-, medium-, long-term
Relation to business process	Primary, secondary, tertiary process

Source: Gareis 2005.

Table 3.9   Projects by industry type

Sector	Industry
Engineering and construction	Building
	Infrastructure
	Process plant
	Defence
	Aerospace
	Environmental, waste, sewerage
Information and telecommunications	E-commerce
	Information technology
	Information systems
	Telecommunications
Services	Arts, entertainment, broadcasting
	Recreation and sport
	Business and consulting
	Education and training
	Financial services and insurance
	Health and social services
	International development
Industrial	Automotive
	Electronics
	Manufacturing
	Chemicals and pharmaceuticals
	Food
	Research and development

Source: Adapted from Turner et al. 2010.

Differentiation by industry: Table 3.9 provides an overview of industries that perform projects. There is obviously a strong correlation between the industry and the technology applied. The construction industry tends to do construction projects. In some industries such as the defence industry, the pharmaceutical industry, or research and development, a range of types of projects is performed. However, there are specific features of the projects particular to the industry, such as specific technology and specific markets.

Differentiation by location: National and international projects can be differentiated (Gareis 2005). Turner (2009) further differentiates national and international projects. For international projects, it is necessary to consider if the customer is in their home territory and the contractor is foreign, or if the contractor is in their home territory and the customer foreign, or if both are foreign to the country where the project is taking place. Specific challenges for managing international projects exist, such as in Gareis (2005). There are specific requirements for the project personnel, such as competencies like language, cultural awareness or mobility of project personnel.

Differentiation by investment type: A differentiation of projects according to their contents an indication of the type of investment that the project is related to. Gareis (2005) differentiates customer relations-related projects, which are contract projects, versus product and market-related projects, infrastructure-related projects, and personnel and organization-related projects.

Differentiation by investment phase: This entails differentiation of projects according to the investment phase to which they are contributing. It provides project types such as feasibility study, conception, realization and re-launch projects. This perception is closely linked to the notion that projects segment investments. In combination with the type of investment, for example, in a customer-related investment, we may differentiate bid projects and contracting projects.

Differentiation by degree of repetition: This relates to the nature of projects that are relatively unique. There is a continuum of unique projects to repetitive projects. The performance of a contracting project by a constructing company is a repetitive project, since all of their projects have fundamentally the same processes. Nevertheless, it is worthwhile using a project, as the customer is always different, the location is always different, and so on. In repetitive projects, project performance takes a rather routine character. Very unique projects are based on processes that are not known by the company and are one-and-only types. A specific form of a unique project is a pilot project (Gareis 2005). A project typology based on the level of uniqueness, and the extent to which the work of the project is familiar, classifies projects as runners, repeaters, strangers and aliens (Turner et al. 2010), as demonstrated below:

- Runners: These are very familiar projects, done repeatedly. Thus, standard processes can be applied;
- Repeaters: The organization has run projects quite similar to these in the past. Most of the parts are known to the organization, some parts of the project are new. But generally, there is knowledge within the organization on which the project can draw;
- Strangers: The organization has never done a project like this before. There are familiar parts, but the overall project is novel;
- Aliens: The organization has never done anything like this before. There is high risk and uncertainty.

Differentiation by customer: Projects can be differentiated based on the relationship with the customer, or whether a customer is internal or external to the company, or based on internal versus external projects (Gareis 2005). Typical internal projects are organizational development, product development, and so on. In external projects (contracting projects), the customer external to the company assigns the company to perform a service or deliver a product against a payment. It is important to stress that the assignment needs to have a certain scope and complexity to be performed in project form.

Differentiation by duration: Projects can be differentiated based on the project duration into short-term, medium-term and long-term projects (see Table 3.10). What is short-term, medium-term, and long-term is relative to the relation of the investment type. In product development, projects tend to become shorter and shorter, and short-term projects of 6–12 weeks are quite common. Infrastructure projects are generally considered to have a longer duration. Long-term projects have a duration of more than one year up to around three years.

Table 3.10   Perception of short-, medium- and long-term

	Gareis (2005)	Turner et al. (2010)	Cook-Davis (2000)
Short-term project	6–12 weeks	A couple of months	Less than one year
Medium-term project	3–6 months	Between a couple of months and one year	Two to three years
Long-term project	7–12 months*	More than one year	More than three years

Note: *With a few exceptions, for example, infrastructure projects tend to be longer.

Differentiation by relation to business process: Project types may be differentiated according to the business processes of the company to which they are linked (Gareis/Stummer 2008). Internal projects are performed to carry out support for business processes, which are, for example, organizational development, personal development and product development. External projects are performed to carry out primary processes, such as delivering products and services to external customers.

3.5 Consequences

In this chapter, I have introduced different theoretical perceptions on a project. I differentiated the perspectives of project as a task, project as a temporary organization and project as a social system. Despite projects being distinct temporary organizations and social systems, they are dependent on the project-oriented organization(s) by which they were created. Their purpose serves this higher social system or several higher systems. The purpose of the project is the contribution to an investment process, which may be, for example, a product investment or an infrastructure investment. A project as a social system is a construction that needs to be differentiated from its context, but is determined by and closely related to its context. The project boundaries are formed in a negotiation process at the project start, and must be re-negotiated during the course of the project. By these boundaries, the project reproduces itself as a distinct social system and distinguishes itself from its context and from the project-oriented organization by which it was created.

The purpose of the project is to perform a business process for which the project is organized. The business process is characterized by criteria such as uniqueness, scope and strategic importance. Projects are explicitly created to carry out business processes that cannot be carried out adequately in the permanent line organization. The project needs to draw on different competencies of personnel, who may be located in different organizational units of the company or even in different companies. To enable this co-operation, the project is established. The project delivers a tangible or intangible product, created by the members of the project in interaction with other relevant project stakeholders.

Table 3.11 shows the basic working definition of a project as a temporary organization and a temporary social system.

The specifics of the perceptions of a project as a temporary organization are summarized in Table 3.12.

The focus of this chapter was the project, which is one of the 'constituting' features of the project-oriented organization. In the next chapter, I will turn to the project-oriented organization.

Table 3.11   Definition: Project

> **DEFINITION: PROJECT**
> A project is a temporary organization for the performance of a relatively unique, short- to medium-term, strategically important business process of medium or large scope. A project is a temporary social system distinct and related to its time, content related and social context.

Table 3.12   Specifics of a project as a temporary organization

Project as a temporary organization	
Time	• Temporary, duration is planned at the beginning of project and the end is inherent in the project start • Short- to medium-term orientation • Temporality creates urgency, rhythm driven by project end date and milestones
Business process	• Relatively unique • Short- to medium-term • Strategically important • Medium or large scope • High result orientation to achieve project objectives, as this is the raison d'être of the project • Contribution to project result (even when intangible as a feasibility study) is visible for the project personnel
Personnel	• Personnel are selected based on the competency requirements of the project • Often needed for different competencies to reach project objectives • Personnel may even be integrated from external organizations, for example partners, suppliers and customers
Team	• Team structures are central to a project • Different teams within one project possible • Temporary teams
Change	• Dynamic, as projects organize change • Change object is the project itself • Change object is also the organization(s) for whom the project is delivered
Identity	• Temporary, needs to be created for the specific project • Relatively autonomous but embedded in the context • May be influenced by several organizations

The Project-Oriented Organization

4

4.1 Introduction

In this chapter, I discuss the organization that is equipped to conduct projects, the project-oriented organization. The chapter draws on early management theories to clarify the origins of the project-oriented organization and then provides an overview on the different approaches to the organization, which performs projects as a central option of organizing business processes. I describe the project-oriented organization with its specific strategy, structures and culture.

To deal with high diversity due to the temporary character of projects, project-oriented organizations also apply specific permanent structures, such as a Project Portfolio Group (PPG) and a Project Management Office (PMO). These specific permanent structures are discussed in this chapter. In addition, as personnel may be organized in expert pools rather than in functional departments, the difference between expert pool and traditional department is interpreted.

I suggest a definition of the project-oriented organization and use its specific features to describe the organization to which the HRM system will be related in the following chapters.

4.2 Origins in Organization and Management Theory

It has been widely claimed that there is a paradigm shift in the nature of twenty-first-century organizations towards a post-bureaucratic mode of organizing, with projects as a specific and significant characteristic (Clegg 1990; Whittington et al. 1999). In project management research, the company that carries out projects came to prominence at the beginning of 1990. In management literature there is a somewhat longer tradition of research into this type of organization (Galbraith 1977; Mintzberg 1979; Sayles/Chandler 1971).

Thus (at least) two streams of literature have looked at project-oriented organizations and have analysed the structural and cultural impact on organizations if they apply temporary organizations such as projects and programmes to perform business processes. The origins of the model of the project-oriented organization lay in organization theory and management studies (for an overview see, for example, Artto/Wikström 2005; Davies/Hobday 2005; Morris 1997). Here, I will concentrate on some of the central theories and models in order to theoretically underpin the project-oriented organization.

4.2.1 THE PRODUCTION PROCESS DETERMINES THE ORGANIZATION FORM

A seminal study done by Joan Woodward was based on the premise that industry organizations that design their formal organization structures to fit the type of production technology they are using are likely to be successful. Woodward (1965) suggested that technology, or more specifically the production process required, has an impact on the adequate organization form. In her traditional classification framework, she differentiated organization forms along the criteria production system and volume of output into:

- Unit;
- Small batch;
- Large batch;
- Mass production;
- Continuous process.

Figure 4.1 provides examples of products differentiated according to the volume of output and the adequate organization form for producing it. Unit and small batch production represent bespoke products with the customer, and require production to be in the form of projects (Davies/Hobday 2005: 23; Turner/Keegan 2001). There are specifics of the unit and small batch production which differ to other production systems. In the case of unit or small batch, the product is sold before the product is developed and built, and there is, necessarily, more intensive communication between the task functions as the product is unique and bespoke to the customer (Woodward et al. 1965).

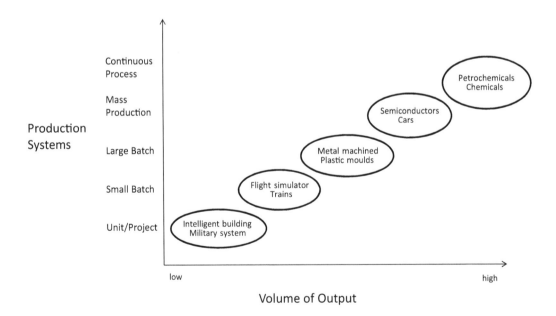

Figure 4.1   Woodward's classification of organization forms
Source: Davies/Hobday 2005: 23.

4.2.2 MINTZBERG'S BASIC TYPES OF ORGANIZATION

While Galbraith (1971) describes a continuum of organization forms, Mintzberg (1983; 1989) suggests different basic types of organizations, which are:

- Entrepreneurial organization: the simple structure;
- Machine organization: the machine bureaucracy;
- Professional organization: the professional bureaucracy;
- Diversified organization: the divisionalized form;
- Innovative organization: the adhocracy.

To differentiate between these basic types, he distinguishes five co-ordinating mechanisms: mutual adjustment, direct supervision, standardization of work processes, standardization of outputs and standardization of worker skills (Mintzberg 1979: 3ff). Later he adds a sixth co-ordination mechanism, the standardization of norms and values (Mintzberg 1983: 294). Table 4.1 provides an overview of the organization forms as suggested by (Mintzberg 1983; 1989). The innovative organization, earlier labelled as adhocracy, is the organization form that sees the project as a central form of organizing. Thus, the adhocracy comes closest to the project-oriented organization, which we will discuss later in more detail.

Mintzberg outlines the innovation power of the adhocracy, which is based on the possibility of creating configurations of experts from different disciplines who work together in projects. Burns and Stalker (1961) suggest that mechanistic forms of management in hierarchical, functional organizations are adequate for stable conditions, while organic forms are better in rapidly changing environments. Projects can be considered as organic forms, where people work together in a flatter structure and more adaptive way in contrast to hierarchical permanent structures (Bennis 1966).

Mintzberg differentiates the adhocracy into the operating adhocracy and the administrative adhocracy. The operating adhocracy solves problems for its clients, thus focusing on contract project work, such as an engineering company building a new wind power farm for an investor. The administrative adhocracy, in contrast, does projects for internal purposes. The organization uses projects for its development work, for example product development, while the production of goods and services for the clients is organized into routine processes. Mintzberg suggests that the adhocracy is an important organization type and states:

> Every one of its characteristics is very much in vogue today: emphasis on expertise, organic structure, project teams, task forces, decentralization of power, matrix structures, sophisticated technical systems, automation, and young organizations. Thus, if the entrepreneurial and machine forms were earlier configurations, and the professional and the diversified forms yesterdays, then innovative is clearly today's. (Mintzberg 1979: 209)

> While the organization forms are described as pure types, the existence of hybrid organizations is also suggested. Such hybrid forms draw on more organizational forms and combine them; for example, for very large multinational firms, there is the divisionalized adhocracy hybrid (Mintzberg 1983).

In line with Mintzberg's differentiation into the operative and the administrative adhocracy, many writers distinguish between organizations that do most of their contractual work in projects, versus organizations where clients' work is done in routine-type processes, while projects take place in the back office to support the functionally-based front office (Lindkvist 2004; Turner/Keegan 2001). The latter are organizations, for example from the banking and insurance industries that have (mainly) routine, primary processes, such as selling a bank account to a customer. But still, the same company may have a need for product development projects or organizational change projects.

Table 4.1   Overview on the basic five types of organization

Original label*	The simple structure	The machine bureaucracy	The professional bureaucracy	The divisionalized form	The adhocracy
Structure	• Simple, informal, flexible, with little staff or middle-line hierarchy • Activities revolving around the chief executive, who controls through direct supervision	• Centralized bureaucracy • Formal procedures, specialized work, sharp division of labour, usually functional groupings, extensive hierarchy • Key is techno structure, standardizing the work • Extensive support staff to reduce uncertainty	• Bureaucratic, yet decentralized; dependent on training to standardize the skills of its many operating professionals • Individual professionals work autonomously, subject to controls of the profession • Wide spans of control over professional work; large support staff to support professionals	• Market-based divisions loosely coup-led together under central administrative headquarter • Divisions run business autonomously, subjected to a performance control system that standardizes outputs • Tendency to drive structures of divisions towards machine organization	• Fluid, organic, selectively decentralized 'adhocracy' • Functional experts deployed in multidisciplinary teams of staff, operators, and managers to carry out innovative projects • Co-ordination by mutual adjustment, encouraged by liaison personnel, integrating managers and matrix structures
Context	• Simply and dynamic environment • Strong leadership, sometimes charismatic, autocratic • Start-up, crisis and turnaround • Small organizations, 'local producer'	• Simple and stable environment • Usually larger, more mature organization • Rationalized work, rationalizing (but not automated) technical system • Common in mass production, mass services, organizations in business of control and safety	• Complex yet stable • Simple technical system • Often but not necessarily service sector	• Market diversity, especially of products and services • Typically for largest and most mature organizations, especially business corporations, but also increasingly for government and other public organizations	• Complex and dynamic environment, including high technology and frequent product changes; short- and long-term projects • Typically young organization, due to bureaucratic pressure with aging • Common in young industries • Two basic types: operating adhocracy for contact project work; administrative adhocracy for own project work

Original label*	The simple structure	The machine bureaucracy	The professional bureaucracy	The divisionalized form	The adhocracy
Strategy	• Often visionary process, broadly deliberate but emergent and flexible in details • Leader positions malleable organization in protected niches	• Strategic programming • Resistance to strategic change • Hence, quantum pattern of change: long periods of stability interrupted by occasional burst of strategic revolution	• Headquarter manages 'corporate' strategy as portfolio of businesses, too • Strategies made by professional judgement and collective choice, some by administrative fiat • Overall strategy very stable, but in detail continually changing	• Many strategies, largely fragmented, but there are forces for cohesion, too • Strategies made by professional judgement and collective	• Strategies evolve by decisions that determine which projects are undertaken • Primary learning process • Largely emergent, evolving through a variety of bottom-up processes • Cycles of convergence and divergence in strategic focus
Advantages	• Responsive, sense of mission	• Efficient, reliable, precise, consistent	• Resolves some problems of machine structures by spreading risk, moving capital, adding and deleting business	• Advantages of democracy and autonomy	• Combines more democracy with less bureaucracy; fashionable structure • Effective at innovation
Challenges	• Vulnerable, restrictive • Danger of imbalance towards strategy or operation	• Obsession with control • Human problems in operating core • Co-ordination problems in administrative centre • Adaptive problems	• Sometimes costly and discouraging innovation • Performance control system risks driving organizations towards unresponsive or irresponsive behaviour	• Problems of co-ordination; reluctance to innovate • Unionization exacerbates problems	• Effectiveness achieved at the price of inefficiency • Human problems of ambiguity and danger of inappropriate transition to another configuration

Source: Adapted from Mintzberg 1979; 1983; 1989.

Notes: * Later, Mintzberg used different labels: the simple structure he called the entrepreneurial organization; the machine bureaucracy he called the machine organization, the professional bureaucracy he called professional organization, the divisionalized form he called diversified organization; the adhocracy he called the innovative organization.

** Mintzberg added two further types: the missionary and the political organization, both usually overlaid on the basic types of organization. The missionary organization has a rich system of values and beliefs and is co-ordinated through the standardization of norms and values. The culture of the organization is very strong and clearly differentiates it from other organizations. It often overlays the five organization types introduced earlier; most commonly entrepreneurial and innovative organization. The political organization expresses itself in political games. It may overlay the conventional organization. Sometimes both may evoke their own organization forms (Mintzberg 1989).

Projects can be differentiated according to the relationship that the company has to the business (Gareis/Stummer 2008). Internal projects are performed to carry out support processes, for example organizational development, personal development and product development. External projects are performed to carry out primary processes to deliver products and services to clients.[1]

The project-oriented organization does not need to be a legal entity. It can be a department or group within a larger organization (Hobday 2000; Turner/Keegan 2001). Thus, a department in a back office doing repositioning or renewal work for a routine front office is a project-oriented organization by strategic choice, even if the front office is a routine organization by strategic choice. A typical example is the product development of an automotive manufacturer: while the product development is organized by projects, the manufacture of cars as routine processes is performed by the permanent organization (Midler 1995). An organization following the strategy *Managing by Projects* may deploy both project-oriented divisions and functional divisions, according to the requirement of applying the adequate working form. Many organizations have made a strategic choice to perform their primary business with clients as projects, but do not consider that they may need professional project management for internal projects. However, these organizations may still be considered to be project-oriented, but they have some development potential. Table 4.1 summarizes the five basic types of organization.

4.3 A Continuum of Organizational Forms to Organize Projects

The existence of different adequate organization forms is in line with Galbraith (1977), who suggests that there is a continuum of organizational forms for any organization, ranging from the functional organization through the matrix organization to the project. The functional organization is best suited for high volume production of standardized products. It supports economies of scale and is characterized by stability and functional specialization. The other extreme is the project organization, originally called product organization, for one-off and small batch production to deal with uncertainty and novelty (Woodward et al. 1965). Interestingly, the product and the project were originally used synonymously, which indicates that the project and the investment were not differentiated. See Figure 4.2 for illustration.

Traditionally, functional, matrix and project form are differentiated (Marquis/Straight 1965) (Cleland/King 1983). The differentiation of these organizational forms is based on the distribution of the authority between the permanent line organization and the temporary project organization. The two extremes are the functional line organization and the pure project organization.

FUNCTIONAL   MATRIX   PROJECT

high-volume production   one-off and small batch production
product standardization   product complexity
economies of scale and scope   bid and project efficiency
stability and functional specialization   uncertainty and task novelty

Figure 4.2   Project versus functional capabilities
Source: Adapted from Davies/Hobday 2005: 23; Galbraith 1971: 114.

---

1   See Chapter 4 for types of projects.

In the functional line organization, a project is conducted within a single function and the line manager has all the authority for the project personnel, which comes from the single function. This organization form can be found in small projects. The functional line is challenged as soon as project personnel are drawn from different functions. When applied to a project that needs to draw on different functions, the project is divided into single function work packages and assigned to relevant functional groups. The heads of the functions are responsible for their part of the project, which leads to small projects within one function, the co-ordination between the functions is then provided by upper management.

In the pure project organization, all necessary project personnel are separated from the functional organization and transferred to the project, which is established as an organizational unit. All of the authority for the project personnel is with the project manager. Often, this project unit, also called project department, has a rather long-term character as it is established for the whole investment, which is conducted in different project phases.

In between these two forms lies the matrix organization. Instead of dividing the project into parts or establishing a dedicated project unit, the functional structures are integrated with horizontal project structures. The matrix organization is defined as a 'mixed' organizational form in which the normal functional hierarchy is 'overlayed' with some form of lateral authority or communication (Larson/Gobeli 1987). Cleland and King (1983) even suggest the matrix organization as a central feature of project management, and describe the matrix organization in which the members of the project organization come from functional departments to work on the project. Two chains of command exist: one along functional line and one along project line. Thus, the project and functional line managers share responsibility for the management of the project and its personnel. Different forms of the matrix organization exist, depending on how the authority is distributed between line managers and the project manager. Larson and Gobeli (1987) differentiate the functional matrix, the project matrix, and in between, the balanced matrix.

In the functional matrix, most of the authority remains with the functional managers, while the project manager has a co-ordination function. The functional manager takes responsibility for the assignment of people to project tasks. The project manager passes responsibility for the completion of a package of work to the functional manager, and the functional manager assigns people from within his or her function to the work. Thus project team members receive instruction from their functional managers. This form is useful if the personnel from the functions are working on several projects simultaneously and also have functional duties. The functional manager can then balance their workloads while meeting the delivery dates for the project work packages (Larson/Gobeli 1987; Turner et al. 2010).

In the balanced matrix, the authority is balanced between line and project manager. Based on a very traditional project management understanding, the project manager defines the overall project plan, integrates the contributions of different functions, sets schedule and monitors progress. The functional line managers are responsible for the project personnel, and how and to what degree of quality the work is accomplished (Larson/Gobeli 1987).

In the project matrix, most of the authority is with the project manager. The project personnel are seconded onto the project for the duration of their involvement with the project. While seconded onto the project, they receive instruction from the project manager. The project manager has direct authority to make decisions about the project personnel and manage the project. The project personnel may only be seconded part time, and they may only be seconded temporarily, but on the project they receive instruction from the project manager (Larson/Gobeli 1987; Turner et al. 2010). See Table 4.2.

Each form of organizational designs has a set of advantages and disadvantages (Galbraith 2001; Larson/Gobeli 1987), as summarized in Table 4.3.

Table 4.2   Traditional project organizational forms

Form	Description
Functional line	• Project undertaken within a function; small, single function projects • If different functions are required, division into work packages, which are conducted again within the single function • All authority remains with the functional manager
Matrix organization	• Authority distributed between line and project manager; different forms **Functional matrix** • Project personnel remain in functions • Project divided into single discipline work packages • Project manager co-ordinates projects across different functional groups • The functional mangers remain responsible for their functional work package • Strong function, weak project **Balanced matrix** • Project manager co-ordinates the project and shares responsibility on an equal base with the line managers from different functions • Constructive conflict between function and project **Project matrix** • Personnel resources seconded full time or part time to project • Project manager has authority over project personnel • Mixed discipline work packages • Strong project, weak function
Pure project organization	• Project is established as an organizational unit, often as a project department • Large dedicated project organization • All authority with the project manager

Source: Adapted from Larson/Gobeli 1987; Turner et al. 2010.

Table 4.3   Advantages and disadvantages of traditional project organizational forms

Organization form	Advantages	Disadvantages
Functional line	• No reintegration efforts of project personnel after projects are finished	• No concentration on project work as project is no temporary organization
Matrix organization	• Efficient use of resources • Ensured quality input from the different functions • Flexibility • Information flow • Discipline retention • Improved motivation and commitment	• Power struggles • Strong conflict over scarce resources • Slow reaction time • Difficulty in monitoring and controlling • Excessive overheads • Stress
Pure project organization	• Concentration on the project work	• Often no differentiation between the object (project result) and the project • Need for reintegration of project personnel after project is finished • Knowledge management challenged

These traditional forms resemble the understanding of a project as a complex task. In the case of the project as a pure project organization, a distinct temporary organization is created as a temporary unit in the organization. We may assume that in this way, the organization tries to treat the temporary project like a functional unit.

Scholars are very sceptical that the balanced matrix works at all in practice (for example, Turner et al. 2010). In practice, project matrix organizations often overcome the formal structures by informally working together as temporary organizations. In line with the cultural value of empowerment of employees, Gareis (2005) questions the matrix organization, as the project team member is not considered to take on any responsibility for his or her work contribution to the project. In line with Senge (1994), who perceives organization as competitive advantage, the organization of the project can be explicitly designed for a specific purpose in contrast to applying standard organization forms. In the project-oriented organizations, the explicit organizational design of the project is encouraged by adding organizational design elements such as empowerment, integration and partnering and virtuality (Gareis 2005).

4.4 Project-Based or Project-Oriented?

4.4.1 DIFFERENT DEFINITIONS AND APPROACHES

The organization conducting projects has become a central object of consideration in project management and management research, with increasing interest. The labels for describing organizations that carry out projects vary, as do the underpinning theoretical concepts and perceptions. These types of organizations are called projectified (Youker 1977), project-based (Turner 2009), or project-oriented (Gareis 1990; 2005).

Different perspectives are taken by researchers, for example: learning and knowledge management (Bakker 2010; Defillippi 2001; Love et al. 2005; Prencipe/Tell 2001), innovation (Blindenbach-Driessen/Van Den Ende 2006; Gann/Salter 2000; Hobday 2000), governance (Lindkvist 2004; Müller/Turner 2010; Turner/Keegan 2001), organizational structures (Engwall 2003; Gareis 2005; Hodgson 2004; Sydow et al. 2004), strategy (Artto/Wikström 2005; Shenhar et al. 2001), and capabilities and maturity (Andersen/Jessen 2003; Cooke-Davies 2005; Davies/Hobday 2005). These perspectives reflect some of the challenges as well as potentials found in the project-oriented organization.

Different approaches can be identified. Organization theory provides a theoretical foundation for the organization, which uses projects for achieving business objectives (Artto/Wikström 2005). In organization theory, the organization is the unit of analysis. Only relatively recently has project management broadened its horizon to 'multi project settings', such as the project portfolio and the project-oriented organization (Söderlund 2004). Lately, project management scholars stress the industry specific context and express it by the term 'project business' (Artto/Wikström 2005). Thus, approaches exist that concentrate on the perspective of an organization that performs projects (such as Gareis 2005; Hobday 2000; Keegan/Turner 2003; Lindkvist 2004), while other approaches focus on the co-operation between organizations, using project networks or joint ventures as the unit of analysis (Artto/Wikström 2005; Grabher 2002; Windeler/Sydow 2001), often within a particular industry context. The focus of this study is the organization.

Hobday (2000) defines the project-based organization in contrast to other companies, and suggests the projects as core units of the organization. He further points to the inherently flexible and reconfigurable advantages for innovation processes. 'In contrast to the matrix, functional and other forms, the project-based organization is one in which the project is the primary unit for production, organization, innovation, and competition' (Hobday 2000: 874). In his perception, the project-based organization only consists of projects without any functional co-ordination (Hobday 2000).

Lindkvist (2004) offers a broader definition including the fact that there is a permanent part of the organization. He defines project-based companies as companies that do most of their work in projects or have a main emphasis on the project dimensions rather than the functional dimensions of organizational structure and processes. In line with Sydow (2004), who suggests that there is a need for organizations to adopt appropriate structures to respond to their customers' 'highly differentiated and customized nature of demand', Turner and Keegan (2001) define the project-based organization as an organization that is project-based perforce because of the customized nature of the demand from their customers. 'The majority of products made or services delivered are against bespoke designs for customers' (Turner and Keegan (2001: 256).

Project-oriented organizations include permanent and temporary structures, thus 'single-project organizations', where the entire organization is dissolved after completion of a project (Whitley 2006), are not considered to be project-oriented organizations, but they are a form of temporary organization.

4.4.2 THE ESSENCE OF PROJECT-ORIENTATION

While in English the term *project-based* is used for the organization that is conducting projects, German-speaking authors often use the term project-oriented (*projektorientiert)*. The terms project-based and project-oriented are often used synonymously. But there are differences between the concept of the *project-based* and the *project-oriented organization*. I clarify these differences to make the concept of the project-oriented organization more concrete, see Table 4.4.

Traditionally, the project-based organization is an organization that carries out contract projects for external customers, which is in line with management theory which says that the production process determines the form of the organization (Woodward 1965). The project-based organization is project-based *perforce* because of the customized nature of the demand from their customers (Turner/Keegan 2001). On the other hand, Gareis (1990) suggests that the project-oriented organization is such by *strategic choice*, based on the organizational strategy of *Management by Projects*. The project-oriented organization carries out projects or programmes for performing business processes, whenever adequate. Thus, these projects may be external contract projects or internal projects such as product development, organizational development or change.

Project-oriented organizations acknowledge projects as temporary organizations and allow for adequate autonomy of the projects. A project as a temporary organization leads to rethinking of structures in the permanent organization to support project-orientation, but permanent structures stay important and provide a certain stability to this organization. In the project-oriented organization, permanent (functional) structures and temporary project structures co-exist. The project-oriented organization can deal with these tensions between permanent and temporary.

Another differentiation between the concept of the project-based and the project-oriented organization is the paradigm on which the concepts are based on. The project-oriented organization is explicitly framed as a construction, and therefore includes a description how a project-oriented organization is capable of performing projects.

Table 4.4   **Project-based versus project-oriented**

	Project-based organization	Project-oriented organization
Reason for projects	• Projects are performed *per force* because of the customized nature of the project	• Projects are a *strategic choice* • Projects are one option for the organizational design
Relation	• Projects relate to production processes	• Projects relate to business processes
Type of projects	• Mainly external projects	• External (if adequate) and internal projects
Management logic	• Predominantly functional line organizations • Projects are forced to fit functional logic, as disturbances are not allowed, large projects are turned into temporary functions	• Permanent and temporary organizations have different management logics • Organization can deal with these contradictions
Understanding of project management	• Operational capability • Project management as tools and control	• Operational and strategic capability • Project management as leadership
Paradigm	• Prevailing mechanistic planning paradigm • Project is considered as complex task or system	• Systemic-constructivist • Project is considered as a temporary organization

4.4.3 BENEFITS OF PROJECT-ORIENTATION

In practice, many organizations have a demand for projects, but may not be project-oriented enough (Lampel 2007). They may not have the adequate and corresponding structural and cultural prerequisites to perform projects and manage a project portfolio professionally. Organizations remain or even enforce a traditional bureaucratic management paradigm to deal with the organizational tensions temporary structures bring to an organization (Hodgson 2004). They enforce hierarchies and bureaucracy *for disciplining the professionals* (Hodgson 2002) on the temporary projects, instead of balancing the organizational needs and requirements of permanent and temporary structures. In these organizations, project management is often considered only from an operational perspective for delivering projects, but the strategic perspective of managing projects (and thus the specific organizational structures and a specific culture to support project-orientation) is not created.

These organizations have the potential to develop further towards the construction of the project-oriented organization with its organizational strategy *Managing by Projects*. Despite their demand for projects, these organizations are not al all or only partly and slowly reacting to equip the organization to perform projects. Thus, they can only partly raise the benefits that projects and project management bring to their organization. Ideally, in a project-oriented organization, the demand for projects is in relation to the organizations' potential/capabilities to perform the projects professionally.

In a large-scale study on the value of project management, Thomas and Mullaly (2008) show that the higher the maturity and the better the organizations are equipped to perform projects professionally, the more intangible benefits can be raised. Intangible benefits include:

- Improvements in decision making;
- Enhanced communications and collaboration;
- Improvements in effective work cultures;
- Alignment of approaches, terminology and values within the organization;
- Overall effectiveness of the organization and its management approach;
- Improved transparency, clarity of structures, roles and accountability.

Further, they suggest that at almost any level of maturity the implementation or further development of project management in an organization leads to tangible benefits. See Table 4.5 for a summary of tangible and intangible benefits.

4.5 The Construct Project-Oriented Organization after Gareis

Roland Gareis (1990; 2005) explicitly considers the project-oriented organization as a construct, and defines the project-oriented organization as an organization that:

- Defines *Management by Projects* as its organizational strategy;
- Applies projects and programmes for the performance of complex processes;
- Manages a project portfolio of different internal and external project types;
- Has specific permanent organizations like a project portfolio group or a project management office to provide integrative functions;
- Applies a management paradigm which reflects the ability to deal with uncertainty, Contradiction, change and collaboration;
- Views itself as being project-oriented.

This definition applies a much broader view than most other definitions, explicitly including internal projects and programmes. It stresses the strategic choice of applying projects for performing business processes of medium to large scope, expressed in the strategy *Management by Projects*. The project-oriented organization therefore makes the strategic choice to apply projects as a central working form.

Table 4.5   Benefits of project-orientation

Tangible benefits	Intangible benefits
• Increased customer share	• Attainment of strategic objectives
• Cost savings	• More effective use of human resources
• Revenue increases	• Staff retention
• Customer retention	• Improved reputation
• Greater market share	• Improved corporate culture
• Reduced write-offs and rework	• Greater social good
	• Improved overall management
	• Improved quality of life
	• Improved regulatory compliance
	• Improved competitiveness
	• New product/service streams

Source: Adapted from Thomas/Mullaly 2008.

Table 4.6   Trends towards project-orientation

From	To
Contracting, research and development	Contracting, research and development, bid, marketing, public relations, personnel development, organizational development, events
Few projects of high complexity	Many projects of different complexities and programmes
Primarily projects for external customers	Projects with external and projects with internal customers

Source: Gareis 2005: 27.

In addition to the traditional project-oriented industries such as construction and engineering, which traditionally perform large contracting projects, contemporary types of internal projects such as strategic planning, marketing, personnel development and organizational development also evolve. The development goes from performing a few projects to many different projects with different size and complexity. Overall, a trend towards flatter network structures is observable (e.g., Morgan 1997; Whittington et al. 1999).

In his works on the project-oriented organization, Roland Gareis starts with the basic assumption that organizations need more differentiations to deal with the increasing complexity of the environment. According to Ashby's law that 'only variety can absorb variety', projects may be considered as a means of organizational differentiation to absorb the complexity of the environment. However, projects are not only a means of differentiating and focusing, they at the same time allow for different integrations the permanent organization cannot provide. For example allowing for goal-oriented co-operations between different functional departments such as for example representatives of the marketing and technical departments in a product development project. Thus, projects organize goal-oriented and temporary integration within a company and may go beyond the single company including for example representatives of partner and supplier organizations onto the project. However, at the same time projects as temporary organizations add additional differentiations in a company.

Figure 4.3   Strategy, structure and culture of the project-oriented organization
Source: Gareis 2005: 26.

Gareis explicitly refers to the project-oriented organization as a social system (Luhmann 1995) and frames it as a construct (Von Glasersfeld 1995). The project-oriented organization is a construction that is viable in practice, but organizations may be more or less well equipped to perform projects. In earlier works, Gareis (1990) refers to organizational fit theory (Bleicher 1991) and describes the specific strategy, structure and culture of the project-oriented organization. In later works, a competence approach (Gareis/Huemann 2007) and business process perspective (Gareis/Stummer 2008) are added.

The project-oriented organization simultaneously performs projects for internal and external customers, small projects, as well as projects of medium or high complexity and projects with different objectives (Gareis 2005: 27). It is perceived as an organization with permanent and temporary structures and a specific management culture. It can be described by its strategy, structure and culture (Gareis 2005; Gareis/Huemann 2007). See Figure 4.3.

4.5.1 MANAGEMENT BY PROJECTS AS STRATEGY

In 1990, a seminal *IPMA World Congress*[2] on the topic *Management by Projects* was performed in Vienna (Gareis 1990). This congress can be considered as a central step forwards in the Project Management Research and Practice Community, by focusing on the organization performing projects as a central object of consideration. The project-oriented organization applies the organizational strategy *Management by Projects* as a strategic choice. Not 'everything' is a project, but the essence of the organizational strategy *Management by Projects* is that the organization applies a project or a programme for the performance of a business process, when adequate. Process management is considered as a prerequisite, as organizations require an understanding of their processes to really apply the strategy *Management by Projects*. Thus, an organization must understand its business processes in order to explicitly choose which of these should better be performed as projects and which should be taken over by the routine permanent organization. Thus, projects and programmes are strategic options for the organizational design of the organization.

In practice, many organizations apply *Management by Projects* not explicitly, but implicitly, as there may be a demand from the customer to carry out projects. As consequence, these organizations may not have the adequate and corresponding structural and cultural prerequisites to perform projects. Ideally, the strategy *Management by Projects* indicates that the project-oriented organization has specific structures and shapes a specific culture to support project-orientation.

4.5.2 TEMPORARY AND PERMANENT ORGANIZATIONS

Generally, different organization forms allow for adequate differentiation and integration in the organization (Burns 1961; Chandler 1962; Galbraith 1977; Lawrence/Lorsch 1967; Mintzberg 1979). Project-oriented organizations apply temporary structures such as projects for organizational differentiation and integration, as well as permanent structures for organizational integration.

While in a traditional management paradigm, hierarchy is the central integration instrument whereby co-operation is organized by the management of interfaces, the project-oriented organization applies projects and programmes as a temporary way of facilitating co-operation between functions and with partners, suppliers and other relevant stakeholders. Despite projects bring the flexibility to organize temporary and goal oriented integration beyond functions

---

2   The International Project Management Association back then called itself INTERnational NETwork-INTERNET, so it was the INTERNET´90 World Congress on Project Management in June 1990, Vienna, Austria.

(Youker 1977) and also sometimes beyond the company boarder, overall introducing projects in an organization leads to more organizational differentiation. (Morris 1997). Project-oriented organizations are highly differentiated, with temporary and permanent structures (Sydow et al. 2004), and perform a number of different internal, external, small and large projects at the same time. To cope with this organizational complexity means that different forms of differentiation and integration are required (Gareis 2005; Morris 1997).

Integration is necessary between projects and between projects and the permanent organization, to ensure synergies and strategic alignment. Forms of integration between projects are, for example, to cluster projects into chains of projects, project portfolios and networks of projects (Gareis 2005).

Figure 4.4 visualizes an organization chart of the project-oriented organization, which shows projects and programmes as temporary organizations, as well as the permanent structures. The permanent structures are, for instance, business units and departments, but also specific permanent structures such as the Project Management Office and the Project Portfolio Group as well as Expert Pools (Gareis 2005). The Project Management Office and the Project Portfolio Group perform essential integration tasks in the project-oriented organization, which I discuss in more detail later in this chapter.

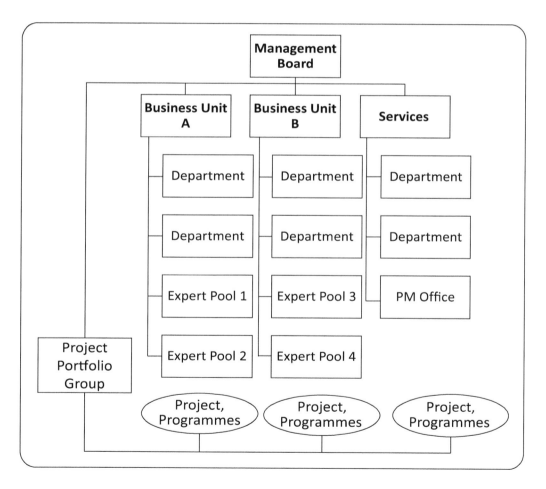

Figure 4.4   Organization chart of the project-oriented organization
Source: Gareis 2005: 31.

Integration between projects and the permanent organization is reflected in governance of the projects and the governance of the project-oriented organization, for instance in the provision of guidelines and rules for projects in the form of project and project management standards (Müller/Turner 2010). Further integration is necessary between the single project and the permanent organization to allow enough alignment as well as enough autonomy for the project. The organizational design of the project takes care of the necessary coupling between the project and the permanent structures of the company.

4.5.3 PROJECT-ORIENTED CULTURE

The culture of an organization is defined as 'the pattern of values, norms, beliefs, attitudes and assumptions that may not have been articulated but shape the ways in which people behave and things get done' (Armstrong 2007: 303). The culture expresses itself in artefacts, visible and tangible aspects of an organization that people hear, see or feel. (Armstrong 2007). The project-oriented organization characterizes itself by an explicit project management culture; that is, by a set of project management-related values, norms and rules (Gareis 2005). Table 4.7 provides an example of specific values of the project-oriented organization.

While traditional project management approaches are based on a mechanistic paradigm and emphasize detailed planning methods (Maylor 2001), the project-oriented organization rather advocates a contemporary project management approach and culture. The management culture of the project-oriented organization is based on the management paradigm such as Lean Management (Womack/Jones 1996; Womack et al. 1990), Total Quality Management (Deming 1986), Business Process Reengineering (Hammer/Champy 1993) and the Learning Organization (Senge 1994) – but it may also be seen in the more contemporary context of sustainable development (Gareis et al. 2013). Table 4.8 provides an illustration of values in selected management approaches.

Based on the cultural values advocated by these management approaches, the culture of the project-oriented organization can be described with values such as empowerment of employees and projects, customer-orientation, teamwork, process orientation, networking between employees and with clients and suppliers, encouraging continuous and discontinuous change (Gareis 2005; Gareis/Stummer 2008). Further organizational values may be stressed or added, such as learning/innovation (Mintzberg 1979) and trust (Bredin/Soderlund 2006). Overall, the project-oriented organization requires a culture that is able to deal with uncertainty, contradictions and change. All of these values fit the contemporary context of sustainable development (Gareis et al. 2013).

A special remark warrants empowerment. Galbraith (2001) describes new product developments as requiring more decision-making and information processing than a functional organization can provide. Product development projects require cross-functional collaborations. The decision-making power at lower levels of the organization is increased without losing the inputs of all affected levels.

> The purpose was to make as many decisions as possible at lower levels with the people most knowledgeable. This should reduce the delays and yet ensure that all the information inputs were considered. (Galbraith 2001: 32)

As organizations act in the context of industries and societies, further industry-specific values such as safety/health-orientation for the project-oriented construction industry are of relevance for project-oriented construction companies. Every project-oriented organization has its own blend of values (Paauwe 2004), deeply dependent on their own contexts and maturity as a project-oriented organization. Nevertheless, Gareis (1990; 2005) draws our attention to a suitable culture that supports *Managing by Projects*. Table 4.9 summarizes selected cultural values that support project-orientation.

Table 4.7 Specific values of the project-oriented company

Project-oriented culture
• Projects are strategically important. On the one hand, projects allow implementation of business strategies; on the other hand, projects influence business strategy
• Top management and management promotes the autonomy and self-organization of projects in order to support the performance of projects
• Leadership is, among other things, understood as the ability to create visions and strategies and to communicate these to the projects
• Continuous organizational development shall ensure the survival of the company. Projects are important in this development process, as they allow for organizational learning based on new experience from interactions with varying environments
• Project management is not a qualification of specialists, but as a general management qualification

Source: Gareis 1990: 40.

Table 4.8 Organizational values in selected management approaches

Values in selected management approaches			
Lean management/ production (Womack/Jones 1996; Womack et al. 1990)	Total Quality Management (Deming 1986)	Business Process Reengineering (Hammer/Champy 1993)	Learning Organization (Senge et al. 1999; Senge 1994).
• Concentration on core competences • Customer-orientation • Process-orientation • Integration • Participation • Team-orientation • Empowerment of employees • Flat organizations	• Customer-orientation • Continuous improvement and learning • Process-orientation • Search for the true reason • People-orientation • Team-orientation • Quality-orientation	• Change-orientation/ flexibility • Innovation • Quality-orientation • Customer-orientation • Process-orientation rather than department orientation	• System-thinking and self-management • Change-orientation • Learning • Team-orientation • Empowerment of employees and teams • Organization as competitive advantage • Trust

Source: Adapted from Gareis/Stummer 2008.

Table 4.9 Project-oriented culture

Project-oriented culture	
Empowerment	• Increased autonomy and responsibility of personnel • Empowerment involves project, project team and project team members
Team-orientation	• Projects require teamwork • Problem solving through teams and projects instead of excessive functional differentiation
Stakeholder-orientation	• Projects create value for customers and other stakeholders • Co-operation with customer, suppliers and other stakeholders on a project

Table 4.9   *Continued*

Project-oriented culture	
Process-orientation	• The characteristics of the process as the basis for organizational design • Processes as the basis for project work • Project management, programme management, portfolio management as processes
Diversity	• Diversity as differences and commonalities • Diversity as a potential for project work
Learning-orientation/ innovation	• Projects promote learning and innovation • Encouraging co-production of knowledge on the project with customers, suppliers and partners
Change-orientation	• Encouraging continuous and discontinuous organizational change

4.6 Specific Integrative Permanent Structures

Specific permanent structures for the project-oriented organization discussed in the literature include the PPG, the PMO and expert pools. These structures are described below.

4.6.1 PROJECT PORTFOLIO GROUP

The PPG is defined as 'a specific, permanent communication structure of medium-sized to large project-oriented organizations' (Gareis 2005: 506). The PPG steers the project portfolio, which may be considered as all the projects held by the company at a certain point in time (Gareis 2005). Services offered by the PPG include (Blichfeldt 2008; Gareis 2005; Turner et al. 2010; Unger et al. 2012):

- Assigning a project or programme; aligning project objectives with company strategy; deciding the organization form for initializing an investment; nominating the project owner;
- Project portfolio co-ordination such as co-ordinating (human) resources used in projects; determining project priorities; stopping and interrupting projects and programmes; determining strategies for designing relations with relevant project or programme stakeholders;
- Networking of projects, such as organizing learning of and between projects; using synergies.

4.6.2 PROJECT MANAGEMENT OFFICE

In contrast to project or programme offices that are set up to support single, usually very large projects, and have no life beyond the single project, the Project Management Office is set up to be a permanent structure in the project-oriented company. However, research has indicated that Project Management Offices, if they do not fulfil the expectations of the company and add value, only have a life-span of several years (Aubry et al. 2010). The objective of the Project Management

Office is to ensure a professional project, programme and project portfolio management in the project-oriented company. Project Management Offices are a central means of integrating an organization's strategic priorities, permanent structures and temporary projects (Aubry et al. 2007). Services offered by the PMO include (Aubry et al. 2010; Gareis 2005; Huemann et al. 2004; Julian et al. 2008; Turner et al. 2010):

- Services for project and programme management such as providing project management guidelines, standards, forms, and so on; organizing management auditing and consulting to ensure management quality in projects and programmes;
- Services for project portfolio management such as providing project portfolio guidelines, standards, forms, and so on; maintaining a project portfolio database, developing project portfolio reports; initializing project networking;
- Services for project management personnel: organizing training and coaching, exchange of experience for project management personnel, further developing and marketing of the profession project management; support in recruiting, selecting, evaluating and determining salaries for project managers.

4.6.3 EXPERT POOL VERSUS TRADITIONAL DEPARTMENT

In the project-oriented organization, the personnel qualified to work in projects and programmes can be organized in expert pools[3] (Bredin/Soderlund 2006; Midler 1995). The tasks of the expert pool comprise especially competency development of the personnel managed by the expert pool, process management and knowledge management. Depending on the business within one organization, different expert pools exist. In an engineering construction company, technical expert pools such as mechanical engineering, electrical engineering and project management can be differentiated (Gareis 2005: 504). Table 4.10 illustrates the traditional department in comparison to the expert pool.

Table 4.10   Traditional department versus expert pool

	Traditional department	Expert pool
Empowerment	• Employees not necessarily empowered to take on responsibility for quality of their work	• Pool members are empowered to take on responsibility for their work in projects and programmes
Perception of manager role	• Manager is the content expert and responsible for the quality of work of the experts	• Pool manager is not necessarily content expert • Pool manager has HRM and managerial responsibilities • Pool manager is not responsible for work quality of pool members

Source: Adapted from Gareis 2005.

---

3   The expert pool is known by different names, such as resource pool or centre for excellence.

4.7 The Tension between Temporary and Permanent Structures

Applying permanent and temporary structures leads to a highly differentiated form of organization. This differentiation allows the organization to play with increasing and decreasing organizational complexity to react to its relevant environment. It further leads to the need of balancing centralization and decentralization (Geraldi 2009).

The project-oriented organization chooses to apply either temporary or permanent structures to perform a certain business process. According to the character of the business process, the organization may decide whether a business process is carried out as a temporary organization, such as a project or programme, or whether the permanent organization is with its standard business processes and structures can carry out the particular business process. This makes the project-oriented organization more dynamic than other organizations, which do not apply temporary structures as a strategic option. We may coin the term project-oriented managing.

A central feature of the project-oriented organization is a relatively stable permanent organization and a flexible temporary part of more or less concurrent projects within their project portfolio, depending on their need. This also means that the size of the temporary part of the organization and the number and size of projects in the project portfolio may vary considerably over time. Thus, the project-oriented organization has dynamic boundaries and contexts. This dynamism accelerates when projects that are organized in co-operation with other partners, suppliers or customers go beyond organizational boundaries.

As a highly differentiated organization, the project-oriented organization is challenged in managing the integration between temporary and permanent structures. Different means for integrating include specific structures such as Project Management Office or Project Portfolio Group, or different coupling mechanisms to link projects and temporary organizations as outlined in this chapter earlier. Nevertheless, tension and different management logics exist in temporary structures in comparison to the permanent parts of the project-oriented organization.

Table 4.11   Management logics

	Temporary project	Permanent line organization
Time	• Temporary, duration is planned at the beginning of project, end is inherent in the project start • Short to medium-term orientation • Temporality creates urgency, • rhythm driven by project end date and milestones	• Permanent organization is planned, unlimited in time • Short, medium and long-term orientation • Time is cyclic, driven by rhythm of the annual budgeting cycle and related to quarterly reports
Business process	• Relatively unique, short- to medium-term, strategically important, medium or large scope • High result orientation to achieve project objectives, as this is the raison d'être for the existence of the project	• Routine, short-term, not strategically important, small scope • Result-orientation may vary considerably

	Temporary project	Permanent line organization
Personnel	• Personnel are put together on a project-based on a project requirement • Personnel may even be integrated from external organizations, for example, partners, suppliers, customer • Contribution to project result (even when intangible as a feasibility study) is visible for the project personnel	• Personnel with similar competences are organized in functional departments or in expert pools • Relation between own contribution and company result may not be so clear for the single employee
Team	• Team structures are central to a project • Different teams within one project possible • Temporary teams	• Team structures possible • Teams then have the character of permanent teams
Change	• Dynamic, as projects organize change • Change object is the project itself • Change object is also the organization(s) for whom the project is delivered	• Often also increasingly dynamic, as change is common in the contemporary organization • Change for the permanent organization often organized by projects
Identity	• Temporary, needs to be created for the specific project • Relatively autonomous but embedded in the context • May be influenced by several organizations	• Is created and shaped over time, embedded in its context

However, the structural tension between the temporary and permanent part of the organization is imminent and challenges managing the project-oriented organization arise in very different aspects, including HRM. These structures follow different management logics. As discussed earlier in this chapter, I concluded that projects as temporary organizations can be described with specific features. Here, I add a description of the contrasting permanent organization in order to summarize the differences between the temporary project and the permanent line organization, which both co-exist in project-oriented organizations (see Table 4.11).

4.8 Consequences

In this chapter, I have discussed the construct of the project-oriented organization and made a differentiation to the concept of the project-based organization. Table 4.12 provides the working definition for the project-oriented organization.

Table 4.12   Definition: Project-oriented organization

> **DEFINITION: PROJECT-ORIENTED ORGANIZATION**
> A project-oriented organization applies the strategy *Managing by Projects*, holds permanent and temporary structures (project and programmes) and has shaped specific structures and values that supports project-orientation.

In comparison to the classical hierarchical organization, specific features characterize the project-oriented organization. These features relate especially to the specific strategy, structure and culture of the organization. In contrast to the concept of the project-based organization, the project-oriented organization has made an explicit choice to be project-oriented, and understands that it needs to be equipped accordingly in order to manage projects and gain the benefits that projects can bring to an organization. Table 4.13 summarizes specific features of the project-oriented organization.

Table 4.13   Specific features of the project-oriented organization

	Description	Consequence
Strategy	• Managing by Projects as making adequate choice of organization to perform business processes	• A highly differentiated organization that requires balancing of centralization and decentralization
Structures	• Temporary projects in addition to permanent structures	• Projects constitute an additional secondary organization, consisting of temporary organizations as coupled sub systems of the project-oriented organization • Tensions between permanent and temporary structures, for example different management logics between temporary and permanent structures • Possibility of building up adequate complexity in the organization to deal with the complexity of the environment and to suit different contexts
Culture	• Project-oriented culture	• Values that fit project-orientation enable dealing with uncertainty, contradictions, change

Project Personnel and their Challenges

5.1 Introduction

In this chapter, I clarify the term project personnel, which is a major but heterogeneous group of personnel in the project-oriented organization. What they share is that they work on projects, either on one or several projects, either solely on projects or also in the permanent organization. I then describe the challenges that arise for project personnel in project-oriented organizations. I reflect on positive and negative aspects of these challenges, and derive HRM-related potentials of project-oriented organizations, while considering employee well-being.

5.2 Project Personnel

Personnel, as human capital of an organization, are considered to be one potential source for creating sustainable competitive advantage (Pfeffer 1994). The other potential source for creating competitive advantage is a viable HRM architecture (Boxall 2010) to attract, develop, maintain and motivate the members of the organization. Davies and Hobday (2005) conceptualize project-oriented organizations as knowledge intensive as they apply projects to integrate knowledge in a fast and flexible way in order to reach defined objectives within a given period of time. Thus, project-oriented organizations, being knowledge-intensive, need highly qualified and competent project personnel (Alvesson 2001). Project personnel are frequently referred to as knowledge workers (Garrick/Clegg 2001). This makes HRM for project personnel strategically important in the project-oriented organization.

A differentiated workforce is common to contemporary organizations (Lepak 2010). Different groups of personnel are of different strategic importance to the organization (Lepak/Snell 1999), and many have different expectations and needs as other relevant stakeholders. In the HRM system, core versus non-core employees are differentiated and managed differently according to their contribution to the organization (Delery 2001). Personnel can be differentiated into different groups, which include the value of the personnel for the organization, competency of the personnel, hierarchical position, the working contract arrangements and the relation of the personnel to temporary and permanent structures.

According to the individual competency required for performing professional roles, management, expert personnel and project management personnel can be differentiated (Huemann 2005). Management personnel are those who have management responsibility and personnel authority (Walker 1992: 211). Typical traditional roles in the project-oriented organization include different line managers, department heads, but also board members, who need to draw on their management competencies to fulfil their roles. Expert personnel are those personnel who bring in their competencies to fulfil their roles. These competencies may range from functional competencies such as marketing and accounting, to technical competencies like programming or engineering. Project management personnel may be defined as those human resources who need to draw on project management competency to fulfil their roles such as the project manager (Huemann 2002).[1] Career systems, as outlined later in this chapter, often follow differentiation into career fields that are based on competence, leading to management, expert and project management career fields (Hodgson 2011; Hölzle 2010).

Another relevant differentiation for project personnel in the project-oriented organization takes a contractual perspective. Personnel in the project-oriented organization may have permanent or temporary contractual arrangements with the project or the project-oriented organization. Depending on the industry, the percentage of temporary personnel may vary considerably in one company over time, as well as from company to company. In project-oriented organizations, there can be between 20 per cent and 40 per cent temporary contract personnel, or even up to 80 per cent temporary contract personnel involved in projects (Keegan/Turner 2003). In the context of project-oriented organizations, which quite often are knowledge intensive companies (Sydow et al. 2004), the relevance of this often highly qualified external temporary workforce (including contractors, freelancers, employees of service firms) is increasing (Storey et al. 2002).

Another possible criterion is the relation of the personnel to the temporary or the permanent structures, which leads to the differentiation into project and line personnel (Gareis/Titscher 1992). As personnel often have multiple roles in a project-oriented organization, this differentiation is not as clear-cut as it may seem.

In addition to traditional line management roles such as department head, project-oriented organizations assume specific roles in the permanent structures, including those personnel contributing to the project management office or project portfolio group. Project office personnel include, for instance, a project management office manager and project management office members. The project portfolio group members take the responsibility to manage the project portfolio from a strategic perspective. Further, specific quality management roles such as project or project management or project auditors and reviewers, project coaches and project consultants may be identified in project-oriented organizations. The latter roles often offer job enlargement for senior project managers.

Personnel with different competencies work together on projects, and what they should share is the competency to manage the project (Huemann 2002) – this especially includes social competencies to be able to work on projects and deal with dynamic environments. Project personnel are knowledge workers. Because of the (relative) uniqueness of projects no project is exactly the same as the previous one. Project personnel need to draw on their knowledge and combine it in different ways in order to create project deliveries. Often, not only is the project outcome novel, but the process used to develop it is created as part of the project.

I use the term project personnel not only for the personnel who are members of a particular project, but more broadly for the personnel of the project-oriented organization that frequently engage in projects and thus become members of project organization in particular project roles. The most important roles that project personnel fulfill on a project are project manager, project team member, project contributor and project owner. All personnel working on a particular project may be considered as the personnel of a particular project, or more precisely the members of the project organization. Project personnel may be solely engaged on one or several projects. In addition, they may have roles in the permanent organization.

---

1   While I acknowledge the increasing importance of programmes and programme management in project-oriented organizations, I do not explicitly include programme management personnel such as programme managers in this research.

5.3 Project Roles

Different competencies are required on a project, thus projects need to draw on project management personnel, expert personnel and management personnel. Expert personnel are contributing to the project as project team members or as project contributors. Management personnel from the permanent organization take on the role as project owner, or for internal projects, also as project team members. In the following sections, I describe the roles that project personnel fulfil on projects.

5.3.1 PROJECT MANAGER

One of the first descriptions of the role of project manager is provided in a classic article by Gaddis (1959) in the *Harvard Business Review*, where he states that the project manager is:

> *A man of action, a man of thought, and a front man. (Gaddis 1959: 91)*

As man of action, a project manager is responsible for keeping the project moving, establishing and preserving the sense of momentum throughout the project. As man of thought, a project manager is responsible for advance planning of the project to avoid project crisis and to focus on the project structures and shaping the project team. As front man, the project manager has selling responsibilities to different stakeholders. The project manager helps to shape and reshape the policies that affect the project; and sells the project to acquire scare resources, such as funds, human resources and material (Gaddis 1959). Gaddis summarizes the role of the project manager as a 'man in between'.

> *He is the man in between management and the technologist – the one man in the organization who must be at home in the front office talking about budgets, time schedules, and corporate policies and at home in the laboratory talking about technical research and development problems. But he is not a superman. He cannot be expected to double as a member of the executive committee and as a scientist equally well. Being a little of both, he is different from both – and it is precisely this quality which makes him so valuable. (Gaddis 1959: 93–94)*

Project managers use project management processes to interest and attract project team members as well as stakeholders, owners and other powerful players to the project, and to shape the project results in a political power process (Blackburn 2002). The project manager ensures that the project realizes a result that achieves the benefits defined in the business case (OGC 2009).

The role of the project manager depends on the form of the project organization, the project management approach applied, as well as the importance of the project manager in the particular organization. The latter may be considered as related to the size and autonomy of the project as well as to the maturity of a project-oriented organization. A wide understanding of the role of project managers exists. The understanding ranges from task co-ordinator and administrator to manager and entrepreneur (Hodgson 2002). Project managers mostly have expert authority, often they also have budgetary authority and on rare occasions they have disciplinary authority. Only in some organizations, is the project manager considered a true manager with disciplinary and budget authority, others see their project managers more as responsible for the execution of the project management guidelines (Hölzle 2010).

In organizations with a traditional project management, the role of the project manager is seen as task co-ordinator and administrator (Hodgson 2002). Then, the main responsibility of the project manager is to enforce the project management guidelines that are in place in the particular organization. Executives may perceive project managers as more tactical and expert than themselves, as project managers concentrate on monitoring and control of cost and time and the delivery of results (Crawford/Pollack 2004; Thomas et al. 2002), which is related to the perception of a project as a task. The incongruence between authority and responsibility is an ambiguity that project managers often face (Fabi/Pettersen 1992).

However, although contradicting practices exist to paint a more comprehensive picture of the role of the project manager, we may draw on role descriptions. Table 5.1 offers a generic role description of the project manager in an empowered project organization (Gareis 2005). The role description relates the tasks of the project manager to the project management process, such as project starting, project co-ordinating, project controlling, solving a project discontinuity and project closing down. The objectives of the role of project manager are to realize the project interest, to ensure the realization of the project objectives, to lead the project team and the project contributors, to represent the project towards representatives of the project stakeholders, and to design the project management process and develop the project management documentation.

Table 5.1   Role description: Project manager

Role: Project manager

Objectives

- Realizes project interests
- Ensures the realization of the project objectives
- Leads the project team and the project contributors
- Represents the project towards representatives of relevant project stakeholders
- Designs project management process and develops the project management documentation

Position in the Organization

- Reports to the project owner
- Is member of the project team
- Leads the project team, the project team members and the project contributors

Tasks

Tasks in project starting

- Designs the project start process (possibly together with selected project team members)
- Transfers know-how from the pre-project phase into the project (together with project team members and project owner)
- Agrees on the project objectives (together with project team members)
- Develops adequate project plans (together with project team members)
- Designs adequate project organization (together with project team members)
- Performs team building and develops the project culture (together with project team members)
- Performs risk management (together with project team members)
- Designs project context relationships (together with project team members)
- Performs initial project marketing (together with project team members)
- Develops project start documentation

Tasks in project co-ordinating

- Dispositions project resources for work packages (together with project team members)
- Controls the work package results and accepts work packages
- Gives feedback to project team members
- Communicates with representatives of project stakeholders and performs project marketing

Tasks in project controlling

- Designs the project controlling process (possibly together with selected project team members)
- Determines the project status (together with project team members)
- Agrees on and performs controlling measures (together with project team members)
- Further develops the project organization and project culture (together with project team members)
- Adapts project objectives (together with project team members)
- Develops project progress reports (together with project team members)
- Redesigns the project context relationships (together with project team members)
- Performs project marketing (together with project team members)

Tasks for resolving a project discontinuity

- Proposes the definition of a project discontinuity to the project owner
- Designs the processes for resolving the project discontinuity (together with the project owner)
- Performs cause analysis and develops immediate measures and alternative strategies (together with project team)
- Performs measures to resolve the discontinuity and controls success (together with project team)
- Ends the project discontinuity (together with project owner and project team)

Tasks in project closing-down

- Designs the project close-down process (possibly together with selected project team members)
- Plans the post-project phase
- Transfers know-how into the permanent organization (together with project team members and representatives from the permanent organization)
- Gives feedback to the project team members, contributors and project owner
- Performs final project marketing (together with project team members)
- Performs emotional close-down of the project (together with project team)
- Develops the close-down report

Stakeholder Relationships

- Project owner, project team members, project contributors
- Co-operation partners, suppliers, media, etc.

Formal Authority

- Holding of project owner team meetings and project team meetings
- Purchasing decisions up to EUR …
- Co-ordination of the project team members and the project contributors
- Selection of the project team members (together with the project owner and the expert pool/line managers)

Source: Gareis 2005: 80.

5.3.2 THE COMPETENT PROJECT MANAGER

Project management scholars have researched competencies of project managers quite extensively (e.g., Aitken/Crawford 2007; Cheng et al. 2005; Morris/Pinto 2004; Thamhain 2004), and in contrast to most of the project management standards, their focus is on the behaviour that the project managers show. In recent years, project management scholars have started criticizing the assumption that there is a positive relationship between the generic standards and effective workplace performance of project managers or project success (Müller/Turner 2010). The feasibility of generic project management standards across industries, organizations and regions has been questioned (Wirth 1996). It is suggested that different competency profiles (Crawford 2005) and leadership styles (Müller/Turner 2010) are appropriate for different project types.

Table 5.2   Behavioural competencies of project managers

El-Sabaa (2001) Human, conceptual and organizational skills	Cheng et al. (2005) PM behavioural competency model	Aitken and Crawford (2007) Project manager personality characteristics and behavioural competencies	Muzio et al. (2007) Soft skills quantification (SSQ)
• Strong goal orientation	• Achievement orientation	• Delivering results	• Results orientation
• Communication: listen, persuade, and understand what others mean by their behaviour	• Impact and influence	• Persuading and influence	• Interpersonal skills
• Delegating Authority: participative decision making	• Teamwork and co-operation	• Deciding and initiating action	
• Mobilizing energy in the project organization	• Directiveness	• Supervising	
• Enthusiasm	• Team leadership initiative	• Leading	
	• Information seeking		
	• Focus on client's needs	• Meeting customer expectations	
• Coping with situations: flexible, patient and persistent	• self-control		• flexibility
	• flexibility		• personal accountability
• Planning	• analytical thinking	• planning and organizing	• planning and organization
• Organizing	• conceptual thinking		
• Strong problem orientation			• problem solving
• Ability to see the project as a whole			
• Ability to visualize the relationship of the project to the community industry			
• Political sensitivity			
• High self-esteem			

El-Sabaa (2001) identifies project management competencies of effective project managers. He differentiates human, conceptual and organizational, and technical competencies and finds that the human competencies the most important one. Cheng et al. (2005) present a PM behavioural competency model, which includes the following 12 behavioural competencies for project managers: achievement orientation, initiative, information seeking, focus on client's needs, impact and influence, directiveness, teamwork and co-operation, team leadership, analytical thinking, conceptual thinking, self-control and flexibility. Aitken and Crawford (2007) assess personality characteristics and behavioural competencies of project managers and identify a set of competencies of successful project managers. Their behavioural competencies are similar to those offered by (Cheng et al. 2005). Muzio et al. (2007) suggest a soft skills quantification (SSQ), including results orientation, interpersonal skills, personal accountability, flexibility, problem solving, and planning and organization. For IT projects, Starkweather and Stevenson (2011) suggest that the most important competencies of project managers are the ability to communicate at multiple levels, leadership and the ability to deal with ambiguity and change.

Table 5.2 presents selected behavioural competency definitions of project managers by scholars. The comparison between the approaches is difficult as the wording and the degree of detail differs. Nevertheless, the behavioural competencies for project managers as outlined in selected empirical studies are mapped against each other to visualize commonalities and differences.

There is a shift towards a more comprehensive understanding of project management competencies including especially behavioural competencies (Muzio et al. 2007; Müller and Turner 2010) observable. While Table 5.2 suggests that there is no shared understanding on the wording, some commonalities can be derived. These are for example the high result orientation and social competence to fulfill the required HR related tasks and relate to the project stakeholders. All definitions show that planning and organizing are central competency elements, which relate the core of understanding project management as plans and planning. In addition, there is an emerging understanding of differences of required competencies in different project types, which I will discuss in more detail next. Different competency profiles may serve as a basis for recruiting, developing and assigning project managers and other project personnel to specific projects.

Hauschildt et al. (2000) identified five types of project managers based on the ratings of their superiors. Using the criteria of organizing under conflict, experience, decision making, productive creativity, organizing with co-operation, co-operative leadership and integrative thinking they differentiate the following types of project managers: project start, project newcomer, focused creative expert, uncreative decision maker, and thick skinned pragmatist; and set these types in relation to project types and success (personal as well as project success). Their results suggest that different types of project managers are likely to be found in different contexts, associated with different project types, however, they cannot prove causality.

Turner and Müller (2006) conducted a comprehensive quantitative study to explore the leadership competency profiles of successful project managers and found differences in project types. Consistently with the general management literature, they suggest that emotional competencies are the most significant for project managers. They develop competency profiles for different project types and make the following recommendations:

• Be aware of appropriate leadership competencies, when selecting and assigning project managers;
• Develop within the pool of project managers appropriate leadership competencies to serve different types of projects performed in the company;
• Appreciate project managers for their contribution to project success within the organization.

The competence profiles developed indicate that ideal senior project managers should bring high scales in often contradicting dimensions, including, for example, result orientation and process orientation, task orientation and team orientation, detail view and holistic view (Huemann/Lauer 2004), which is in accordance with the findings of (Thomas/Buckle-Henning 2007).

In addition to the project type, the adequate competency profile depends on the company context as such. As suggested earlier in Chapter 4, every project-oriented organization has its own blend of cultural values, which ideally at its core would support project-orientation. Competencies of project managers reflect the project type and the culture of the project-oriented company. To perform projects within a specific industry, project personnel require, in addition to the project management competence, specific industry competence, comprising technology and market competence, which may also lead to rather industry specific careers of project managers (for example IT project manager, construction project manager) (Morris/Pinto 2004).

5.3.3 PROJECT TEAM MEMBER

Project team members are part of the project team and may lead sub teams within the project. The objectives of the role project team member include: to realize the project interests, to contribute to the realization of the project objectives, to fulfill work packages with the required quality and quantity, the possibility of leading a project sub-team and contributing to project management (Gareis 2005).

Project team members are also referred to as core team or project management team members. In an empowered project organization, project team members engage in project management and contribute to project starting, project co-ordinating, project controlling, solving a project discontinuity and project closing down. While the project team member, who is part of the project team, requires project management competency in addition to his/her technical/contents competency, the project contributor or project worker only contributes his/her technical/contents expertise to the project.

5.3.4 PROJECT TEAM

Contemporary project management is based on team structures to achieve collective work efforts. Teams are central to projects, but the team is not synonymous to project, in the notion of a temporary organization. Larger projects consist of several teams (Hoegl/Proserpio 2004), for example, a project (management) team and several (technical) sub teams. A large project may have 200–300 people engaged and working in different team structures. In this section, I further discuss the project team as a central unit of the project as a temporary organization (Lundin/Söderholm 1995), and describe the project team as a team role.

Project teams are especially conceptualized as units for collective learning, as they are designed to solve problems that cannot be solved by a single person. More explicitly, the project team is viewed as an 'elementary learning arena of projects' (Grabher 2004: 1492).

Hoegl and Parboteeah (2006: 79) define teamwork quality based on elements such as:

- **Communication**: The team members communicate mostly directly and personally with each other. Project-relevant information is shared openly by all team members. The team members are happy with the usefulness of the information received from other team members.
- **Co-ordination**: The work done on subtasks within the project is closely harmonized. There are clear and fully understood goals for subtasks within the team.

- **Balance of member contributions**: The team recognizes the specific potentials (strengths and weaknesses) of individual team members. The team members are contributing to the achievement of the team's goals in accordance with their specific potential.
- **Mutual support**: The team members help and support each other as best they can. Discussions and controversies are conducted constructively. Suggestions and contributions of team members are discussed and further developed.
- **Effort**: Every team member fully pushes the project. Every team member makes the project highest priority.
- **Cohesion**: It is important to the members of our team to be part of this project. All members are fully integrated in the team.

The importance of the project team for project performance/success has been widely discussed by scholars (Hoegl/Gemuenden 2001; Pinto et al. 1993; Zwikael/Unger-Aviram 2010). Gareis and Huemann (2007) suggest the maturity of the project team based on the individual team members' competencies, and the competency of the team to create a 'Big Project Picture', create commitment, assure synergies, learn and innovate, solve conflicts and commonly design the project management process. Table 5.3 provides a comparison between effective and ineffective project team.

5.3.5 PROJECT OWNER

There is an increasing research interest in the role of the internal project owner, also named project sponsor (Crawford et al. 2008; Hall et al. 2003; Helm/Remington 2005; Kloppenborg et al. 2009). In accordance with Andersen (2012) I use the term project owner, as it expresses that the project owner is not only providing financial resources in cash or kind to the project, but is responsible for strategic project decisions, and assigns and approves a project.

Table 5.3   The effective versus ineffective project team

The effective project team	The ineffective project team
• High performance and task efficiency	• Low performance
• Innovative and creative behaviour	• Low commitment to project objectives
• Commitment of the team members	• Unclear project objectives and fluid commitment
• Professional objectives of team members fit with project requirements	levels from key players
• Team members highly interdependent but interface effectively	• Manipulation of others, hidden feelings
	• Conflict avoidance at all costs
• Capacity for conflict resolution present in team	• Subtle sabotage, fear, disinterest, or foot-dragging
• Conflicts are dealt with and lead to beneficial results	• Cliques, collusion, isolation of members
• Effective communication	• Unresponsiveness
• High levels of trust	
• Results orientation	
• Interest in membership, commitment	
• High energy levels and enthusiasm	
• High morale	
• Change orientation	

Source: Adapted from Kerzner 2006: 216.

Table 5.4   Comparison: Project owner and project manager

Project owner	Project manager
• Realization of project-related company interests	• Realization of project interests
• Strategic project management	• Strategic and operative project management
• Engages with the project from time to time	• Engages on the project rather continuously
• Provision of context information	• Ensuring project information

Source: Adapted from Gareis 2005.

The project owner realizes the project-related company interests, co-ordinates project and company interests, provides context information and gives feedback to the project team on the project deliverables. The project owner leads the project manager and carries out marketing tasks for the project and communicates with relevant stakeholders (Gareis 2005; OGC 2009).

To better clarify the role of the project owner, it can be compared to the role of the project manager (Andersen 2012; Gareis 2005). The project owner is a manager, or in strategically important projects, a group of managers, who are most interested in the project results. The project owner is not a super project manager, but has a kind of counterpart role in regard to the project manager. While the project manager represents the project interests, the project owner represents the project related company interests. While the project manager is responsible for strategic and operative project management, the role of the project owner is solely strategic. The project owner only engages with the project from time to time, while the project manager is continuously engaged on the project. In the project owner meetings, in which the project manager and project owner meet, the project owner provides context information, while the project manager provides project information, such as the status of the project. The comparison of the project owner and the project manager is illustrated in Table 5.4.

The internal project owner provides a structural link to the permanent organization, which maintains the project's alignment to the company strategy and interest. The role can be considered as a 'liaison position' between the temporary project organization and the permanent line (Andersen 2012; Mintzberg 1979). The project owner provides the critical link between the permanent organization and the project, ensures that governance requirements are met, and that support is provided to projects (Crawford et al. 2008). The project owner is the least explicitly established project role in many organizations, although it is considered of high importance for project success (Bryde 2008).

5.4 Some Challenges for Project Personnel

Project personnel are considered as essential human resource/capital for the project-oriented organization. The higher the demand for projects and their strategic importance to the organization, the more valuable project personnel are for the project-oriented organization. Project personnel spend their time on projects, see Table 5.5. Thus, the project is their specific working environment. Projects as temporary organizations are described with specific features, such as time limited, task oriented, team as central unit and dynamic (Lundin/Söderholm 1995). The challenges for project personnel arise from the project itself as well as from the need for changing between permanent organization and project organization. Project personnel need to have not only the content competencies and expertise to fulfill the project objectives, but must also be equipped to deal with discontinuity, dynamism and other challenges for employee well-being that project work may bring. Table 5.6 summarizes the specifics of projects and indicates HR related issues. Table 5.7 summarizes relevant studies.

Table 5.5 Overview on roles of project personnel

Characteristics	Project owner	Project manager	Project team member	Project team	Project contributor
Names	• Project owner, project sponsor, project steering committee, project supervisory board, etc.	• Project manager, project leader, project co-ordinator, project director etc.	• Project team member, project core team member, project management team member project engineer, etc.	• Project team, project management team	• Project contributor; expert, project worker etc.
Importance for project success	• Very high	• Very high	• High	• Very high	• High
Objectives	• Realization of project-related organization interests • Strategic project management • Provision of context information relevant for project	• Realization of project interests • Strategic and operative project management • Ensuring project information	• Fulfilling work packages • Possibly leading a sub-team • Participating in project team meetings • Contributing to project management and project marketing	• Developing the 'Big project picture' • Ensuring synergies • Solving conflicts • Ensuring commitment • Organizing learning in the project	• Contributing to work packages • Participating in sub team meetings
Non-objectives	• Performance of the tasks of the project manager • Arbitrator for the project team	• Only work on the project content • Expert on the project content	• Only tasks as expert	• Individual work	• Participating in project team meetings
Number of persons	• One (for small projects) or two to maximum four (for larger projects) • Same or higher levels in the hierarchy	• One person • In practice sometimes two persons	• One person	• 3–12 persons	• One person
Competencies	• Industry • Company/organization • Project management • Strategic orientation and decision-making abilities • Social competence	• Project management • Company/organization • Industry • Product • Social competence	• Expert • Project management • Social competence	• Team work competence, project management competence	• Expert • Minimum understanding of project management • Social competence
Recruiting	• Managers affected by the project results	• PM expert pool • Sometimes: external market	• Expert pool (or department) • Sometimes: external market	• Is temporary, thus needs to be developed on a project	• Expert Pool (or a department) • External market

Source: Adapted from Gareis 2005.

Table 5.6   **Specifics of a project and HRM consequences**

	Specifics of a project	HR-related issues
Time	• Temporary, have start and end • Duration is planned at the beginning of project, end is inherent in the project start • Often high time pressures • Short- to medium-term orientation	• Transient work processes • Uncertainty for personnel about future assignments • Temporary nature of project creates urgency for the project personnel to work for the project • Less time for training and explicit development of project personnel in traditional training settings
Business process	• Relatively unique, short to mid-term, strategically important business process of medium or large scope • High result orientation to achieve project objectives, as this is the raison d'être for the existence of the project	• Relatively unique and novel work, which often involves innovation and learning for project personnel • Changing targets and uncertainty for project personnel • Different competences of project personnel required • Personnel may even be integrated from other companies, for example partners, suppliers, customers • Project result (even when intangible as a feasibility study) is visible for the project personnel at the end of the project
Team	• Team structures are central • Different teams within one project possible	• Teams on projects are temporary and need to be explicitly created for the specific project • Team as well as individuals are objects for HRM on a project
Change	• Dynamic, organize for change, change object is the project and the organization(s) for whom the project is delivered	• Project personnel needs to deal with dynamic, ambiguities, uncertainty, discontinuities

Table 5.7   **Relevant studies of HRM in project-based/project-oriented organizations**

	Midler (1995)	Hobday (2000)	Lindkvist (2004)	Thomas/Mullaly (2008)	Bredin/Söderlund (2011)
Aim	• Study of the change in Renault from a strongly functional organization to a project-based organization	• Study of different types of project-organizational solutions and the advantages and disadvantages of organizing versus a strongly project-oriented organization	• Study the logic of project-based organization, in particular the governance process Combination of hierarchical principles with market principles	• Study on the value project management can create in organizations	• Study analyses the interplay between HR department, line manager, project manager and project worker in the project-based organization

Methodology	• Retrospective and longitudinal case study over a period of almost 40 years. Comparison of the different types of project co-ordination used by the company	• Comparative case study of two projects in the same firm	• A single case study investigation of a unit with the Tetra Pak group, a Swedish company operating in the packaging material industry	• Large scale international study with quantitative and qualitative parts, mixed methods approach	• Multiple case
Industry context	• Automotive, R&D	• Advanced, high-cost scientific, industrial, and medical equipment	• Packaging material, market-based R&D	• Multiple context industry and country contexts	• Multiple context
HRM findings	• Engineers were not prepared for cross-functional collaboration. Vague responsibility for the skill-based functional departments. Difficulties to maintain the long-term technical learning when organizational structures focused short-term and project-oriented objectives. Staff rotation had dysfunctional effects on project convergence. The dismantling of a team at the end of a project was a complicated issue, since permanent structures or new projects rarely produced satisfactory job opportunities at the right time	• A strong emphasis on the project dimension can breed insecurity concerning career development. Cross-functionality leads to both opportunities and problems, including learning from other disciplines and a local focus, but also a lack of professional connections with experts in the same field and an ignorance of the global processes and systems within the firm	• Project teams hardly became 'well-developed groups' in the traditional sense with shared values, shared understandings, and shared knowledge base. Organizational structure becomes 'individualized', making the firm reliant upon the abilities of the employees to self-organize. Internal labour markets become more important and individuals feel more like 'free agents'. To build a reputation for a willingness to contribute and help others becomes essential	• Mature project-oriented organizations can raise intangible HR-related benefits, like improvements in effective work cultures, alignment of approaches, terminology, and values within the organization, overall effectiveness of the organization and its management approach, improved transparency, clarity of structures, roles, and accountability	• They differentiate two typical organizational settings they could identify in project-based organizations and describe in the HR quadriad the different interplay

5.4.1 HIGH GOAL ORIENTATION

Project-orientation creates pressures on individuals (Packendorff 2002), caused, for instance, by the very temporary nature of the work and its dynamic work boundaries and contexts. Project management is considered as a rather self-selecting profession (Turner et al. 2008b). Project managers and, more broadly speaking, project personnel enjoy working on projects, but the strong focus and task orientation that result may bring side effects.

> The very vocabulary of project-based management seems laden with connotations: surpassing of oneself, challenging, initiative, personal achievement, professional development, employees working in projects become actors, a choice of language that emphasises the autonomy they are supposed to enjoy in order to get involved and bring projects to their conclusion. (Asquin et al. 2010: 166)

Asquin et al. do not deny the value of projects for company performance, but critically investigate the side effects. Projects are recognized as a means for high levels of commitment because of their intrinsic characteristics. The time-limitation of projects creates urgency and stirs individuals into action, giving them clear objectives to be fulfilled through teamwork and offering a break from the daily work routine. A similar conclusion is drawn by Lindgren and Packendorff (2006) who studied project personnel in an IT-consultancy context and contributed to an understanding of how project work is related to the on-going construction of femininity and masculinity. They find that the current project work practices entail reproduction of masculinities such as rationality, efficiency, control and devotion to work.

5.4.2 UNCERTAINTY

Every time a new project starts or an old one finishes, the human resource configuration changes. Personnel are transferred from one project to the next, from the permanent organization to new projects or from old projects back to the permanent organization. The temporal nature of projects brings a degree of uncertainty for project personnel, who cannot be sure what kinds of projects they will be assigned to, the location of future projects, or their future work colleagues (Turner et al. 2008b). Projects are dynamic because they are created to deal with complexity; thus, projects often include high uncertainty. The job requirements on projects may be neither well-defined nor stable (Keegan/Turner 2003), which may lead to role ambiguity and role conflict.

5.4.3 FRAGMENTED CAREERS

While some organizations can still provide a person with a (lifelong) career, a project being temporary cannot. Careers are characterized by hopping from one project assignment to the next (Jones/DeFillippi 1996). Because of these varied and fragmented careers, project personnel can get easily lost between projects.

The project-oriented career fits into the concept of modern career research. Project-oriented careers are rather fragmented, and the nomadic lives of project personnel are plain to see. Project personnel move from one project to another, which take place in different contexts. This creates a picture of *project nomads*, who can be considered as adventurous. The project-oriented career is characterized by a series of projects in different contractual arrangements; periods of permanent employment contracts and temporary employment contracts are interweaved (Lang/Rattay 2005), as shown in Figure 5.1. A career thus becomes a succession of projects (Jones/DeFillippi 1996), not a series of steps up a career ladder. A high percentage of personnel in project-oriented organizations may be working in projects. Experts and line managers are contributing to the project, for example, as project team members or as project owners. Thus, the careers of most of the personnel in the project-oriented organization – not only of the project manager – may relate more or less to project work.

Schein (1978: 37) differentiates between vertical, horizontal and centripetal career movements. In the case of vertical career movements, promotion is associated with a hierarchical advancement. In the case of horizontal career movements, no hierarchical advancement is performed. Centripetal career movements indicate changes towards the inner core of the organization. An example of a centripetal career movement in the project-oriented organization is where, for example, in addition to a management role, a person may take on a membership role in the project portfolio group, which includes taking on the responsibility for strategic decisions in the project-portfolio of a project-oriented organization.

Turner and Keegan (2003) coined the term staircase career for the project-oriented organization. Career movements can advance up the career ladder, but also along the career ladder, which is known as horizontal and centripetal career movement. Possible movements along the career ladder prevent the so-called *Peter Principle*, which says that persons are promoted until they reach their level of incompetence. If an employee finds himself/herself in a position not fitting, he/she can make a sideways career movement, which is not negative compared to a step down the career ladder.

The project-oriented career is not defined according to the increased number of subordinate employees, but rather as a personal development process and the attainment of competencies (Keegan/Turner 2003). Careers may be perceived as a series of projects for competency development of the individual, which may lead to role differentiation instead of hierarchical steps in careers. Projects may be considered as stepping stones in the course of the project manager's career (Jones/DeFillippi 1996). See Table 5.8.

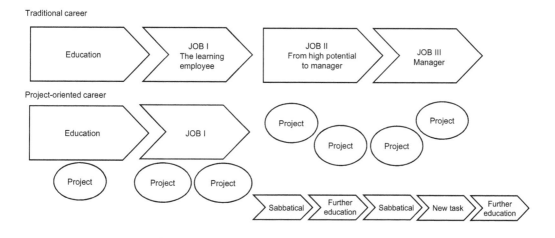

Figure 5.1   Traditional versus project-oriented career
Source: Adapted from Lang/Rattay 2005: 36.

Table 5.8   Career of project managers versus functional line managers

Career	Project manager	Functional line manager
Average age	• About 35 years	• About 42 years
Mobility/stability	• Greater mobility across projects and companies and less stability, stay in one field: 4.3 years	• Less mobility, greater stability, stay in one field: 20 years
Career motives	• Teamwork • Creativity • Own further development	• Stability orientation (maintaining a position) • Leadership
Key competencies	• Collaborative and self- governance • Communication • Skill diversity	• Knowledge-based technical spatiality • Efficiency and accuracy
Strategy	• Self-managed	• Regulated by organization
Incentives	• Bonuses • Job rotation • Learning	• Promotion • Bonuses

Source: Adapted from El Sabaa 2001: 6.

There are differences between careers of project managers and functional line managers, including average age, mobility, stability, career motives, key competencies, strategy for career management and incentives (El Sabaa 2001). Project managers are generally younger than functional managers, have greater mobility across projects and companies, and have less stability (i.e., maintaining a position) compared to functional managers. Essential career motives of project managers include: teamwork, creativity and a desire to further develop oneself; while line mangers are attracted by the stability of a position and the leadership role that they can play there. While the career strategy pursued by a project manager is characterized by self-management, the career strategy of a functional manager is characterized by being rather paternalistic. Thus, the latter may rely much more on the career system offered by the company. Project managers are assuming greater individual responsibility for planning their career moves and identifying the steps that are required to achieve them.

Project managers take a much greater responsibility for their career. In planning their development to progress their career, they need to look for projects that will give them those development opportunities (Skilton 2008) and bring them visibility and reputation. In line with Schein's (1978) centripetal career movements, Hodgson (2002) suggests that project management is a path to power which over the years leads to roles on larger, more costly, or strategically more important projects.

> But career development is not only a question of the challenges one meets and the responsibilities one holds. It is also a question of whether one is involved in project management, is visible to others and enjoys a certain level of prestige ('prestige' in the sense of being involved in prestigious projects).(...) [career] success seems to be enhanced by factors, such as: range of responsibility, budget controlled, access to top management, and personal reputation. (Larsen 2002: 34)

Thus, reputation is an issue for project personnel – especially for project managers – forcing them to not only acquire project management competencies, but even to sell themselves and to promote their careers.

Keegan and Turner (2003) coined the *no home syndrome*. Project personnel spend their working lives moving from one project to another. They work on one project for several months, then that project breaks up and they move to a new project. This creates a nomadic life, and it also increases the need for team building on projects to create a sense of belonging to the project (Reid 2003). Project managers may feel that they do not have a permanent professional home when they are not spending time in permanent structures. They may lack a permanent sense of belonging to a company.

5.4.4 MULTIROLE CHALLENGE

Closely related to project overload, stress for project personnel may specifically derive from their engagement in many projects at the same time, which is more often the case when the company undertakes many small to medium-sized projects (Turner et al. 2008b; Zika-Viktorsson et al. 2006). Project personnel can work in different projects at the same time, even in different project roles. A person may have a role in the permanent organization, as well as in one or several projects. These multi-role settings not only challenge human resource planning and may lead to project overload for the person, but they can lead to very stressful role conflicts (Rau/Hyland 2002).

Personnel planning and allocation to projects is challenged in the project-oriented organization, as the number and size of projects performed in a company may vary considerably, making predictions of future resource and competence requirements for the organization difficult (Engwall 2003; Eskerod 1998). The sharing of personnel in concurrent projects is found to be challenging (Yaghootkar/Gil 2012). Challenges of human resource planning especially refer to the necessity to consider different levels of aggregation in the project, the project portfolio and the company.

Peaking workloads may make it difficult to achieve a work–life balance for project personnel. Gällstedt (2003) explores the impact of working conditions-related problems of resource allocation and priorities within the project organization on the motivation and stress of project personnel. She suggests if not managed properly these could have an impact on project performance.

Challenges of project overload for project personnel are especially high in organizations that perform small to medium-sized external projects, where project personnel work simultaneously in more than one project, and unexpected projects add on to the workload (Blichfeldt 2008). In particular, contract organizations often cannot precisely predict the levels of resource requirements into the immediate future (Keegan/Turner 2003), which suggests that the problem of project overload is most significant in companies undertaking projects for external clients (Lindgren/Packendorff 2006).

The following reasons for project overload are named for external projects lasting three to nine months, which include: challenged resource planning, multi-role assignments and unrealistic promises to clients (Turner et al. 2008b: 581). These projects often cannot be planned as part of the annual budgeting cycle because most of them are not known at the time that the budgets are prepared, so it is more difficult to ensure that there are sufficient project personnel for the encountered project workload. The resource demands for successive projects might be wildly different, and that makes it difficult to plan for the required number of project personnel. It is possible to employ temporary workers, but it can take time to find appropriate temporary personnel, which may happen once it is too late for projects that only last a few months. Project personnel work on more than one project at once, so there is a chance that two or more projects will peak simultaneously. Resource demands will peak at commissioning, but now that this is occurring many times per year, these times are less easy to plan and balance. With much shorter timescales on projects, it is not so easy to give the project personnel two weeks off to pursue other non-work interests, either immediately before or immediately after the peak.

Finally, to compete on the market and to win the work, contracting companies deliberately underestimate the required workload, and then project personnel have to work long hours in order to complete the project on time. In any case, the clients have tight timescales, so the projects require intensive work all the way through. If these problems are left unmanaged, they can lead to greater inefficiencies, exacerbating the issues of employee well-being (Zika-Viktorsson et al. 2006).

5.4.5 HIGHER DEGREE OF RESPONSIBILITY

Project personnel take on higher responsibility for their work, in the notion of empowerment (Gareis 2005) and for themselves (Bredin/Söderlund 2011). The latter refers in particular to their own responsibilities regarding a work–life balance (Turner et al. 2008b) and to their careers. Project personnel need to take responsibility for planning the development that they need and for finding projects that will give them learning and career opportunities. For project managers, this refers to their project management competences. Keeping state of the art competences and getting them certified becomes an issue, even for those who have unlimited contracts with a project-oriented organization. Project personnel take on the responsibility for the acquisition of the competences demanded, as well as of his/her professional development in order to remain employable.

5.5 Raising the Potential Projects Bring

The literature provides evidence for challenges, and most of the scholars take a critical perspective on those. But any challenge has both a positive and a negative side. Whether a challenge turns to a threat or creates potential depends on the person as well as on the organization that provides or doesn't provide structures to deal with these challenges. Table 5.9 provides an overview of the challenges, and shows the positive as well the negative aspects for the project personnel.

HRM-related potential of project-orientation include projects as an attractive working form and source of motivation and commitment for project personnel. If project-orientation is introduced in an organization commitment, dynamism, support and solidarity can be expected to increase (Hovmark/Nordqvist 1996).

Table 5.9   Positive and negative aspects of project work

Positive side	Challenges	Negative side
Intrinsic motivation Source of commitment Providing sense	High goal orientation	Over commitment, burnout
Adventure Learning possibilities	Uncertainty/novel	Stress
Possibility for time outs without harming professional career	Fragmented careers	Getting lost in transition
Variety of roles	Multi role assignments	Project overload, stress
Freedom and empowerment	Higher degree of responsibility	Left alone, no support

If we accept the evidence that project personnel in the project-oriented organization are especially challenged and put under pressure by the high resulting focus, uncertainty and discontinuity projects bring, then the question arises as to how a HRM system can support the employee well-being of the project personnel to decrease the negative aspects, increase the positive aspects and by that raise the HR-related potential projects bring to the personnel and to the project-oriented organization.

5.6 Consequences

This chapter has defined project personnel and discussed the challenges that arise for project personnel working in project-oriented organizations. Table 5.10 provides the definition of project personnel.

The roles taken on the projects were discussed, and the project team as an essential unit of consideration in a project described. The discussion of the competencies of project managers provides evidence that project managers require leadership/people competencies to manage projects successfully.

Nevertheless, because of the specific features of projects, there arise HR-related challenges for personnel that can either threaten employee well-being or may be bring potential, if the HRM system provides viable structures.

Table 5.10   Definition: Project personnel

DEFINITION: PROJECT PERSONNEL
Project personnel are those persons that are frequently members of projects, in the role as project managers, project team member, project contributor and project owner. They derive from project management, technical expert personnel and management personnel.

6

HRM for the Project-Oriented Organization

6.1 Introduction

In Chapters 3, 4 and 5, I described the project, the specific features of the project-oriented organization, the project personnel and the challenges project work bring and in doing so I have created a comprehensive picture of the project-oriented organization. In this chapter, I relate the HRM system to the project-oriented organization. To do that, I introduce a working model based on social system theory as theoretical lens. The working model serves the purpose of observing the HRM system for the project-oriented organization. The *Working Model: HRM system in the context of project-oriented organization* is described with propositions.

6.2 Working Model: HRM System in the Context of Project-Oriented Organization

By using Social System Theory[1] after Niklas Luhmann (1995) as the theoretical lens, I conceptualize HRM as a self-referential HRM system, which comprises HRM-related decisions/communications, manifested in the internal structures of the HRM system distinct from its environment, and (more or less adequately) related to its relevant context (environment).

In essence self-referential systems are autopoetically closed; that means that they are producing the elements of which they actually consist. Social systems consist of communications/decisions and because of being operationally closed, they can interact with their environment. The way the system interacts is determined by the internal structures of the social system itself. Social systems are structurally coupled with their environment via persons (more precisely, psychic systems). The persons who are members of the social system interpret the environment and try to initialize communication processes in the system. Luhmann places persons as a relevant environment outside of the social system, in that they lose their place in the system, but as internal environment, they gain a central position in the social context of the system.

Managing happens by communication/intervention whether the system reacts or not (that means whether the communication produces connecting communications/decisions and the system depends on the system) (Kasper 1990; Willke 2005). That might be part of the reason why many

---

1   For more information on Social System Theory and Radical Contructivsm see Appendix.

project-oriented organizations do not have viable HRM systems, as they might consider project management only as a competency area for the project personnel and provide according services in training, but do not perceive projects or project-orientation as relevant for the HRM system.

HRM is defined as a bundle of HRM practices or components of a HRM system, which are carried out by different actors, such as the members, the CEO, board of directors, work council/ trade activist, government/legislation and HR managers/experts (Paauwe 2004). More specifically for project-oriented organizations, by the relevant players are those of the HR quadriand, the HR managers, line/expert pool managers, project workers and project manager (Bredin/Söderlund 2011). These are important players in HRM and they are of relevance in my research, but are positioned as internal social environments of the HRM system. They are of essential importance, as they are the 'eyes and ears' of the HRM system and they need to understand and interpret the context adequately to provide the HRM system with information that 'makes a difference'. In other words, they allow for adaptation of the structures of the HRM system to be and keep on being viable to its context.

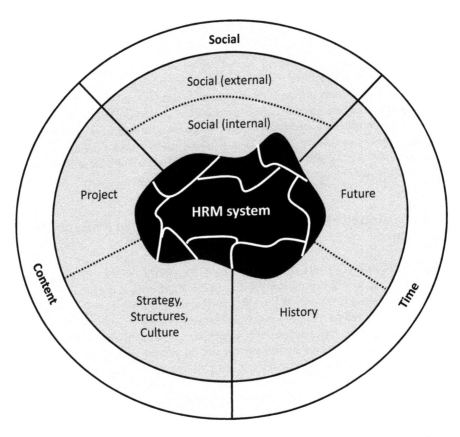

Figure 6.1   Working model: HRM system in the context of the project-oriented organization

I have chosen this theoretical position to look more closely at the structures, independently of persons. I am interested in the internal structures of the HRM system that come into existence by the reproduction of communications/decisions. Further, I am interested in how far these internal structures are viable to its context, more specifically how they relate/or not relate adequately to the project-oriented organization.

Mayerhofer and Steyrer (2004) point to the advantages of analysing HRM with the lens of Social Systems Theory. It allows for analysing the social sphere, which emerges even in the simplest form of social system, the interaction between two persons. Thus, this theoretical lens allows the internal structures that emerge in a social system to be analysed, independently of the persons. But it also provides the option of a multilevel analysis considering context and relation to contexts (Mayrhofer 2004).

Figure 6.1 visualizes a working model to analyse the HRM system in the context of the project-oriented organization. The units of analysis are the context (social, content and time-related context), the internal structures of the HRM system and possible relations between the system and its environment, whereas the latter are part of the internal structures.

Following, the elements of the working model are described more comprehensively with propositions based on the literature that was presented in earlier chapters of this book.

6.3 Context: Content-related Social and Time-related

6.3.1 CONTENT-RELATED CONTEXT

The internal structures of a social system can only be understood in its context. For content-related context, I concentrate on the specific features of the project-oriented organization, and on the projects.

As described at length in Chapter 4, the project-oriented organization based on the strategy *Managing by Projects* is a highly differentiated organization that requires specific structures.

To deal with diversity, the project-oriented organization develops specific integrative structures for governance, such as the Project Portfolio Group that manages the project portfolio from a strategic perspective, or the Project Management Office that supports the development of project management related capabilities.

Project-oriented organizations develop specific capabilities for managing projects including project management, programme management, assigning a project or programme, assuring quality on a project and project networking.

Fitting values to support project-orientation enable uncertainty, contradiction and the tensions between permanent and temporary to be dealt with.

Table 6.1   Propositions regarding: Content-related context

PROPOSITIONS: CONTENT-RELATED CONTEXT
- Based on the strategy Managing by Project, the project-oriented organization has specific structures and shapes a specific cultural values.
- Different projects are carried out in the project-oriented organization.

6.3.2 SOCIAL CONTEXT

Narrowly defined, HRM could be represented by the HRM department. As discussed earlier, the understanding of HRM has developed further. The HRM function/system includes top managers to establish a strategic link between the HRM system and the company strategy line managers/ expert pool managers to deliver HRM. In the project-oriented organization there are even more 'players'. The social environments of the HRM system including specific ones for the project-oriented organization are:

- HR managers/experts;
- top managers, middle managers, expert pool managers, project managers;
- project personnel which comprises project management, expert and management personnel;
- PMO managers, PPG members;
- Project Academy (as internal training unit in large organizations such as, for example, NASA);
- from a HRM related perspective relevant additional company external social environments are, for example, PM training/education providers, national and international PM associations and certification bodies.

Table 6.2   Propositions regarding: Social context

PROPOSITION: SOCIAL CONTEXT
- Additional stakeholders are of relevance for the HRM system.

6.3.3 TIME-RELATED CONTEXT

In addition to social and content-related context, time-related context is considered. The time-related context includes the history of the HRM system and its future expectations, as well as the history of the project-oriented organization and its future expectations. For example the 'heritage' of the HRM system from the past shapes the possibility of the present HRM system of an organization. Also, future expectations influence decisions made today. These can change or not change the internal structures of the HRM system. If the HRM system, for example, has the future expectation that the demand for projects and project management will increase, well-experienced project managers will be urgently needed in the future, so the HRM system will make different decisions than in a situation when a decline in the project business is expected.

The HRM system requires the strategic information about the future relevance of projects and project-orientation to relate its HRM structures accordingly.

Table 6.3   Proposition regarding: Time-related context

PROPOSITION: TIME-RELATED CONTEXT
- The history and the future expectations regarding the importance of projects are of relevance for the HRM system.

6.4 Structures: HRM Strategies, Goals and Values

6.4.1 HRM STRATEGIES

HRM strategies support project-orientation

The HRM system explicitly recognizes the existence of temporary projects in the project-oriented organization and adapts its HRM internal structures accordingly. The HRM strategy of a project-oriented HRM system considers project-orientation in its services to offer projects some support towards project performance, as well as in the way the HRM system is organized to allow for alignment with the project-oriented organization.

For example, in the development strategy for project personnel, projects may be explicitly used as learning opportunities and stepping stones within career fields the organization offers. Career systems and incentive systems acknowledge the existence of projects and supports project (management) careers and the profession of project management (Hölzle 2010; Jones/DeFillippi 1996; Larsen 2002). Adequate resource planning systems are provided (Eskerod 1998; Engwall/Jerbrant 2003) that are able to capture resource requirements of projects.

Table 6.4   Proposition regarding: HRM strategy

PROPOSITION: HRM STRATEGIES
- HRM strategies support project-orientation.

6.4.2 HRM GOALS

Employee well-being as a dimension of sustainable development of a company is especially challenged in the project-oriented organization, as it is an organization with uncertainty, ambiguity and structural breaks. This organization requires balancing in many aspects, as it is engaged in balancing short-term and long-term orientation, balancing stakeholders with different interests, balancing social and economic interests, balancing individual and organizational interest.

Employee well-being is challenged in the project-oriented organization especially because of the temporary character of projects that creates urgency and high goal orientation, the uncertainty and dynamics on projects, and the challenge of multi role assignments. Nevertheless there is also a positive side of project work, when employee well-being is ensured by the organization. There are HR potentials to be raised when a viable HRM system supports project-orientation. HRM potentials of project-orientation include the consideration of projects as learning opportunities, projects as attractive working form and source of motivation and commitment for project personnel.

Table 6.5   Propositions regarding: HRM goals

PROPOSITIONS: HRM GOALS
- The HRM system understands the HR-related challenges projects bring to project personnel and ensures employee well-being to raise HR-related potential.

Projects are learning opportunities: Sveiby (1997) argued that a key to retaining personnel in knowledge-based organizations is ensuring that personnel have the opportunities to work on interesting projects providing interesting career challenges. It is widely acknowledged in literature that projects bring learning opportunities. I here add that projects may be more explicitly framed as learning opportunities for project personnel. This is also especially true for project managers. The study by El-Sabaa (2001) on the careers of project managers in comparison to line managers pointed out that the project managers are motivated by teamwork, creativity and their own further development.

Projects are motivating and create commitment: Project management is considered as a rather self-selecting profession (Turner et al. 2008b). Persons who do not like to deal with the dynamics and stress leave the profession. I argue not only that project managers enjoy project work, but also that projects may be considered as project personnel. They are an attractive working form for motivating and generating commitment of project personnel (Mayrhofer/Meyer 2002) because of their high goal-orientation. They offer a time-limited challenge, giving the members of the project organization clear objectives to be fulfilled through teamwork.

In that projects can be recognized as a means of high levels of commitment, projects contribute meaning and sense to the members of the project so they can achieve project results. As the organization is relatively small, the members of the project can see their own contribution to the project results. The high goal-orientation combined with team-orientation are specific of project work. Members of the project can work together with others and see the end product of their work. Projects can be considered as an attractive working form for motivation and commitment of personnel (Mayrhofer/Meyer 2002).

Projects are attractive: Projects are modern and attractive working forms and people also enjoy working on projects. In the 'war for talents' project-oriented organizations may actively promote themselves to attract the most competent personnel by showing that the organization applies modern structures and uses project as working forms.

6.5 Structures: HRM Processes and Infrastructure

HRM processes in the project-oriented organization are not novel, but specific adoption of these processes may support project-orientation. These HRM processes include recruiting, managing performance (including developing, appraising, rewarding) and releasing.

Recruiting is the process of bringing new project personnel to the project-oriented organization. It is based on planning and includes selection of new permanent and temporary project personnel. Recruiting is done for a position in an expert pool or directly for a position on a project.

Developing is the process of increasing the competence of an employee. The objective of developing project managers and further project personnel is to improve the competence by supporting the acquisition of knowledge and experience. Development activities are carried out either on the job, in a project or in general outside of project assignments.

An appraisal is the process of evaluating the performance and providing feedback to the employee. This includes future performance planning and improvement, and not just retrospective performance evaluation. The appraisal meeting is a formal review once or twice a year to consider key performance and development issues.

Rewarding is the process of providing financial and non-financial remuneration for personnel according to their contribution to the organization. Reward includes salary, variable pay and benefits, responsibility, career opportunities, learning development, the work itself and the quality of work–life balance (Turner et al. 2008a).

Table 6.6   **Propositions regarding: HRM processes and infrastructure**

PROPOSITIONS: HRM PROCESSES AND INFRASTRUCTURE
- Specific adoptions in the HRM processes in the permanent organization ensure relations to project HRM processes.
- Specific adoptions in the HRM infrastructure support project-orientation.

Releasing is applied when personnel leave the company. The most significant challenge faced by project-oriented companies is loss of knowledge when temporary workers leave the company at the end of projects. With the release of temporary workers, it is also useful to remain in contact in order to maintain the organization's network and to make future co-operation possible.

If HRM takes place on the project and in the permanent organization, then the question arises how are these project HRM processes and the HRM processes in the permanent organization aligned to support each other. Borrowed from business process management (Gareis/Stummer 2008) I draft a process network as shown in Figure 6.2. The process network is applied to analyse and visualize the relations between project and line HRM processes in the permanent organization.

The process network indicates different relationships between project HRM processes and those in the HRM system of the permanent organization. If projects are learning opportunities for the project personnel and particularly stepping stones within a project (management) career, the interplay between developing, appraising and rewarding in the permanent HRM system with the temporary project HRM are essential.

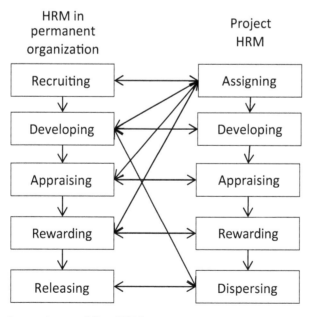

Figure 6.2   Aligning project and line HRM

6.6 Structures: HRM Roles and Organization

In HRM literature, there is an on-going debate on the devolution of HRM responsibilities from the HRM department to the line. It is widely agreed that the HRM department is not the sole deliverer of HRM within an organization, but HRM is carried out beyond the HR department, and by parties other than HR practitioners. Line managers play an essential role in HRM as they bring HRM policies and HR processes as shaped by the HR department into life as they interact with the employees and influence their performance.

While there is a very rich debate on the devolution of HR responsibilities to the line as outlined in Chapter 2, research considering HRM beyond the line is very rare (Bredin/Söderlund 2011; Keegan et al. 2012), but shows that there are explicit or implicit HRM responsibilities project managers have for other members of the project. Further to the role of the project manager, I also consider the project owner as a role with HRM tasks. The roles which take on HRM-related tasks are manifold and include those in the permanent structures:

- HR managers/experts;
- top managers, Project portfolio group (PPG);
- line manager/ expert-pool manager;
- Project Management Office (PMO).

The interplay between these different and partly very specific roles like the PMO or the PPG is challenging for the project-oriented organization. The distribution of the HRM responsibilities between these roles may change overtime. Especially when the company is developing into a project-oriented organization, which leads to a more networked HRM organization.

Table 6.7   Propositions regarding: HRM organization

PROPOSITIONS: HRM ROLES AND ORGANIZATION
• The HRM roles are spread out in the project-oriented organization, which attests to a more networked HRM organization.

6.7 Consequences

In this chapter I have proposed a working model for analysing the HRM system in the project-oriented organization. I distinguished a social, a content-related and a time-related context dimension, and I described the internal structures of the HRM system specifically required to relate the HRM system to its specific context. In the next chapters, this working model will be applied to analyse the empirical data gained from case studies and interviews.

In Chapter 7, I present a longitudinal case study, which shows the change of a HRM system in an organization that developed towards a project-oriented organization. While this case study covers all elements of the working model introduced, I will then focus on particular elements of the working model in Chapter 8, to discuss in particular how the HRM system relates to the temporary project HRM.

A Changing HRM System

7

7.1 Introduction

This chapter presents a longitudinal case study of a company from the telecommunication industry.[1] The case study company investigated is part of the wireline telecommunication industry and is situated in Austria. It was a former state-owned organization that was privatized in 1996 and in 2000 went on the stock exchange. The company was under a lot of pressure and had to transform itself in several ways in order to become competitive on the market. The company had lost their monopoly position in the Austrian market. The number of employees had to be reduced tremendously, while company services were increased and their quality was ensured. The case study covered a period of 12 years.

I use the *Working model: HRM system in the context of a project-oriented organization* to analyse the HRM system in the specific context of a company that developed itself from a former state-owned hierarchical bureaucracy towards a project-oriented company. Thus, this chapter firstly contributes descriptions of the elements of the model in the context of different phases of project-orientation of a company. This allows for comparison of the HRM system in different contexts of project-orientation and for reflection on how and why adaptions in the HRM structures occurred.

I present different phases on their journey to develop towards a modern and project-oriented organization. For each of these phases, I describe the context and the internal HRM structures that were evolving in the course of the development.

7.2 Phase 1: Welcome to the Project Jungle

7.2.1 CONTEXT

Need for projects

After the privatizations, the company was very hierarchical. There was a need for internal projects and for their professional management. One of the first projects was the introduction of an Enterprise Resource Planning System for four million clients, 2,500 workplaces, and 12,000 training days, including changes in processes.

---

1   The chapter builds upon an article which was published in the *IJPM* Huemann, M. 2010. Considering Human Resource Management when developing a project-oriented company: Case study of a telecommunication company. *International Journal of Project Management*, 28(4/2010), 361–369. The article focuses on how the project-oriented company changed and did not take a systemic perspective. The data collection process is described in the appendix: Research objectives and approach.

The technical unit involved in product development started considering the relevance of projects and project management for organizing product development. Product development was conducted within the technical unit without the co-operation of other important units, such as marketing. This resulted in many small 'projects'.

Project management becomes an issue

There was little understanding of what a project was. All temporary work was called project. Looking back in time, a PMO manager, who was then working for that organization as a consultant to manage projects and was later hired by the company, described the project understanding in the following terms:

> Projects? The term project was used for everything that was not routine. There was a tradition of establishing working groups, which met weekly. That was the use of the term project. (PMO manager 2008)

The project management competence depended on the individual, and was different from project manager to project manager. Some big projects were conducted successfully and professionally, others failed completely. There was little overview on the projects, and no project-portfolio management existed.

Relevant stakeholders

The HRM experts were highly qualified in administration; they did not care much about projects and project management, but they were concerned with how they could handle the disturbances that projects bring to administration:

> The HR department was challenged by the projects. They needed to explicitly assign the civil servants to the projects. But in their technical infrastructure, there was no possibility to show temporary projects. The project did not exist in their system. I do not know how they solved that problem. But for them this was a big issue, they could not administrate the personnel that worked on a project. (HR manager 2009)

While the personnel were predominantly civil servants with no experience in projects and project management, project managers and core team members were consultants with temporary assignments.

Firstly, business units became interested in projects and project management and realized they needed adequately trained project personnel who were able to perform the IT projects successfully.

Top management was interested in changing the organization and knew that changes in personnel would be necessary.

7.2.2. HRM SYSTEM: ADMINISTRATION

In this early phase of developing towards a project-oriented organization, HRM was an administrative function (performed by the HR department). From the perspective of project-orientation, specific HRM structures related to the HRM processes: recruiting and training. Therefore, adaptations in the HRM infrastructure were necessary.

Recruiting external project managers

As no qualified project management personnel were available within the company, consultants were recruited as project managers and as core team members, on temporary assignments. Some were offered permanent contracts in the company with excellent functional conditions.

Project management training

Project management training was paid for individuals who requested it. A database was established to administer those individuals who had received project management training. As the HRM department promoted training in general, they also paid for PM training. There was neither a PM-related strategy behind it, nor was there any systematic approach regarding the content or quality of the PM training. There was no active support of developing project managers.

HRM infrastructure

The HRM system was challenged, as their IT infrastructure did not have the option of working on a project. For large projects, pure project organizations were established and personnel were explicitly assigned to the project by the HRM department. This was a challenge for the organization, as technically there was no way to establish such a temporary organization. Thus, the organization needed to turn the project into a quasi-permanent organization. These large projects were organized like pure project organizations and in that way, HRM was able to formally assign the project personnel to these large projects.

HRM as reactive administration function

HRM was a reactive administration carried out by the HR department function to support the bureaucracy of the former public sector organization. The HR department itself was hierarchical organized with HR specialists. There was little interaction between HR managers, top managers and line managers.

7.3 Phase 2: We Make It Work

7.3.1 CONTEXT

Strive for transparency

To become ready for the stock exchange, in 1999/2000 more transparency was necessary. Project budgets became crucial and as the number of projects increased an overview on the activity was required. Thus, there became an increasing need for more professional and more standardized project management to ensure transparency and traceability.

In 1999/2000, top management set an initiative and tried to introduce project management guidelines. This top down approach failed completely because there was still no clear and common understanding of what a project was, and the project management guidelines were not adequately adapted to the organization. But by now, several islands of project management existed in the company, which had developed themselves. One island was the technical unit, another one the IT unit and the finance unit, responsible for conducting organizational development projects.

First benefits of project management

In the technical unit, where product development projects were carried out, the managers found that through project work they could organize work better and employees would be better motivated by working in teams. Still, there was a struggle to co-operate with other departments such as the marketing department – and such co-operation was essential for successful product development projects. Later, they established a project management process for product development, including project team members from other departments. To provide an incentive for the employees to be better able to take over work package responsibility, managers in the technical unit started to promote project management certification. They organized assessment of individual project management competences and supported project management certification. The professional project manager was established. The projects motivated personnel and the idea of teamwork in projects became part of the company's culture.

The establishment of PMOs to formalize project management

Finally, in 2001, three PMOs existed in different units. Project portfolio databases and management were introduced in these three units. Still there was a struggle with the project definition. The different units had different project management approaches, but they started working together.

A small group of project managers, closely related to the PM offices, promoted project management within the company. They were called the 'musketeers', within the company. In 2004, the units performed a maturity assessment and set each other benchmarks to understand communalities and differences. The aim was to establish an overreaching PM office, to standardize the project management approaches where possible and to define a common project management strategy.

Relevant stakeholders

The HRM experts remained hesitant regarding project management and seemed paralyzed by the 'old structures'. They were not hindering nor were they supporting HRM-related developments for increasing project-orientation

Business units interested in project management were IT, finance (where the internal change projects were organized) and the technical unit. These business units wanted project management for product development, and therefore asked for qualified project managers and work package leaders (a project team member who leads a work package). They organized project management training and project management certification.

New stakeholders had evolved with HRM-related interests. First of all, these were the PMOs; strong PMOs who drove the PM-related HRM developments and initiated co-operation with the HRM department.

Project managers increasingly became a personnel group with some importance; they became visible through the PMOs and demanded training, certification and career opportunities.

7.3.2 HRM SYSTEM: ADMINISTRATION WITH SOME CO-OPERATION

In this phase of implementing project management and project-orientation in the organization, HRM remained an administrative function, but HRM-related structures became observable throughout the organization. From the perspective of project-orientation, specific HRM structures were necessary.

Training and certification of project managers and project team members

In 2001, the first pilot project management certifications took place in the technical business unit, and in 2003 they were rolled out through the company.

Career paths

Job descriptions for project managers and, finally, a career path for project managers linked to project management certification levels existed.

HRM infrastructure

To establish large projects as temporary organizations, dummy units were opened up and closed down when the projects were finished. Personnel were explicitly assigned to the project by the HRM department.

HRM organization

The HR department remained hierarchically organized with HR specialists. Some (intensive) interaction between HR managers and PMO managers in informal meetings was observable. Overall, the HRM remained tied by their administrative heritage, and were reactive and not proactive to project management.

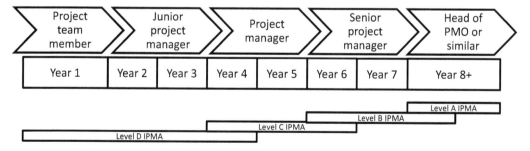

Figure 7.1 **Career path for project managers**

7.4 Phase 3: Professionalization

7.4.1 CONTEXT

More projects!

There was further requirement to reduce personnel, further change projects were conducted which required professional management. Also, customer assignments became more and more complex, as new services like providing infrastructure for workplaces or security services were established. Thus, professional project management became even more relevant, as it was now also of relevance for complex customer assignments. Different internal and external projects were performed. Generally, the demand for professional project and programme management increased. In 2008/2009, a large infrastructure for a modernization initiative was started. By the end of 2009, as personnel were further reduced, the company was challenged to plan resources properly to prevent project overload.

Professionalizing project management

As there was increasing need for projects, project working became more the norm and less the exception. Company-wide definitions of projects and programmes were established to set a shared understanding for projects and project management. A company-wide categorization system for projects was established, and common minimum project management requirements were developed for all project types.

Relevant stakeholders

Because of personnel changes in the HR department, there was the possibility of major changes there. A business partner model was introduced. Some former senior project managers and a PMO manager moved into the HR department and brought project management knowledge with them.

No overreaching PMO was established, but the PMOs remained in existence: one in the technical unit, one in the finance/controlling unit and one in the sales unit, as projects were now also applied to perform complex customer assignments. They required qualified project managers and other project personnel from the HRM function.

The number of project managers had increased within the company and knowledge management of managing projects became a hot topic of conversation. The technical unit started an initiative to establish a company-wide project management community to promote exchange of knowledge between all project managers and to further promote the profession.

A central project portfolio group was established to manage the project portfolio strategically. Current and future needs regarding quantity and quality of project personnel, in particular project managers, became transparent.

7.4.2 HRM SYSTEM: MORE NETWORKED

In the phase of professionalization of project management, HRM had changed into a business partner model aware of the requirements projects and project management bring. HR-related structures relevant for supporting project-orientation became observable throughout the organization. From the perspective of project-orientation, specific HRM structures were now visible in the HRM strategies, goals and processes as well as in the HRM organization.

HRM strategies and goals

The need for growing endogenous project managers who understand the context of the organization was recognized by HRM structures. The PM career path was further enhanced and new services were developed. For instance, incentive packages for project teams to support a proper project team development were offered. Services to line managers to help find adequate project managers were offered, which supported project performance in particular:

> There are less political project manager assignments now. Some years ago, if a project was initiated the line manger often took a person of trust for managing the project. Whether this person had project management expertise or not was considered. After a year or so you could see no project result. Now it this is different for strategic important projects the PMO and the HR department help to find the adequate project manager. (Senior project manager 2008)

Project management training, certification and PM assessment centres

Standardized training of project managers, team members and project owners was established. Project managers were put forward as managers and leaders and received leadership training. While previously the training suggested project management tools and procedures, now project personnel were trained additionally in social competencies and self-competencies as a basis for the leadership tasks in projects. To professionalize the communication between project managers and project owners, specific training and coaching on how they can communicate with each other more effectively were established. Project management training was further formalized, and a standard was introduced to ensure that project personnel will get an adequate project management approach. Project management certification was continued, and assessment centres for identifying potential project managers were developed and conducted.

Support of Project HRM and aligning with HRM system in permanent organizations

Generally, HRM structures started supporting HRM on projects as well as the alignment between the HRM system and project HRM.

HRM infrastructure

Adaptations in the knowledge database were conducted to keep track of the practical experience of project personnel. Proper resource planning is now tackled by a central portfolio-planning database.

Table 7.1   **Distribution of responsibilities in HRM processes for project personnel**

| | **Process: Recruiting** | | |
	HR manager **Process owner**	**Line managers** **Issues demand**	**PMO manager** **Issues demand**
First selection	Yes	No	No
Interviews	Yes	Yes	Yes
Assessment Centre	Yes	Yes	Yes
Decision	No	Yes	Yes
Mentoring	Guidelines	Yes	Yes
	Process: Training		
	Process owner	**Issues demand, delivers input**	**Issues demand, delivers input**
Employee selection	Support	Yes	Yes
Trainer selection	Yes	Proposal	Proposal
Form of training	Yes	Proposal	Proposal
	Process: Performance management		
	Supports processes	**Process owner for expert personnel**	**Process owner for PM personnel**
Career planning	Proposal	Yes	Yes
Successor planning	Support	Yes	Yes
Remuneration	Guidelines	Yes	Yes
	Process: Releasing		
	Process owner	**Issues demand**	**Issues demand**
Debriefing	Guidelines	Yes	Yes
Formal release	Yes	Support	Support

HRM roles and organization

The HRM department was no longer functionally organized, but there were HRM generalists who are themselves responsible for different internal business partner groups. The HRM activities were shaped by the HRM generalist, in co-operation with line managers and the PMOs. In contrast to the previous phase, HR managers took the lead and started actively supporting project-oriented working. Table 7.1 shows the distribution of responsibilities within selected HR processes for project personnel between the HR manager, line manager and PMO manager.

7.5 Reflections

7.5.1 ADAPTIONS IN THE HRM SYSTEM AND THEIR INITIATORS

The company overall had to change from a hierarchical former state-owned company to a modern project-oriented organization. The company was very hierarchical, and projects and project work were new and thus irritated the established structures, including the HRM structures. For example, the HR database was not equipped to administrate HR personnel.

What becomes obvious in this case study is that HRM managers neither drove the development of the organization towards project-orientation, nor did they consider adapting the HRM system because of project-orientation. In phase 1 and phase 2, the HRM department as such was not a viable option to support project-orientation, but remained caught in its heritage as an administrative function. Project-orientation of the company seemed not to be of relevance for them. For a long time, the HRM department did not relate to the developments towards project-orientation that were going on in the organization.

The HRM system was rather 'forced' to provide adequate HRM structures by its content-related context and by social environments such as the PMO and the business managers. The PMOs had an interest in adapting structures in the organization to make them fit and support project-orientation. The PMO acted as a 'chameleon' function, and fulfilled a lot of HRM-related services/goals processes that were necessary from the perspective of project management and project-orientation, but were not provided by the HR department.

Only in phase 3 was the HR department ready to take the initiative. The new structures of the HR department had brought in some flexibility, and the HRM department was ready to not only better fulfil the business managers' need for qualified personnel, but also to adapt new services for projects and project personnel.

7.5.2 PROJECT HRM AND MUTUAL ALIGNMENT TO PERMANENT HRM

Project managers carried out HRM tasks for project team members, even if they have no personnel authority. Table 7.3 shows the development over the time period under consideration. It seems that project managers took even more responsibility than line managers towards the development of personnel, for a purpose beyond their own temporary project.

7.5.3 PROJECT-ORIENTED HR DEPARTMENT

The HR department started to be organized in a project-oriented way. Many of the HR managers already had project management competencies and thus they implemented *Managing by Projects* as a strategy for organizing HRM. Examples of relevant projects are the development and implementation of assessment centres for project managers; or the development and implementation of a new career system. By understanding project-oriented working, HRM can better support the project-oriented company and its requirements. Table 7.2 provides an overview on the different development phases and the viability of the HR department and the HRM system for the case study company.

Table 7.2   Viability of the HRM department/system in different phases

Viability for project-orientation	Phase 1	Phase 2	Phase 3
HR department	no	no	getting there
HRM system	no	About yes	yes

7.6 Conclusion

This chapter offered a case study of the HRM system in the context of a company that progressed itself towards a project-oriented organization. For the analyses of HRM, the *Working model: HRM system in the context of a project-oriented organization* was applied and descriptions of the different elements were produced (Tables 7.3, 7.4 and 7.5). This allowed for comparison of the HRM system in different contexts of project-orientation, and for reflection on how and why adaptions in the HRM structure occurred or did not occur.

The case shows evidence that project-orientation is a relevant context to HRM, and why HR related structures need to adapt in order to support project-orientation. The case provides further evidence that the HRM system was not viable for project-orientation in all phases of development. Initiated by the PMO rather than by the HR managers themselves, the HRM system has since developed structures to support project-orientation.

In general, the two main roles of HRM in a project-oriented organization can be differentiated: on the one hand, the HRM takes an active role in developing a company towards a project-oriented organization by offering, for instance, adequate training for project management personnel, career and incentive systems, and support for project HRM.

On the other hand, the HRM system has to adapt its HRM processes and the organization as such, in order to acknowledge project-orientation. Thus, new HRM processes like assigning and dispersing project personnel to a project need to be considered, as well as project HRM processes being aligned to those in the line. A more networked form of HRM with a clear interplay between PPG, HR managers, PMO and project managers is a viable structure by which to increase HR-related potentials, which in this particular case included the possibility of teamwork in projects, project as learning opportunities, projects as sources of motivation and offering interesting working forms to employees.

Table 7.3 Development of the HRM system 1997–2009

Phases	Context of the HRM system	Internal structures of HRM system
Phase 1: Welcome to the project jungle (1997–1999) After privatization need for change to become competitive in market	**Content-related context** • Need for organizing internal IT/ organizational development projects • Single large internal projects were professionally managed (mainly by consultants) • Very little HRM on projects **Social context** • HRM experts: highly qualified in administrators • Consultants: were hired as project managers and core team members on projects • IT unit: became interested in projects and project management, need qualified project managers • Project personnel: predominantly civil servants • Top management: interest in changing the organization **Time-related context** • No experience with project and project management in the company/HRM system • Expectation of company/HRM system that demand for projects will increase	**HRM strategies and goals** • Not explicit existing and no relation to project-orientation **HRM processes and infrastructure** • Recruiting external consultants as project managers • Assigning to projects, establishment of project organization to be able to assign civil servants to projects • PM training not standardized • IT system does not make projects visible **HRM roles and organization** • Functionally organized • Reactive administration function • Little contact beyond the HR department
Phase 2: We make it work (2000–2004) Company prepares and goes to stock exchange	**Content-related context** • More need to change the organization by projects • Technical unit sees advantage of projects and PM for product development and infrastructure projects • Need for transparency and traceability of projects required because company goes to stock exchange Project budget was established, which provides a certain autonomy to the project • PMOs were established in several units • Portfolio management in units started • PM promoted by PMOs • Project HRM takes place	**HRM strategies and goals** • Reduction of personnel • HRM strategy related to project-orientation not explicit existing • Beginning of no project-orientation related HR goals, end of period active support in training of project manager • PM career path **HRM processes and infrastructure** • PM certification • Assessments for project managers and team members (in technical unit) • Promotion of PM profession

Table 7.3   Continued

Phases	Context of the HRM system	Internal structures of HRM system
Phase 2: Continued	**Social context** • HRM experts: hesitative behaviour but not hindering developments • Project managers increasing group with some relevance, become visible because of PMOs • Projects team members: receive PM training • PMOs: strong and active • PMO and heads of technical units driving PM development, initializing PM training and certification • Project personnel mixture between civil servants and top management: introduce PM guidelines which first fail **Time-related context** • Some experience with project and project management had been gained, organization had become more dynamic • More relevance of projects and project management was expected	• Standardized PM trainings started • Job description for project managers • Project performance considered in performance contracts • Administration of persons who did PM training in database **HRM roles and organization** • Functionally organized • HRM as functionally organized unit. • More interaction between HRM experts and PMOs, but still main part of PM-related HRM actives driven by PMOs and project managers
Phase 3: Professionalization (2005–2009) Even higher competition on market	**Content-related context** • Need for further change projects • A large infrastructure programme is carried out • Customer assignments get more and more complex, some are to be organized as projects • Company-wide portfolio management • Company-wide minimum PM standard started • Establishment of project owner role started **Social context** • HRM manager with PM competence • PMO professionalized, but lost power • Project managers: many left company • PM community established **Time-related context** • Experienced with PM and project-orientation • Clear about future need of projects	**HRM strategies and goals** • Further reduction of personnel • Identify high potential project managers • Balancing the different career paths **HRM processes and infrastructure** • PM certification continued • Standardized PM training • Leadership training for project managers started • Proper company-wide resource planning started with database linked to portfolio management • Clear understanding of how many project managers needed in future • Aligning HRM system with project HRM: Support of selection of project managers, incentive packages for project teams **HRM roles and organization** • HR as business partner • HR generalists • Development towards a project-oriented HR unit

Table 7.4   Project HRM

Phase	Assigning	Developing	Appraising	Rewarding	Dispersing
Welcome to the project jungle (1997–1999)	• Consultants as PMs and core team members recruited from outside the company	N/A	N/A	• Pay for temporary assignment	• Performed together with releasing from company for the external project managers
We make it work (2000–2004)	• Voluntary assignments for internal projects • Often rather political assignments of project managers • Selecting and Assigning partly supported by PM Office	• Projects as development chances for employees	• Feedback in projects, often informal, depending on project manager and project owner, • No formal link to appraising in line	• Non-monetary team rewards	• Seldom performed
Professionalization (2005–2009)	• Voluntary assignments for internal projects • Selecting and assignment of PM supported by HRM and or PM Office • Selection core project personnel Key personnel project supported	• Projects as development chances for employees • Team development supported	• Formal feedback established • Formally linked to appraising in the line	• Non-monetary team rewards	• Performed for key personnel

Table 7.5   HRM processes in the permanent organization

Phase	Recruiting	Developing	Appraising	Rewarding	Releasing
Welcome to the project jungle (1997–1999)	• PMs and core team members are recruited as consultants from outside the company • External project managers are offered permanent contracts	• Little developing efforts for PM personnel	• Not formally performed for project managers, as they were external	• External project managers rewarded with bonuses	• External project managers are released from the company or offered permanent contracts
We make it work (2000–2004)	• Recruiting of potential project managers • Recruiting project personnel for specific project is still possible	• Training for project managers and team members • Some assessment of project managers and project team members • PM certification	• Annual appraisals	• Rewarding system recognizes projects as variable part of performance contract	• Not specific for pm personnel, • Sometimes still external project managers get specific project assignments, • Network of freelance project managers
Growing a project management community (2005–2009)	• Little recruiting of new PMs from outside the company	• Assessment centres for project managers • Training for project managers, project team members and project owners • Developing leadership competence of project managers • Coaching of project managers and project owners • PM certification	• Annual appraisals linked to the appraising (formal feedbacks) in projects	• Rewarding system recognizes projects as variable part of performance contract	• Not specific for PM personnel, • Sometimes still external project managers get specific project assignments, • A network of freelance project managers is available

8

Towards a Project-Oriented HRM System

8.1 Introduction

After tracing the development of a HRM system in the context of an organization that was working towards becoming a project-oriented organization, I focus here on the findings from five case studies in which I studied the HRM system in the context of (relatively) mature project-oriented organizations. The companies studied derive from different backgrounds and industries. See Table 8.1.

What they shared was a (relatively) high maturity as project-oriented organizations. Following the Working model: HRM system in the project-oriented organization, I firstly describe the contexts, then the structures of the HRM systems and then I will reflect on the findings.

Table 8.1   Overview case study companies

Case	Company	Projects	Locations
Case 1	Telecommunication company Wireline part	Small to large projects/programmes mostly internal small external projects	Austria
Case 2	IT consultancy Subsidiary of inter-national company	Many small projects Mostly external projects	Austria
Case 3	Transportation systems International division of global company	Small to large projects Mostly external projects	Germany
Case 4	IT consultancy	Many small projects Mostly external projects	The Netherlands
Case 5	Division of a public sector organization involved in aerospace research and development	Medium size to very large projects/ programmes Investment projects	US

8.2 Context

8.2.1 PROJECT-ORIENTATION OF COMPANIES AND THEIR PROJECTS

As a means of analysing HRM systems of project-oriented organizations, the case studies have been selected in such a way that they all present companies which possess a (relatively) high maturity in managing projects. Nevertheless, there are some differences regarding the type of projects that they conduct and their approach to project management, as well as how well their cultural values fit project-orientation. See Table 8.9.

8.2.2 RELEVANT STAKEHOLDERS

Relevant stakeholders of the HRM system are Project Portfolio Group (Top management), Project Management Office, line managers/expert pool managers, project managers, project owners and project personnel. All of the cases had established most of the PM-related roles, such as Project Portfolio Group and Project Management Office as well as project managers. What was missing in most of the cases was the role of the project owner. See Table 8.9.

8.2.3 HISTORY AND FUTURE EXPECTATIONS REGARDING THE IMPORTANCE OF PM

Some of the case companies had a long tradition in managing projects. There were differences regarding the future expectation of their project business or internal demand for projects. For example, Case study 2 had the future expectation of project management becoming less important. The HRM system started giving less attention to training and certification of project managers. See Table 8.9.

8.2.4 HRM STRATEGIES AND GOALS

All case study companies had more or less an explicit strategy to support project-orientation. Specific goals were the further development of the profession of project manager, formalizing/ further developing career paths for project managers and taking care of young consultants working on projects to sustain them in the company and in the profession. See Table 8.9.

Most of the case companies had understood that there is HRM on projects and recognized that the HRM system relates to this temporary part of the organization.

8.3 HRM Processes: Assigning Project Personnel to and Dispersing from a Project

Assigning and dispersing are the processes that establish or dissolve the temporary project. These processes relate the permanent organization to the project that is created existence in the case of assigning, and the project that is being dissolved in the case of dispersing.

8.3.1 PURPOSE OF ASSIGNING PROJECT PERSONNEL

Project personnel are recruited by the project within the organization or outside the organization, and assigned by the permanent organization to a project. The purpose of assigning personnel to a project is to equip the project with adequate resources to fulfil the project objectives and deliver project results. The permanent organization creates a temporary organization for a certain purpose, in essence for the delivery of project results according to the project assignment. The permanent organization, or organizations if there are more than one involved, supply the project with adequate project personnel.

Thus, the process of assigning personnel to a project is initiated in the permanent line organization and leads to the establishment of the project. To show this relation between project and permanent organization, I have explicitly chosen to label this process 'assigning of project personnel to the project', and have not named it 'recruiting of personnel to the project'. There may be a strong sense of urgency to recruit project personnel to the project, as the project is competing with other projects and probably line tasks for adequate personnel; nevertheless, 'assigning' better expresses the creation of the project by the permanent line organization.

In addition to the establishment of the project comes the assignment of the project personnel, which happens in stages. Firstly, a project manager and sometimes a core team is assigned to the (potential) project to prepare the first project plans or to detail existing plans, as in the case of contract projects when a bid process has taken place to win the contact. However, this first step includes preparing or detailing a project plan, including a resource plan for project personnel required on the project. Based on the project plans, the project manager negotiates with the permanent organization, often specifically with the line managers or expert pool managers, for the personnel resources required on the project. The project personnel are then assigned by the permanent organization to the project, either full time or part time.[1]

The basis for the assignment of personnel is the project resource planning, related to the resource planning in the project initiation, and to matching the availability of personnel in the permanent organization, which assigns the personnel to a project. Nevertheless, the project manager has an active role in finding adequate project personnel for the project that he or she is going to manage.

A more specific practice is voluntary enrolment. This form of assignment is dependent on employees voluntarily responding to internal advertising of projects. Some companies have established internal marketplaces, where project assignments are posted and persons can offer themselves, see Table 8.2. Despite that, all of the case study companies in this sample had some sort of internal market for projects, one reported an issue of employee well-being associated with internal project marketing:

Table 8.2   Voluntary enrolment as challenge for employee well-being

---

CASE 4: VOLUNTARY ENROLMENT

A Dutch consulting company reported on their experience with voluntary enrolment to projects. They had an internal marketplace. Open positions are posted to the potential project personnel. They had to stop this practice, as young personnel, in particular, eager to get experience and work on projects, enrolled for too many projects. This resulted in lower project performance and burnt out young consultants. The company still has an internal marketplace in which the potential assignments are posted; nevertheless it is combined with young consultants being coached by senior consultants.

---

1   In the case of a project performed with personnel from more than one permanent organization, the personnel are assigned from these different organizations.

8.3.2 ASSIGNING OF A PROJECT MANAGER TO A PROJECT

The role of the project manager is often the first role to be assigned. In mature project-oriented companies, the future project manager is already included in the project initiation process and nominated by a project owner. The practices applied in assigning a project manager to a project may range from informal to structured and formal. A PMO manager describes a structured approach of assigning a project manager to an external project.

> *In the pre project phase the requirements regarding the project manager are defined: for example, which level of competence the project manager should have (certification level B or C), which industry experience is required. A profile is defined and then the databases of the PMOS are searched for a suitable candidate. If no candidate is found a recruiting process within the company group is started. (PM Office Manager, internal and external projects, Case 1 (3))*

A central issue in assigning project personnel is the matching of the adequate project manager to the project, to secure project success (Müller and Turner 2010). Companies use a categorization of project types to explicitly match the project manager with the adequate degree of competences to a particular project. To be able to match project managers to projects, project-oriented companies apply project categorizations and differentiate between project types based on different criteria. Table 8.3 provides, as an example, the categorization criteria for contract projects of one of the case study companies. This case study company uses the criteria financial value, contractual arrangements, technical complexity and organization considerations to distinguish their projects into categories. As categories, they use A to D projects, where A are the most comprehensive and complex projects (or are even considered to be programmes).

The project manager is selected for a particular project in relation to his/her competencies. A measurement this company takes into account is project management certification. The Project Management Office explicitly ensures that projects from level B onwards are managed only by certified project managers who can prove that they have a certain project management competence.

Table 8.3   Categorization criteria for projects

Case 3: Categorization criteria for projects	
Financial	• Order value
	• Total estimated risk volume
	• Project profit gross margin
	• Gross R&D/engineering costs
Contractual	• Contractual position in the project
	• External partners, bound by contract
	• Company internal partners
	• Customer/rep relationship rating (known and co-operative?)
Technical complexity	• Technical complexity
	• Clarity of product/scope of definition
	• New technology development
Organizational considerations	• Type of project
	• Contractual complexity
	• Strategic significance for group level including potential future sales
	• Strategic relevance for customer

The Project Management Office in this company tries to ensure that complex projects are assigned to certified project managers.

Some case study companies tend to see the role of project management shared in a core project team, especially between the technical and the commercial project manager, or the project director and his/her project deputy. Thus, the companies also try to match the competencies of this pair of persons, who need to work closely together on the project. However, in Case 3, the need for different but matching competences is expressed in the labels of their roles. While the technical project manager is responsible for project management and has a technical background, the subordinated commercial project manager is responsible for the commercial part of the project. This company follows a set of predefined project roles that are required on their projects, technical project manager and commercial project manager being two important ones.

In addition to the formal competences, companies consider the social competences and self-understanding of project managers for the assignment to the project. For example, Case 5 explicitly considers, in addition to the competencies required to fulfil the project manager role, the social competences and self-understanding of this person. If the project manager is a very task/result oriented person, the deputy project manager, second in command, is assigned based on the premise that he/she is people-oriented in order to create an adequate mixture for the particular project, and to balance the strong goal orientation on the project, and this might become an issue for employee well-being.

Ideally, the project owner is involved in the decision taken on the project manager. Some of the companies in the sample have the role of project owner in place, and these tend to be the line managers with a major interest in the project results. For an internal project, a senior project manager explains:

> The line manager who is affected most by the project decides on the project manager. Most of the times, several proposals exist. The project owner picks the project manager (Senior PM, Case 1(3))

Methods applied in the assigning process for selecting the adequate project manager may vary considerably within one company. Within a mature project-oriented company, the variations may mostly occur because of the size and strategic importance of the projects. Methods include mostly formal and informal interviews, but also sometimes selection assessment centres for finding the adequate project manager for a strategically important project.

The formality of the process of assigning a project manager varies from company to company, and might even vary within one company. When conducting internal projects, political decisions regarding the project manager happen. In mature project-oriented companies, a particular project manager receiving a strategically important project is related to his/her self-marketing.

Table 8.4   Assigning a project manager

CASE 3: ASSIGNING A PROJECT MANAGER

In Case study 3, the assigning process is mostly dependent on the line managers and in general the maturity of the particular line organization. More mature parts of the organization have a general assigning strategy that is based on the career path for project managers. To identify appropriate project managers, the HRM department can support the selection with their database of project managers and if necessary, recruit within the company or externally. Experience shows that successful assignments are made if the entire context of the specific project was taken into account, that is, beside the hard facts according to the contract, soft issues like related intercultural experience, language skills, sometimes even age, gender, and last but not least, the interrelation with core members of the project.

8.3.3 ASSIGNING OF A PROJECT TEAM MEMBER OR CONTRIBUTOR TO A PROJECT

The assignment of project personnel comes in stages: ideally the project owner assigns the project manager first and he or she might already be involved in the bid process in the case of a contracting project, or in the project initiation in the case of an internal project. In any case, at this stage the project manager asks for further core personnel and details the project management plans. Based on the detailed project management plans the project manager finds further personnel. Despite that project-oriented companies have databases of their project personnel, the project manager very often takes a very active role to get the adequate project personnel assigned to the project. A project manager describes this task:

> I produce a skill matrix. Based on the object of consideration plan I know which skills I need to perform the project (...) Further I say I need this skill in this level ... Is a junior expert sufficient? We have Junior, Expert and Senior Expert. (...) I need to understand the task this person will fulfill on the project (...) I prepare a job description ... Then I go look for people. I approach them directly and then go negotiate with their manager. I approach the persons directly is he available then I get the ok from the line manager. Do I not find somebody through my network, I need to ask the line manager for providing me with a person with the right expertise. (...) If there is no expert available, can I take a junior person and train him? Who is available? (Senior PM, Case 1(3))

This description of a senior project manager is very representative of the practices applied by the project managers interviewed. Methods applied are job description and project management plans. Experienced project managers combine this with knowledge about personnel in the company and the network that they have built. Experience and informal networks seem to be of upmost importance.

> As we have a matrix structure, the project manager negotiates with the line managers. You need experience with projects to know how this works. (...) You need to know the key players (...) As these key players are always asked for personnel it is tricky to get the right people. (Senior PM, Case 1(3))

Very related to how this process works in detail is the project organization form applied for the particular project. However, a core task within this process is the negotiating of the project manager with the line organization to receive adequate personnel for a particular project.

8.3.4 FUTURE PROJECT MANAGER SEEKS PROJECT OWNER

When the project really starts is often blurred in practice. If in a company the role of the project owner is established then the project starts with the assignment of the project to the project manager or the project team by the project owner. As the role of the project owner is relatively immature, even in organizations where this role is formally established, sometimes the project owner does not seek the project manager, but rather it is the other way round: the project manager seeks an adequate project owner to ensure that the project has an adequate liaison to the permanent organization. The project manager of an internal project explains who he looks for as project owner:

Project owners they are line managers … it depends, I have one or two, more than two I do not want, this gets too complicated. At the moment I have one project owner for my project. (…) In a merger project I managed before the project owners were the CEO of the company merged and the line manager, who is especially effected financially from the merger. (Senior PM, Case 1(3))

In many organizations, the role of the project owner is relatively immature, although it is argued that the project owner may be considered as a liaison role between temporary and permanent organization, and thus is important for the relative autonomy of the project and for ensuring that the project relates to the company's interests. Line managers may not be aware of what is expected from them when they act as project owner of a particular project. Thus, project managers have the task of clarifying the role with the project owner and explaining their expectations. This is a rather difficult task, as project owners often come from hierarchically higher ranks in comparison to the project manager. Project managers use, for example, briefings and role descriptions to clarify expectations of the project owner with the person. In the case of an internal project, the project owner can be considered to be the project customer.

I insist to have the project owner engaged in the start workshop to empower the project and the people. (…) Even when he only says some words about how important the project is for the board of directors. I need the project owner for decisions, status meetings as often as possible especially before milestones (…) I am responsible for the process and I lead my project owners to make the project a success. (Senior Project Manager, Case 1(3))

In the case of contracting projects, the project manager's superior may automatically be considered as the project owner, which then might cause friction, as they are not automatically the adequate project owner.

8.3.5 DISPERSING FROM A PROJECT

The purpose of dispersing is to transfer a member of the project back to the permanent organization, to assign this person immediately to another project, or to release him/her from the organization, in one case this is a temporary employee. The process is comparable to assigning staff to the project, as it also takes place in stages.

Other case study (Case 1, 2, 4) companies expect the project personnel to find their next assignment, which makes dispersing the responsibility of the individual, not the company or project.

My last projects were all board level. If you do one right and you do not ruin your reputation, you get the ticket for the next one. (Senior project manager, internal projects Case 1(3))

Table 8.5   Planning the next assignment

CASE 3: PLACEMENT OF PROJECT MANAGER

Case 3 operates a database to remind the HRM manager a couple of weeks before a large project is closed down to get in contact with the project manager and other core project team members to plan for the next project assignment. In doing this they actively ensure the relation to the permanent organization. At the end of project, valuable, highly qualified and experienced project managers might get lost, either to other companies or to other career fields like the management career, which in this company still has higher prestige.

8.4 HRM Project Processes: Developing, Appraising, Rewarding on a Project

8.4.1 PURPOSE

Developing, appraising and rewarding are part of performance management on a project. Before discussing the specific processes of developing, appraising and rewarding on a project in detail, I point out their relations and issues that these HR processes share. We may consider that performance management on a particular project aims at different purposes. I differentiate project purpose and purposes that go beyond the temporary project and relate to the company interests or to the individual interests of the project personnel.

Project purpose: In essence, managing personnel on a project aims to support the achievement of the project results. An example of this is that a project team member is quickly trained in a technology which will be needed on the particular project, and only then can the project team member fulfill the task on the project. The purpose of the training is related to the particular project objectives.

Beyond project purpose: Nevertheless, the purpose of managing the personnel performance may go beyond the project and serve other interests or purposes. This approach represents a rather long-term orientation. Going beyond the project, it contributes to the competence development of a particular individual engaged on the project and in more general terms to the development of company competences.

Although we differentiate these purposes, they are interlinked and they may later indirectly support project purposes. So the question I ask is: For whom? Who is the beneficiary, the project, the company, the individual? And we will find that in many cases it will be more than one.

Another distinction I would like to introduce here is the individual or the team. Developing, appraising and rewarding on the project might either be linked to the individual or to the team. Doubtless, on a project the project team as a collective is a central unit. Some scholars even point out the existence of a temporary project team competence, which needs to be developed in the course of the project, but is of temporary character and comes to an end at the project close down (Gareis/Huemann 2007).

8.4.2 DEVELOPING ON A PROJECT

I explicitly say developing rather than training, as I find that especially on projects there might be little formal training but a lot of developing possibilities provided to project personnel. The purpose of developing project personnel on a project is manifold. We may differentiate whether the development activity is necessary for the purpose of the project and thus support the project performance directly, or the development activity is mainly provided for the purpose of another unit, which can be the individual person or the company.

Development on the project for project purpose: This includes further development of individual competences required on a specific project; examples include learning a new software required by the project, training a junior person to fulfill the task on the project, developing of new project personnel when they join the project to be briefed on the project, training project personnel in new technology developed early in the project to be able to use it later in the project, and finally developing of the project team to better perform the project.

Development on the project for purposes beyond: In addition, we find that project managers who are explicitly organizing learning opportunities on the project contribute to the further development of the individuals assigned to the project. Then, the purpose of developing is not directly to support the performance of the particular project, but it is an offer to a project team member or participant and contributes to identification with the project, thus creating commitment. In addition, we find projects explicitly framed for individual and collective learning, and their prime function is to train people.

8.4.3 BRING THE TRAINING TO THE PROJECT

There is a friction between the urge to perform on a project and the development needs of project personnel. Projects are highly goal-orientated, because they are time limited with deadlines, which means it is not always easy for project managers or core team members to participate in traditional training courses. A common strategy in all of the case study companies is to overcome the time pressures on projects and this means a combination of performing on a project and training.

> *For example, there is t he need to learn a new technology. That means all the project team members need to learn it. We do that 'on the project', that means not as classical training but with the help of a consultant, which teaches them directly on the project. Each of the project participants can learn what he needs. The experts will learn the technical details, the project manager only needs a general understanding and what the new technology means for the scope, timing and duration of the work packages. (PMO Manager, Case 1(3))*

8.4.4 PROJECT AS LEARNING OPPORTUNITY

Strongly related to the leadership role of the project manager, many of the project managers interviewed explicitly create learning opportunities for project personnel, which go beyond the purpose of the particular project. Projects establish exchange relationships with their project personnel by offering competences, knowledge information and participation.

> *I develop my people. (…) What can I offer on the project that you can further develop? Well this is less the technical expertise; this is what the person brings to the project. I might not be able to offer much. (…) I have no budget for this. (…) The person will have the technical expertise, but I can offer to develop social competence: Contact to people, experience with people, interesting work. (…) You need to motivate the people (…) I can offer a lot, the line cannot offer. (Senior Project Manager, Case 1(3))*

Table 8.6   Project failures and training

CASE 4: PROJECT FAILURES AND TRAINING

Due to severe project failures the organization decided to implement a project academy to ensure that the project personnel is adequately trained and failures that happened in the past will not happen anymore. The approach taken by the organization was to improve in particular the leadership competencies of the project managers and the ability of the project team to work together. They offer team development and bring that team development to the project.

This senior project manager clearly points out that he engineers the relation to the project personnel and offers learning opportunities on the project. He neither has a formal training budget nor formal personnel responsibility in the internal projects he manages, which includes mainly organizational development and product development products. He offers development opportunities to the project personnel and herewith tries to create motivation and commitment to the project. He points out that project work in the company offers more interesting tasks in comparison to the line work.

> I enjoy developing people!/./For instance a project contributor, who was only responsible for a single work package was very enthusiastic, wanted to learn and was using project management terms the right away. I thought 'she has just joined the project and is eager to learn' [so] I supported her to get the appropriate training. She was in the accounts department and now she is in the product development department and works in projects as a project team member. She has found her way. (Senior Project Manager, Case 1)

Another project manager from Case 1 said:

> People like to work in my project team. The fact I provide learning opportunities for them is an incentive. Yes, there are people who feel more related to the line than to the project. It is difficult to get them on board. [But] in my projects I have never had to change a project team member. (Senior Project Manager, Case 1)

This particular senior project manager also describes a specific example of organizing a learning opportunity on a project.

> I ask to prepare a presentation and to perform it. I explain how to do it and then observe the person when he gives the presentation. There are different possibilities for presentations within the project. I observe the presentation, tempo of speech, professionalism of performance, behavior, reaction of the audience. (.) At the end of the day I sit down with the person and give feedback. (Senior Project Manager, Case 1)

In Case 5, a team member of a science project explained that to work on the project and to learn something new as an individual is a prime motivator for him.

8.4.5 APPRAISING ON A PROJECT

This is the process of providing feedback on their performance on the project, to relevant project members. The appraisal can be formal or informal. Whether or not appraisals are conducted depends on the duration of the project. Appraisal on the project is necessary for the development and motivation of project personnel, and for cohesiveness of the project team. Appraisals are part of project performance management to ensure the performance of the project. Often project managers implicitly take over appraising and also developing tasks for the project team members, but in general are not aware of it. Project managers do feedback talks with the project team members, but the relevance for the annual appraisal in the line organization is limited.

8.4.6 REWARDING ON A PROJECT

In the case study companies, there was evidence of monetary as well as non-monetary rewards.

Table 8.7   Non-monetary rewards on projects

> **EXAMPLES OF NON-MONETARY REWARDS ON PROJECTS**
> - Social events (dinners, parties, sporting events)
> - Badges, t-shirts, project stationery
> - Award certificates
> - Extra holiday time
> - Additional training or development opportunities
> - Explicit links to future project opportunities

We talk about the double monthly income for the project manager and for time members a bonus oft thee amount of their monthly income. Very seldom the project manager gets up to four times his monthly income as a project bonus. But this is very seldom. (Senior Project Manager, Case 1(1))

8.5 Relating HRM in Line with Project HRM

Since the assignment of project personnel and dispersal of them from a project are related to the start and the close down of a project, these processes must have strong relations to the HRM system of the project-oriented organization that established the project (as a temporary sub-system).

The main appraisal needs to be conducted in the line and this is the case for most companies. The main reason is that the time horizon over which decisions need to be made for career development and succession planning is longer than the duration of projects. There are exceptions where the company undertakes large projects lasting more than a year, where the project manager fulfills the duties of the line manager. But in most cases, the appraisals are only conducted in the line.

Table 8.8   Performance management

> **CASE 3: PERFORMANCE MANAGEMENT – LINKING PROJECT AND LINE**
> As the project durations are by nature not in line with the annual PMP, it is a challenge for the line manager to consider both, i) the overall project goals, where the duration – at least on larger projects – is often between two to four years and ii) appropriate annual goals derived or in line with the overall goals as the basis for the Performance Management Process. One possibility for a regular monitoring can be in the course of the project reporting and related project discussion with the line management. With such regular monitoring, the annual evaluation is adequately supported. In cases where the disciplinary manager is hardly involved in the project, a further person should take that part in the evaluation discussion with the project manager. By experience, such 'three-party-talks' are considered positively by all participants. This three-party constellation can also be used for the evaluation of a sub-project manager with the line manager and the project manager leading the evaluation. It underlines the role of the project manager and is good practice for his/her evaluation skills as well. In the subsequent round table discussion, all line managers of one hierarchy level of that organization meet with HR to present their employees and suggest, for example, development actions, special training courses and salary adjustments. The round table approach also has the advantage that other line managers can give their opinion and recommendation as well, and HR can cluster top, main, and under performers for that organization level and correlate the salary, making it easier to achieve a fair evaluation.

Figure 8.1   Performance Management Process

In Case company 3, the so-called 'Performance Management Process' (PMP) applies to all employees worldwide on an annual basis. The process has the following main phases: target setting, monitoring, evaluation, round table, feedback, action, as shown in Figure 8.1.

There were frictions regarding timing of relating HRM with project HRM. In several case study companies, the project managers found that the HR department was not acting fast enough to be able to assign personnel to the project, especially when the personnel had to be recruited externally.

8.6 HRM Infrastructure

All the case study companies in the sample had a database that provides an overview on the project managers (and core project personnel), their competences and experience which may serve as virtual project manager pools. This competence/skill database provides information about the project managers in a company or department and their resource availability. The benefit of such competence/skill database is that the company has an overview on the existing project management personnel. However, companies report that there are challenges with these competence/skill databases, and the search for project managers internally in the organization just works via informal networks or reputation of the project manager. A project manager for instance points out the limited practical relevance:

> Theoretical it has value, but in practice? We do have a so-called project manager database. But if a project manager puts up his CV there is voluntarily. We (PMO) want to have as many project managers as possible there, to be able to search for a project manager. But I do not know anybody up to now, who has searched for a project manager there. The recruiting of project managers works differently. It does not work with the database of project managers. (PMO member and senior PM; Case 3)

While these databases might not completely serve their purpose, all case study companies had competence or knowledge databases, and all had resource planning systems to be able to manage balancing resources between projects and between permanent organizations and temporary projects.

8.7 HRM Roles and Organization

All case studies showed that the HRM function was aware that managing projects was essential to the organization and that the HRM roles were distributed through the organization and also included temporary projects. Case 1 and 3 in particular had very clear role distinctions. Table 7.1 shows the distribution of responsibilities between HRM department, line managers and Project Management Office of Case company 1.

All cases showed evidence that the HRM system was networked, and differences were visible in the role distribution between the HR department and the PMOs. In Case 5, most of the PM-related services like training for project personnel, support in project team development, or selection of project managers for projects are performed by the PMO or the Project Academy, which is linked to the PMO. The HRM department is not involved in these services.

In Case 1 and Case 3, the HRM department for instance supports the selection of project managers for strategically important projects. In both organizations, the HRM department and the PMO co-operate with each other on a regular basis. In both case study companies, the HRM department has a strategic interest in fostering PM and sustaining/developing project managers internally for future projects.

8.8 Comparisons and Consequences

In this chapter, I reported on five case studies of HRM systems in (relatively) mature project-oriented organizations. All companies had more or less explicit strategies to support or further develop project-orientation. All companies had the role of 'Project Manager' established and at least an informal PM career path (Case 4) for project managers. All companies had quite a mature project assignment process, while the dispersing process was less mature. Some companies cared more for their project managers than others and had explicit placement and career planning strategies in place for the project managers to develop them and keep them in the organization. Others preferred to hand over the responsibility for the career to individuals (Cases 2, 4).

All cases had structures to mutually relate project HRM to HRM. All had databases for resource management, competence management and knowledge management, although in all case studies these were critiqued. Otherwise, the way they related to their projects differed and were often related to the size of the overall company (large companies, for example, Case 3 had more formal structures) and the size and nature of their projects.

All HRM systems were networked, and some applied project management to perform HRM projects. Interestingly, the way the HRM system was organized differed. In some companies, the HR department was driving even the PM-related HR structures in other cases (for example 5) the PMO performed many relevant HR-related support functions for the projects and the project personnel. The HRM department was not involved, except for providing some guidelines.

Table 8.9 gives a summary and comparison of the descriptions of context and HRM structures in the five case study companies.

Table 8.9   Comparison cases: Context and HRM structures

		Case 1	Case 2	Case 3	Case 4	Case 5
Content related context	**Company**	Telecommunication company Wireline part Austrian	IT consultancy Austrian subsidiary of inter-national company	Transportation systems Germany international division of global company	IT consultancy Dutch company	Division of a public sector organization involved in aerospace research and development US government organization
	Projects	Small to large projects/ programmes Mostly internal Small external projects	Many small projects Internal projects	Small to large projects	Many small projects	Medium size to very large projects/ programmes Investment projects
	Project orientation	Strong line structures Relatively, high maturity Modern PM Values not yet fitting for project-orientation	Flexible organization High maturity Modern PM Fitting values	Strong line structures, matrix High maturity Rather traditional PM Strong sustainability approach	Flexible organization Relatively high maturity Modern PM Fitting values	Partly matrix; large projects as pure project organizations High maturity Rather traditional PM Fitting values
Social context	**HRM department**	Business Partner Model	Small HR unit	Business Partner Model	Small HR unit	Traditional and local HRM departments in flight centres
	PPG (Top management)	Several PPGs	Top management team	Several PPGs	Top management team	Several PPGs
	PMO	Several PMOs Project management community	PMO/PM community	Central PMO and PM coaches in units Project management community	PMO	One PMO with Project Academy to train Project management community
	Line managers/ expert pool managers	Strong line managers Virtual expert pools	Expert pools	Strong line managers	Expert pools	Strong project functions
	Project managers	Project management mostly technical some leadership PM community established	Management with consultant/ IT background	Manager with technical background PM community	Consultant with IT background	Strong leadership science/ engineering background PM/Project community
	Project owner	Most of the times established	Established	Not established for external projects	Not established	Not necessary in large project/ programmes. Project director is manager of the quasi business unit

	Column 1	Column 2	Column 3	Column 4	Column 5
Social context — Project personnel	Project managers / Managers / Different experts / External consultants	Project managers / IT consultants	Technical project manager / Commercial project manager / Technical experts	Project managers / IT consultants	Project directors / Deputy project managers / Sub project leaders / Experts scientific/technology / Many temporary workers
Others	PM associations and PM certification bodies / Links to university and PM training/consulting	PM association and PM certification bodies / Links to university and PM training/consulting	PM association and PM certification bodies / Links to university and PM training/consulting	PM association and PM certification bodies / Links to university and PM training/consulting	PM association and PM certification bodies / Links to university and PM training/consulting
History	Some tradition in project management	Long tradition in project management	Long tradition	Tradition in project management (small assignments)	Very long tradition in project management
Future expectations	Demand for project management rather increasing	Importance of project management decreasing, keep maturity	Demand for project management stable	Demand for project management stable	Reduction of funding for programmes: Importance of PM questionable in future
HRM structures — HRM strategies	Explicit strategy to support and develop project orientation	Support of project orientation decreases, project management becomes less unimportant	Explicit strategy to support and develop project orientation	Project management important	Project success is important / Knowledge management
HRM goals	PM is a profession! / Raise potentials of projects for further transforming the organization	Sustain project managers	Support project business / PM as profession	Have qualified project personnel (PMs and consultants) / Care for employee wellbeing	All employees are trained in project management / Knowledge management: Projects are learning opportunities
HRM process	HRM process adapted / HRM and project / HRM processes are related / PM career path with limited relevance	HRM process adapted / PM career path	HRM processes adapted / HRM and project HRM processes related / PM career path	HRM processes adapted	HRM processes need less adaption because projects are like business units
HRM infrastructure	Competence database / Resource planning database	Competence database / Resource planning database	Competence database / Resource planning database	Competence database / Resource planning database	Knowledge database / Resource planning database
HRM roles and organization	HRM Department is aware of project orientation, strong co-operation with PMOs / Projects are applied for HRM	Networked, strong co-operation with PMO / Projects are applied for HRM	Business partner model, strong PMOs taking project management related resources / Projects are applied for HRM	Networked, not so differentiated because small organization	Traditional HRM department but strong PMO / Project Academy taking over project management related HR services

Conclusion

9.1 Introduction

This chapter discusses the results of the research study into constructing a viable HRM system for the project-oriented organization in order to raise the HR-related potential that projects can bring. While the goal of the working model (in Chapter 2) was to provide a structure to analyse a HRM system in the context of the project-oriented organization, the final *Model: project-oriented HRM system* serves as one possible way of describing a viable HRM system for the project-oriented organization. To discuss the *Model: Project-oriented HRM system* I further develop the propositions of Chapter 6 based on the empirical findings, which were presented in Chapters 7 and 8.

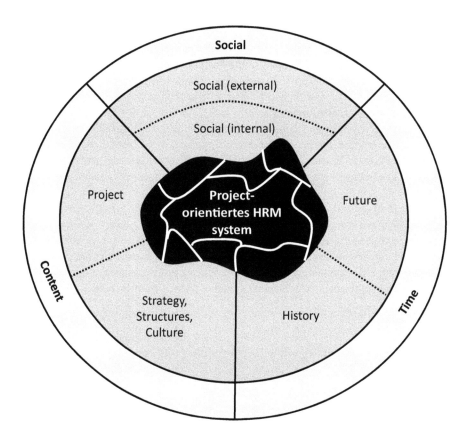

Figure 9.1   Model: Project-oriented HRM system

9.2 Model: A Project-Oriented HRM System

The goal of this study was to construct a model of a HRM system for project personnel that is viable to the project-oriented organization, whereby I applied Social System Theory as the theoretical lens, which has considerable implications on the model. The basic assumption is that a system can only be understood in a particular context. I differentiated between social, content-related and time-related context-dimension, which are relevant for the HRM system. A HRM system is viable if it relates to its specific context adequately. To relate to the context, the HRM system requires adequate structures. As I was interested in the difference that project-orientation makes for the HRM system, the perspective taken was project-orientation.

The empirical findings in Chapters 7 and 8 indicate that the HRM system adequate for a project-oriented organization is rather networked. I call it a project-oriented HRM system. To be viable to the project-oriented organization, it is adequately related to its content-related, social and time-related contexts. That means, in particular, that it has the adequate structures to relate to its context. To describe the *Model: Project-oriented HRM* system, I again use the further developed research propositions.

9.2.1 CONTEXT: PROJECT-ORIENTED HRM SYSTEM

The research propositions give in Table 9.1 regarding content-related context were developed and are interpreted.

As the project-oriented organization applies permanent and temporary structures, the organization is a rather differentiated and decentralized organization. In addition to the permanent line organization, there are projects. Managing in the line and managing on projects follow different management logics. The main difference is regarding timing: while the permanent organization rather follows a cyclic, annual or quarterly time rhythm, the project is driven by its milestones and by the inherent end, which creates urgency.

To deal with these frictions and dynamics that occur because the number and amount of projects will change over time, the project-oriented organization requires structures, culture and personnel that can navigate tensions between balancing of centralization and decentralization, stability and flexibility, between permanent and temporary, short-term, medium-term and long-term orientation.

Project-oriented organizations may perform very different project types, such as internal and external projects. Within a company, the size and duration can be quite different. Especially the size and the duration, as well as the autonomy of the projects make a difference for the HRM system.

To relate adequately to this context, the HRM system requires the Project Management Office as being related to the HRM system to interpret the specifics of project-orientation.

There are several quite distinct additional stakeholders of relevance to a project-oriented HRM system.

Table 9.1   **Final propositions regarding the content-related context**

PROPOSITIONS: CONTENT-RELATED CONTEXT
• Based on the strategy Managing by Project, the project-oriented organization has specific structures and shapes a specific culture.
• Different projects are carried out in the project-oriented organization.

Table 9.2   Final propositions regarding the social context

PROPOSITION: SOCIAL CONTEXT
- Additional internal and external environments/stakeholders are of relevance for the HRM system.

Essential stakeholders of a project-oriented HRM system are the HR department and the Project Management Office. A major difference for the HRM system occurs because of the HRM department and its self-understanding. In organizations where the HRM department is rather traditional and far away from projects or project business there is evidence that the specific project management related HRM structures are more driven by the Project Management Office, than by HR managers. The Project Management Office, which knows the specific features of project-orientation, are closer to the project managers and the projects. They can interpret the content-related context for HRM managers to initialize HRM structures that support project-orientation. In modern HR departments that are more networked, HR managers know projects and project management as they might apply projects for organizing HRM. Then the project-oriented HRM system is driven by the HR managers who co-operate with the Project Management Office managers.

The Project Portfolio Group (if it's a strategic portfolio group) consists of top managers who steer the portfolio from strategic perspective. They are interested by the fact that the HRM system provides project personnel in adequate quality and quantity to resource the projects they select to perform. They are interested in a short-, medium- and long-term perspective.

Project managers play a central role in delivering project HRM, for the purpose of project performance. They expect support by the HRM system so that they can staff their projects quickly and with adequately trained project personnel. They expect that the HRM system recognizes their contribution and supports it.

Project personnel are an important group of personnel in the project-oriented organization. By project personnel, I mean the personnel that are frequently members of projects. The most important roles project personnel fulfil on a project are project manager, project team member, project contributor and project owner. Project personnel have several expectations from HRM. Most importantly, they want the HRM system to offer them a project-related career, for instance via a PM path. Even when they are accustomed to empowerment and taking responsibility, they expect the company to ensure their well-being as an employee.

As project management training is essential, company internal project academies or the relation to PM training providers is of relevance for the HRM system. Project academies can be found in large project-oriented organizations.

Relevant additional company external stakeholders are, for example, PM training/education providers, and national and international PM associations and certification bodies. Most of the mature project-oriented organizations have strong links to PM associations and organize the stages of the PM career path in accordance with the certification levels international PM certification bodies offer.

Table 9.3   Final propositions regarding the time-related context

---

PROPOSITION: TIME-RELATED CONTEXT
- The history and the future expectations regarding the importance of projects are of relevance for the HRM system.

The time-related context includes the history of the HRM system and its future expectations, as well as the history of the project-oriented organization and its future expectations. For example, the 'heritage' of the HRM system from the past shapes the possibility of the present. Strong co-operation between the HRM department and the Project Management Office seem to be creating viable HRM structures for the project-oriented organization, but these must have grown over time.

Future expectations influence decisions made today. These can change or not change the internal structures of the HRM system. If the HRM system, for example, has the future expectation that the demand for projects and project management will increase, then the structures will develop differently in comparison to a situation when the project business or the need for performing internal projects decreases. If well-experienced project managers are needed in the future, the HRM system should build the future into the present (Ehnert 2009) with HRM structures that keep excellent project managers interested so that they remain in the PM career field.

As the HRM system requires strategic information about the future relevance of projects and project-orientation, relations are required with top management and/or the project portfolio group.

9.3 Structure: HRM Strategies

The research propositions given in Table 9.4 regarding HRM strategies were developed and are interpreted. Further developments are made visible in bold.

9.3.1 HRM ACTIVELY SUPPORTS AND IS SHAPED BY PROJECT-ORIENTATION

The HRM system on the one hand has an active role in developing a company towards a project-oriented organization, by offering, for instance: adequate training for project personnel; project career and incentive systems; support for project HRM; and adequate quantity and quality of personnel.

On the other hand, the HRM system has to adapt its HRM processes and the organization as such to acknowledge project-orientation. Thus, new HRM processes like assigning and dispersing project personnel to a project are to be considered, as well as project HRM processes aligned to those in the line. A more networked form of the HRM system with a clear interplay between Project Portfolio Group, HR managers, Project Management Office and project managers is a viable structure for raising HR-related potentials. This in this particular includes the possibility of projects as learning opportunities and projects as a source of motivation and offering interesting working forms to employees.

Table 9.4   Final propositions regarding: HRM strategies

PROPOSITIONS: HRM STRATEGY
• The HRM system actively supports **and is shaped by project-orientation**.
• The HRM system uses Managing by Projects as an organizational strategy.

Besides business strategies, the project-oriented HRM system considers project-orientation as a strategy in the structures and content of the HRM system.

9.3.2 MANAGING BY HR PROJECTS

The HRM system uses *Managing by Projects* as organizational strategy. If project-orientation is a core feature of the organization, then a more networked HRM system could serve the company better.

Managing by Projects is the organizational strategy of the HRM system. Thus, the HRM system makes a strategic choice as to how it would like to organize HRM, whereby projects are one option. *Managing by Projects* means that the HRM system has an overview on its processes and can explicitly choose to organize a process as a project, when adequate. That means not everything the HRM system carries out is a project, but the HRM system may choose to organize a relatively unique process of a certain scope as a project. Routine HRM processes, such as recruiting of a new employee or pay role activities, will remain organized by applying process management, or are even outsourced to a supplier organization that increasingly takes over administrative or routine HRM processes. In contrast, the more strategically important and unique processes, such as the development of a new career system or the conception and delivery of an organizational change, are organized by a project or a programme.

9.4 Structures: HRM Goals

The research propositions given in Table 9.5 regarding HRM goals were developed and are interpreted. Further developments are made visible in bold.

9.4.1 ENSURE EMPLOYEE WELL-BEING TO RAISE HR RELATED POTENTIAL

The challenges of project for project personnel are known, which include high goal orientation, uncertainty/novel, fragmented careers, multi-role assignment and taking higher degrees of responsibility. Nevertheless the HRM system has the duty to ensure the positive potentials that can be raised, which include:

- Motivation and commitment as projects provide sense for the project personnel;
- Projects as developing opportunities;
- Projects as attracting working forms to attract and retain personnel;
- Working in projects to support cultural change;
- Projects are explicitly used in HRM marketing to attract competent personnel.

Table 9.5   Final research propositions regarding: HRM goals

PROPOSITIONS: HRM GOALS
• The HRM system understands the challenges projects bring to the project personnel and ensures employee well-being to raise HR related potential.
• Balancing short-term and long-term orientation.

9.4.2 BALANCING SHORT- AND LONG-TERM ORIENTATION

Project HRM's main purpose is to ensure project performance and is a short-term orientation, while the HRM processes in the permanent part of the organization should also include more long-term orientation to be able to make a career by hopping from one project to the next. The HRM processes in a project-oriented organization should allow for linking short-term oriented project HRM with long-term oriented project HRM.

9.5 Structures: HRM Processes

The research propositions given in Table 9.6 regarding HRM processes were developed and are interpreted. Further developments are made visible in bold.

9.5.1 PROJECT HRM PROCESSES

Project HRM takes place on projects. Project HRM processes are performed for a project manager, a project team member or contributor, or a collective such as the project team. Specific project HRM processes include the following:

- Assigning to the project is the process of assigning project personnel, such as project managers, team members and project contributors to a project. It is similar to recruitment persons to the project-oriented organization. Assignment of project personnel starts in the permanent line organization. The project manager, project owner and initial project team members are identified and assigned. The project manager then identifies additional personnel required and negotiates with the permanent organization for their assignment to the project.
- Developing on the project means individual or team competencies also increase within the project. Development activities include project specific training, which is required by the project, and briefing in the work, which needs to be done on the project. An interesting practice identified is 'Bring the training to the Project'.
- Appraising on the project is the process of providing feedback on the performance of the individual or the team on the project. Appraisal on the project is necessary for development and motivation of project personnel and cohesiveness of the project team.

Table 9.6   Final research propositions regarding: HRM processes

PROPOSITIONS: HRM PROCESSES
- Project HRM processes are assigning, developing, appraising, rewarding and dispersing project personnel.
- Specific adoptions in the HRM processes in the permanent organization ensure relations to project HRM processes.
- Project HRM and HRM processes in the permanent organization are mutually aligned to support each other.

- Rewarding on the project is the process of rewarding members of the project for their performance. Project-specific rewards in the form of bonuses for exceptional performance on the project or non-financial awards (like social events and giveaways) exist. Individual and team rewards on projects can be differentiated.
- Dispersing from the project is applied when members of the project move on. This activity has similarities to, but also substantial differences from, the release from the project-oriented organization. This process is applied when personnel leave the project and this can occur during or at the end of a project.

9.5.2 SPECIFICS OF HRM PROCESSES

The HRM processes are not novel but specific adoptions of these processes support project orientation.

Recruiting is the process of bringing new potential members of project personnel to the project-oriented organization. It is based on planning and includes selection of new permanent and temporary project personnel. Recruiting is done for a position in an expert pool or directly for a position on a project.

Developing is the process of enhancing the competency of an employee. The objective of developing project managers and further project personnel is to improve competence by supporting the drive to increase knowledge and experience. Development activities are carried out either on the job, in a project, or outside project assignments.

Appraising is the process of evaluating the performance and providing feedback to the employee. This includes future performance planning and improvement and not just retrospective performance evaluation. The appraisal meeting is a formal review once or twice a year to consider key performance and development issues, whereas input from the person´s performance on projects is ensured.

Rewarding is the process of providing financial and non-financial remuneration for personnel according to their contribution to the organization. Reward includes salary, variable pay and benefits, responsibility, career opportunities, learning development, the work itself and the quality of work life.

Releasing is applied when personnel leave the company. The most significant challenge faced by project-oriented organization is to lose knowledge as in when temporary workers leave the company at the end of projects. It would be very useful to remain in contact with them in a bid to maintain the organization's network and to make future co-operation possible. Companies with fluctuating demand for project personnel establish pools of potential workers that can be temporarily assigned to projects when required.

9.5.3 ALIGNING HRM PROCESSES AND PROJECT HRM PROCESSES

HRM is executed explicitly in projects. Relations between project HRM and HRM processes in the permanent organization are explicitly recognized. Special solutions are adapted according to the characteristics of specific projects such as project type, size, duration, and so on, of a project. For example, in organizations with many small or medium-sized projects, the appraisal interview includes an employee who worked in several projects as a project member, and the expert pool leader in charge of the employee. The basis for the interview is the collected feedback from closed projects. In organizations where the employee is just working in one project, the appraisal interview includes the expert pool manager and the project manager.

Table 9.7 Relating line and project Human Resource Management

HRM system	Permanent HRM system to support project HRM	Project HRM to support permanent HRM system	Project HRM
Recruiting	Recruiting appropriate personnel Recruiting people quickly enough to meet the needs of project mobilization Ensure all project team members have the same terms and conditions Ensure project team members adhere to the organization's policies Project categorization system to differentiate competences required by the project manager Take account of individual and organizational development needs	Forecast future requirements Maintain a resource management system within the project Take account of individual and organizational development needs	Assigning
Developing	Develop personnel competent to work on the organization's projects Ensure success planning for future project managers Ensure good personnel are not held in inferior line jobs to the detriment of the organization's needs and the individual's career development Provide adequate career path	Ensure focused project development is compatible with the line career development plans Ensure project assignments meet organizational and individual development needs	Developing
Appraising	Incorporate project appraisals for the motivation of project team members and the cohesiveness of the project team Project manager and line manager are doing the appraisal together	Do appraisals/feedback on the project to provide data for the line appraisal; for example provided assessments are documented and collected to be incorporated for the annual appraisal in the line	Appraising
Rewarding	Ensure rewards reflect project performance so that people are motivated to work on projects Ensure people from different departments working on the same project are rewarded in the same way for cohesiveness of the team	Ensure that project rewards and bonuses are compatible with the organization's policies and the line reward system	Rewarding
Releasing	Capture knowledge from temporary workers leaving the organization Retain a network with temporary workers	Capture knowledge at the end of the project, particularly from temporary workers Ensure project workers are returned promptly to the line so they can be reassigned quickly for efficient utilization Try to find development work for project workers without new assignments to go to immediately Inform the line about project workers without assignments to go to immediately so they can be counselled Ensure project workers are moved to projects where their skills are best used	Dispersing

Source: Adapted from Huemann/Turner 2010.

Table 9.8   Propositions regarding: HRM infrastructure

> **PROPOSITION: HRM INFRASTRUCTURE**
> * Specific adoptions in the HRM infrastructure support project-orientation.

9.6 Structures: HRM Infrastructure

The research proposition given in Table 9.8 regarding HRM infrastructure were developed and are interpreted.

The HRM system needs an overview over the project personnel and their competences. Furthermore, they need information about their capacities. For that, the appropriate infrastructure is needed. An overview of the capacity of the project employees is especially challenging. Project personnel can be involved in different projects, as well as in the task of the permanent organization. Additional project work is fluctuant. A project-oriented organization uses a resource-management system. Furthermore, IT systems for competence and knowledge management are used.

9.7 Structures: HRM Organization

The research propositions given in Table 9.9 regarding HRM organization were developed and are interpreted.

Project-orientation accelerates the devolution of HRM responsibilities and HRM goes beyond the permanent organization (Keegan et al. 2012). Thus HRM tasks are performed by different roles, in permanent and in temporary structures. The roles taking on HRM in addition to the HRM department are manifold and include existing in the permanent structures:

* Top managers/ Project Portfolio Group;
* Line managers, expert pool managers;
* Project Management Office managers;
* Project Academy.

Further to the role of the project manager, I also consider the project owner as a role with HRM tasks. Thus the roles taking on HRM in the temporary project are project roles such as:

* Project owner;
* Project manager.

The project-oriented organization is specifically challenged by the interplay of these roles to deliver adequate HRM. The interplay of these different and partly very specific roles like the Project Management Office or the Project Portfolio Group is challenging for the project-oriented organization. There are differences in the role distribution and interplay, depending on the organizational structure of the company; the size of the project and the role understanding of the HRM department. The distribution of the HRM tasks and responsibilities between these roles may change over time, as discussed in the longitudinal case study in Chapter 7. The Project Management Office may play more or less of a role in the HRM system. How much role and which HRM tasks it fulfils depends on the activity and readiness of the HRM department to consider project-orientation.

Table 9.9   Propositions regarding: HRM roles and organization

---

INTERNAL STRUCTURES: HRM ROLES AND ORGANIZATION

- The HRM roles are spread out in the project-oriented organization, which leads to a more networked HRM organization/function.

Finally, the operationalization of *Management by Projects* as HRM strategy impacts the set up of the HRM organization, especially the HRM department. The HR department is no longer a functionally organized administrative unit. But in the context of dissolving HRM departments and understanding that HRM is the task of many in an organization may gain network character. To manage the co-operation in a distributed, networked HRM, the HRM department understands its own need to work in a project-oriented way themselves. HR departments become more project-oriented themselves and apply projects and professional project management to organize the required co-operation.

The reason for this is twofold. As the project-oriented company is applying projects when necessary, this may, in internal projects particularly, include the need for HRM contributions or even for managing internal projects out of the HRM department. This is especially relevant during the establishment of new HRM services, personnel development, or organizational change and development. Last, but not least, the better HRM practitioners live the project-orientation themselves, the better they understand the requirements of project-orientation, and the better they can shape and contribute to the future of the company that they are providing services for.

9.8 Limitations and Research Agenda

There are several limitations with regard to what this research was able to achieve. Taking the perspective of project-orientation, I explore its implications on HRM. The perspective of project-orientation is considered as *one* possible way of analysing and interpreting the HRM system in the project-oriented organization – not more, but also not less. In a constructivist approach the limitations lay in the constructs of the researcher and observer.

This was an explorative study. Nevertheless, several topics emerged during the course of the research study, which I was not able to cover, but which have potential for further research, such as:

- To explicitly analyse the challenges of project HRM and its alignment with several organizations, when the project personnel derive from different (partnering) organizations. This would require a different research design, with focus on the project, while in this research study the focus was the project-oriented organization and its organization of HRM system.
- The complexity of the interplay between the different roles in the HRM system is not yet fully understood and warrants further research.
- Career and career paths: Better understanding of project (management) careers in the context of project-oriented organizations and society. The establishment of an adequate career path with an explicit project management career in balance with other career paths.
- Most project managers have to do their job, which leads to the question what are the motives of persons who start a project management career. Why do they seek this challenge, what is the psychological contract (Rousseau 1995), is this with the project-oriented organization or is there another one with the project, that steers the project managers into action?

- More work is needed to optimize HRM planning in terms of competencies and project resource allocation. Not only will this prevent project overload, but it will also ensure employee's well-being through active measures which promote a work–life balance, even though this is almost always challenging in a project context.
- Better understanding of the management paradigm and development of the culture of the project-oriented organization, including values like sustainability and diversity, as project work not only requires diverse personnel, but sustainable development is a key challenge of contemporary organizations and society.

This is a relatively new research field and there is much to be done. So let's continue!

Appendix:
Research Objectives and Approach

A.1 Introduction

This appendix provides a description of the research objectives and the research approach taken. The appendix explains the underpinning research paradigms, which represent the theoretical stance of this research study. After that, the context and structures of the research study are described. The research process is outlined and the research methods are explained. The appendix concludes with a section on viability, which summarizes the assurance of viability of the research results gained and the limitations of the approach that was taken.

A.2 Context and Research Question

The research study was performed between 2004 and 2012 and is related to other research studies on HRM in the project-oriented organization in which I was involved (Huemann et al. 2007; 2004; Keegan et al. 2012; Turner et al. 2008a; 2008b).

Recent and not so recent studies have indicated challenges for HRM in the project-oriented organization. While most of these studies describe the challenges for the project personnel in project-oriented organizations I here propose a more comprehensive approach to the HRM system and indicate the HRM related potentials that can be raised if the HRM system is viable for the particular context of the project-oriented organization.

The main assumption put forward in this book is that in the context of the project-oriented organization a viable HRM system explicitly acknowledging project-orientation can raise potentials for the project personnel as well as for the HRM system as such. The viable HRM system can contribute to sustainable development of the project-oriented organization. Thus, the research study discusses the research question:

> *Which HRM System is Viable to the Project-oriented Organization in Order to Raise the HR Related Potential That Project-orientation Can Bring?*

For answering this research question I analysed the project-oriented organization as a specific context that impacts the HRM system in the project-oriented organization, as well as HRM-related potentials that may arise if the HRM system fits its purpose to support and shape project-orientation. The following research objectives were pursued in the course of the study:

* Analyse HR related potentials;
* Describe the specific social, content-related and time-related contexts of a HRM system in the project-oriented organization;
* Analyse changes in a HRM system when developing into a project-oriented organization;

- Analyse possible mutual relations of the permanent HRM system in the project-oriented organization and the temporary HRM system on a project;
- Develop the *Model: Project-oriented HRM system*.

A.3 Working Model and Initial Research Propositions

The research analyses the HRM system in the context of the project-oriented organization. In particular, I am interested in the HRM system for project personnel. With project personnel, I mean the personnel who frequently engage in projects of the project-oriented organization.

I use Social System Theory (Luhmann 1995) to describe the HRM system in the project-oriented organization. The application of a self-referential system theory is not completely new to HRM, and especially in German-speaking countries, this theoretical lens has been applied to HRM (Hauschildt 2004; Mayrhofer 1996), but it is a new endeavour for analysing the HRM system in the context of the project-oriented organization.

Figure A1.1 visualizes the working model used to analyse a HRM system. The elements of the working model are the:

- context, with its three context dimensions:
  - content-related context
  - social context
  - time-related context;
- and the internal structures of the HRM system, including those structures that make relation/ aligning to the different relevant contexts possible.

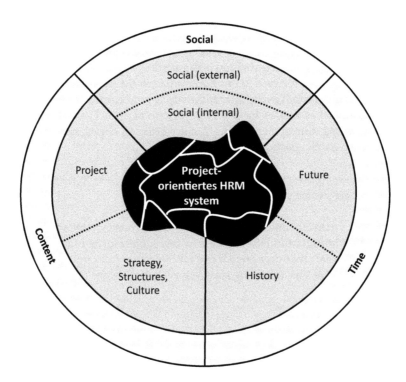

Figure A.1.1   Working model: HRM system in the context of the project-oriented organization

Table A1.1   Initial propositions regarding: Context of the HRM system in the project-oriented organization

Initial Research Propositions Regarding the Context of the Hrm System in the Project-Oriented Organization
Proposition: Content-related context
The project-oriented organization has specific strategies, structures and culture. Different projects are carried out in the project-oriented organization.
Proposition: Social context
Additional stakeholders are of relevance for the HRM system.
Proposition: Time-related context
The history and the future expectations regarding the importance of projects are of relevance for the HRM system.

Table A1.2   Initial propositions regarding internal structures of the HRM system in the project-oriented organization

Initial Research Propositions Regarding the Internal Structures of the Hrm System in the Project-Oriented Organization
Internal structures: HRM strategies
HRM strategies support project-orientation. HRM recognizes the temporary part in projects.
Internal structures: HRM goals
The HRM system understands the challenges projects bring to the project personnel and ensures employee well-being to raise HR-related potential.
Internal structures: HRM processes infrastructure
Specific adoptions in the HRM processes in the permanent organization ensure relations to project HRM processes.
Internal structures: HRM infrastructure
Specific adoptions in the HRM infrastructure support project-orientation.
Internal structures: HRM roles and organization
The HRM roles are spread out in the project-oriented organization, which leads to a more networked HRM organization/function.

The working model is described by the initial research propositions in Tables A1.1 and A1.2. These research propositions are further explained in Chapter 6, when the *Working model: HRM system in the context of the project-oriented organization* is more comprehensively introduced.

The research propositions are revisited in the course of the research and the final set of research propositions are discussed in Chapter 9.

A.4 The Underpinning Research Paradigms

Research paradigms address basic questions of how we perceive reality and how we create knowledge (Kilduff et al. 2011). Different paradigm stances exist and must be combined with methodological choices within a research study. An increasing need for engaging with practice is suggested in management research (Corley/Gioia 2011; Van De Ven 2007), which stresses the utility dimension of research studies. Research results and models are measured regarding their usefulness and potential for problem solving (Kilduff et al. 2011; Von Glasersfeld 1995). Thus, the quality criterion is viability to practice. Viability can be considered as a social construction. Research therefore requires exchange not only within the scientific community, but also engagement with the practice community to develop research solutions that are viable to practice.

I consider the theoretical as well as practical relevance of research, and to achieve the purpose of the research study, I have chosen a systemic-constructivist research approach as developed by the Project Management Group of the WU Vienna University of Economics and Business (Fiedler 1996; Gareis et al. 2013; Huemann 2002). It is based on the epistemological paradigm of Radical Constructivism (Von Glasersfeld 1995), the understanding of organizations as social systems (Luhmann 1995), and the methodological paradigm of Qualitative Social Research (Yin 2009; 2011). These are compatible with each other (Fiedler 1996; Kasper 1990) and are operationalized through a qualitative iterative research approach, which supports knowledge creation.

A.4.1 RADICAL CONSTRUCTIVISM: CREATING KNOWLEDGE

Different strands of constructivist approaches have been developed and are being developed, which break with the traditional understanding of truth and lay out how knowledge can be understood and created. All constructivist approaches refer to the idea that reality is constructed and the observer plays a vital role in this construction. However, the strands differ in how far they take the idea that reality is constructed (for a detailed discussion of different strands of constructivism see Riegler 2012).

This research applies the epistological paradigm of Radical Constructivism as its basic stance of creating knowledge. Radical Constructivism was developed by Ernst von Glasersfeld (1995) who claims that reality cannot be the subject of perception in the notion of a picture. This stance is well expressed by Gregory Bateson, who is said to have told a little story about Picasso and his pictures:

> Somebody was saying to Picasso that he ought to make pictures of things the way they are – objective pictures. He mumbled he wasn't quite sure what that would be. The person who was bullying him produced a photograph of his wife from his wallet and said, 'There, you see, that is a picture of how she really is.' Picasso looked at it and said, 'She is rather small, isn't she? And flat?' (Ralston 2010: 35)

Perception and knowledge are bound to the observer and related to the experience and expectations of the observer, leading to the impossibility of grasping reality as an objective picture or even describing reality objectively. With 'radical', von Glasersfeld (1995) expresses that there is no possibility of even finding out whether a reality exists, as reality is considered to be bound to the observer.

> Objectivity is the delusion that observations could be made without an observer. Heinz von Foerster. (Epigraph in Ernst von Glasersfeld 1995)

Heinz von Foerster (1984) considers an observation as identifying a difference. This brings the assumption that any observation is in relation to a prior observation, and thus bound to the observer. Or as Gregory Bateson puts it:

Information is a difference that makes a difference. (Bateson 1972)

This difference is a construction of the human brain, just as perceptions of the world are constructions of the human brain. The reasons are the specific way that human perception functions, and the idea that the human brain considered a self-referential closed system without the possibility of a direct contact with the environment (Von Glasersfeld 1995). Von Glaserfeld thus vehemently disagrees with Wittgenstein, who suggests the possibility of comparing one's own knowledge with reality:

In order to discover whether the picture is true or false we must compare it with reality. (Wittgenstein 1933: proposition 2.223)

Von Glaserfeld suggests that reality is bound to an observer (who is a closed system), and therefore cannot be compared with the reality, but only with the perception of reality of the observer. Pointing to Piaget, von Glasersfeld further suggests that knowledge is not a picture of reality, but the value of knowledge lies in its function. While Piaget uses the term 'adequate', von Glaserfeld suggests the term *viability* and states:

Actions, concepts, and conceptual operations are viable if they fit the purposive or descriptive contexts in which we use them. Thus, in the constructivist way of thinking, the concept of viability in the domain of experience, takes the place of the traditional philosopher's concept of truth, that was to indicate a 'correct' representation of reality. (Von Glasersfeld 1995: 14)

The validity criterion for reality constructions, and therefore also for research models, is viability. Viability describes how far the findings and models of a research study fit reality. It cannot be the extent up to which the model matches reality, as the latter cannot be established. Viability does not mean true or false, but comprises the explanatory and prognostical potential for the research question itself, and the potential for further development of the research object regarding new questions or applications in other research areas. Von Glasersfeld summarizes the fundamental principles of Radical Constructivism as:

1. Knowledge is not passively received either through the senses or by way of communication; knowledge is actively built up by the cognizing subject.

2. The function of cognition is adaptive, in the biological sense of the term, tending towards fit or viability; cognition serves the subject's organization of the experiential world, not the discovery of an objective ontological reality. (Von Glasersfeld 1995: 51)

Therefore, models and propositions that are developed based in the stance of Radical Constructivism cannot represent reality objectively, but are always actively built by the researchers, and remain their interpretations. The propositions and models are not created for their own sake, but rather to serve a purpose and contribute to problem solving. Thus, the models and propositions contain the potential to challenge existing practice. The roles of a researcher therefore are observer, interpreter, and most importantly, also creator.

A.4.2 SOCIAL SYSTEMS THEORY: ORGANIZATIONS AS SOCIAL SYSTEMS

The research study builds upon the understanding of organizations as social systems (Luhmann 1995). While there are different strands of systems theory, I use Social Systems Theory as developed by the German sociologist Niklas Luhmann as a theoretical lens to approach organizations. Kasper (1990: 220) argues that the Social Systems Theory is well suited for analysing organizations, as system relations in organizations are neither linear nor monocausal, but selective, discontinuous and non-linear. The consideration of organizations as social systems influences the research study fundamentally, and therefore I introduce it as one of the fundamental paradigms of the research taken. As a 'Grand Theory', it is impossible to describe Luhmann's system theory comprehensively here, I will therefore only describe the pieces that are of particular relevance to this research study.

Organizations as a type of social systems

Luhmann (1995) differentiates systems as machine, organism, social systems and psychic systems. Social systems are further differentiated into interactions, organizations and societies. In this research, I concentrate on social systems in particular organizations.

Luhmann (1995) describes social systems with specific characteristics, such as the environment and system difference, self-reference and communications/decisions as elements. In essence, Luhmann positions his theory as a theory of system/environment difference as well as a theory of self-referential systems.

> There are systems that have the ability to establish relations with themselves and to differentiate these relations from relations with their environment. (Luhmann 1995: 13)

Willke (1987) suggests that one of the strengths of Luhmann's theory is *differentiation*. Differentiation may be drawn between the environment and the system and between the elements of that system and their relationships. While the first kind of differentiation leads to a theory of system differentiation, the other leads to a theory of system complexity (Luhmann 1995: 21).

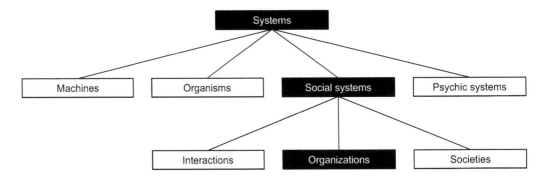

Figure A1.2   Systems
Source: Adapted from Luhmann 1995: 2.

(...) For the theory of self-referential systems, the environment is, rather, a presupposition for the system's identity, because the identity is possible only by the difference (1995: 177). (...) This difference is not an ontological one (...) It does not cut all of the reality into two parts: here system, there environment. It's either or is not an absolute, it pertains only in relation to the system (...). It is correlative to the operation of observation, which introduces this distinction (as well as others) into reality (1995: 178). (...)They (social systems) constitute and maintain themselves by creating and maintaining a difference from their environment, and they use their boundaries to regulate this difference (...). In this sense boundary maintenance is system maintenance. (1995: 17)

Luhmann radializes the biological concept of self-reference developed by Maturana and Varela (1991) and applies it to social systems. According to Luhmann, social systems are closed systems, that is, they are not open to their environment as the environment produces only a stimulus for the system. The construction of 'information' completely depends on the system's specific structures and processes. An organization as a self-referential system creates the elements it consists of with the help of these elements.

A social system consists of communications. Therefore, a social system is a communication system that reproduces itself based on its elements; in particular, a social system reproduces communications. For an organization, these communications are a specific form of communication, notably decisions under the pressure of expectations (Luhmann 2006). From this theoretical perspective, an organization is not constituted of persons, or their actions, but of their decisions. Persons are important, and without them the social system cannot exist, but they are considered as 'relevant internal environments' to the social system. To fulfill its objectives/functions, the organization requires persons. There is a structural coupling between an employee and the organization. The coupling exists for the duration of that employee's membership to the organization (Fuchs 1999).

In the case of a project, the project manager, project team members, project owner and project contributors are the personnel engaged in the project. These are considered as the 'internal project environments'. The 'external environments' include, for example, business units of the company conducting the project, other organizations like clients or suppliers, competitors, community, media and so on. In project management, the relevant internal and external environments are referred to as project stakeholders.

Decisions are events that are transitory. A decision realizes a certain option and excludes other possible options. Based on the reproduction of decisions, the organization shapes structures that are of essential importance to that organization. Structures such as communication rules, roles, processes and strategies reduce uncertainty, as they offer pre-selected options (Fiedler 1996; Kasper 1990).

In this research, I consider organizations, projects and project-oriented organizations as well as the HRM system as social systems. Project-oriented organizations differentiate themselves and use projects as temporary sub-systems to fulfill distinct purposes. The project-oriented organization can be further differentiated into permanent organizations and temporary organizations such as projects and programmes.

More precisely, a project is a distinct form of a social system: an organization (Gareis 2005; Lundin/Söderholm 1995). The project, as well as the project-oriented organization that created the project, are distinct social systems and organizations, but relations between them exist. The project-oriented organizations are differentiated by projects. The project-oriented organization creates the project. As Luhmann describes:

System differentiation is nothing more than the repetition within systems of the difference between system and environment. Through it, the whole system uses itself as environment in forming its own subsystems and therefore achieves greater improbability on the level of those subsystems by more rigorously filtering an ultimately uncontrollable environment. (Luhmann 1995: 7)

A project is a sub-system of the project-oriented organization. It is related to one or more organizations, for example, to one or more investor organizations and to supplier organizations.

As opposed to trivial systems, which always react in a predictable way, social systems are dynamic. They can surprise the observer by their reactions. Interventions from the environment don't pass the system linearly, but are broken, changed and directed in new directions. Therefore, social systems can take on a high number of possible alternative states. The structures of a social system created by communications/decisions, along with the context in which the system operates, determine its identity (Gareis 2005: 49).

The relevant context dimensions of social systems are its content-related context, its social context stakeholders, and its time-related context and expectations regarding the future. External stakeholders of a company are, for example, clients, suppliers and competitors. There are also internal stakeholders, such as the employees and the managers, of the organization. Social systems are shaped by their histories. Many specifics of a system can only be understood and interpreted through knowing the history of the system. On the other hand, the expectations regarding the future development of a system determine current decisions.

Dimensions of the internal structures of an organization are, for example, its objectives and strategies, its services, products and technologies, its organizational structures and cultures, its personnel and infrastructure, as well as its budget and financing.

The dimensions influencing the identity of a social system are illustrated in Figure A1.3.

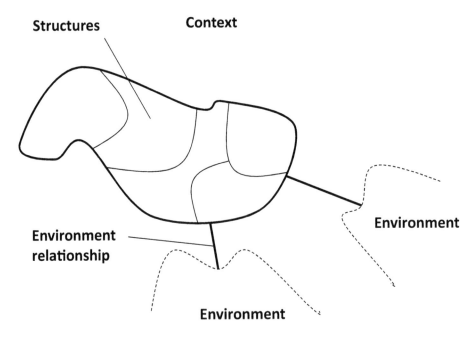

Figure A1.3   Identity model to describe social systems
Source: Gareis/Stummer 2008.

A.4.3 QUALITATIVE SOCIAL RESEARCH APPROACH

Consistent with radical constructivism and social systems theory, this research follows a qualitative research approach. This is because the project, the project-oriented organization and project personnel construct their own realities. The understanding of these construction processes and their underlying structures is the major challenge for the researcher who constructs their own perception. This requires interpretation of verbal or observational data, considering not only the content, which in this study are HRM processes, roles and strategies, but also contextual information. To avoid the danger of reductionism and the loss of relevant information, a variety of qualitative research methods are combined to be able to interpret research objects in context, which are specifically the features of projects as temporary organizations and the features of the project-oriented organization. Yin (2011) stresses the advantages of qualitative research, which include the understanding of the context of the phenomenon studied and the possibility and requirement of a multi-method, multi source approach to understand the development of the HRM organization and the interplay of different roles contributing to HRM over a period of time.

A.5 Consequences for the Research Study

Following the fundamental paradigms radical constructivism, social systems theory, and the application of a qualitative social research approach has an impact on the research process, the research methods applied, as well as on the findings expected from the research study. Due to the complexity of the research, and in order to avoid the danger of reductionism and the loss of relevant information, the research process applied the same distinct principles.

A.5.1 CONSEQUENCES: RESEARCH PROCESS

The research followed a cyclic research process (see Figure A.4), while data collection and data analysis were iterative. Several methods for data collection and analysis were applied. Analyses of findings and model development were carried out in an open and cyclic way. It consisted of several loops of proposition generation, data collection, interpretation of propositions/models and reflection. For the data collection and interpretation of propositions, several methods were applied as a multi method approach was followed (Yin 2011).

The propositions were generated based on prior studies and the literature research. However, in the centre of the multi-method approach was a case study approach, constituting a long-term case study and four further in depth case studies. In each case study, several methods like documentation analysis, interviews, and sometimes presentations and workshops were applied.

In addition to these case studies, more than 40 qualitative interviews with different informants such as project managers, HR managers and line managers were performed. These interviews served two purposes: while the first interviews aimed for additional understanding of HRM system in the project-oriented organization, the later ones rather aimed to validate the propositions and models developed.

I perceive research as a communication process with practitioners and other researchers. As the aim was to further develop HRM in the project-oriented company, engaging with practice was essential to ensure the relevance of findings (Van De Ven 2007). The engagement with practice was in particular organized in the case studies and the interviews conducted, but also in practice conferences. Communication with other researchers was organized in individual conversations and at research conferences, with researchers working on similar topics.

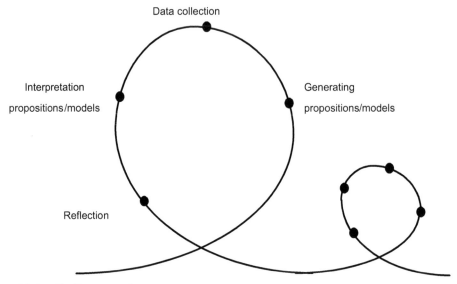

Figure A1.4   Cyclic research process

A.5.2 CONSEQUENCES: RESEARCH CONTENT

* **Project-orientation as one possible perspective to approach the HRM system:** I take the perspective of project-orientation and explore its implications on the HRM system. The project-oriented organization is the context within which HRM is studied. Nevertheless, to consider the perspective of project-orientation is only *one* way of looking at the HRM system in an organization. This perspective was chosen because projects are a relevant working form with increasing importance in contemporary organizations.
* **Organization:** Radical Constructivsm and social systems theory are considered in the understanding of projects and the project-oriented organization. Both are considered as constructs and social systems, specifically as organizations. Projects are considered as sub systems of a project-oriented organization. In particular, the project is considered as a temporary organization.
* **Structures:** To understand the behaviour of a social system, the decision patterns over time are of relevance. These are observable in structures evolving in the organization, such as processes, roles and strategies.
* **Differentiation as a leading principle:** I explicitly distinguish permanent and temporary organizations, and I distinguish system and contexts. For example, the temporary project and the permanent organization in the project-oriented organization are differentiated, which then constitute different contexts for HRM on the project and HRM in the permanent organization and question how the HRM system of the permanent organization is mutually related to the temporary HRM system of the project.
* **Personnel and HRM system:** According to social system theory, the unit of analysis of an organization is a decision, which is a specific form of communication. Persons are not the smallest elements of the organization. Project personnel are the internal environment of the organization, and include persons in the role of project managers, project team members, project contributors and project owners. These are coupled for the duration of the membership to the social system. Thus, the objective of the HRM system is designing and managing the relationships between the personnel and the organization, which is in line with modern HRM theories.

A.5.3 CONSEQUENCES: RESEARCH RESULTS

• **Propositions and models:**The research focused on the generation of research propositions and models and their discussion. The research study was explorative. By research propositions, I mean statements to describe and interpret the research object. By models, I mean constructs that fit reality (Von Glasersfeld 1995). These models and propositions are explicitly perceived as social constructs, and are discussed and further developed in the course of the research and represent the results of the research study. The models that are suggested build upon theories which are viable to practice.

A.6 Case Study Approach

A case study research involves the study of an issue explored through one or more cases within a bounded system (Creswell 2007: 73). The case studies served the purpose of observing HRM system in practice and further developing the HRM propositions and working models introduced earlier in this chapter. One case was investigated in depth over an extended period of time. This enabled in particular the investigation of the change of the HRM system in a particular organization over an extended period of time when the demand for projects raised and the company was becoming more and more project-oriented.

A.6.1 SAMPLING OF CASE STUDIES

The case study organizations represent a purposive sample (Yin 2011), as they were examples of project-oriented organizations with a medium to relatively high maturity in project-orientation. Furthermore, I was able to determine from the initial interviews that the HRM system of these organizations was at least partly aware that they too support project-orientation (Huemann et al. 2004). They are all rather large companies and conduct a variety of project types, from simple to complex projects for both internal and external customers. The five companies are from different industries, including telecommunications, information technology, engineering, and science, and are from a variety of locations (Austria, Germany, USA and UK).

A.6.2 DATA COLLECTION IN CASE STUDIES

All case studies followed a multi-method approach, which included documentation analysis, single and group interviews, and partly observations, presentations and workshops. The documentation analysis comprised publicly available company documents as well as company internal HRM and PM documentations to better understand the case study company as well as the structures of the HRM system and project management.

While access was organized through senior project managers or Project Management Office managers, these contact persons organized for further access to different case study representatives who were suitably knowledgeable about HRM and its role in the company and in projects. Single and group interviews were conducted. To gain multiple perspectives, case study company representatives in different roles were interviewed. These included HR managers, line managers, Project Management Office managers, project managers, project team members, and if possible, representatives of a Project Portfolio Group. Different informants as described in Table A.3 above were interviewed in each case. Some companies were revisited several times to make follow up interviews and to see if and how the HRM system was changing. The individual and group interviews were semi-structured according to the propositions. The interviews for the case studies were all recorded, and field notes were taken during the interviews.

The interpretations of the findings were presented to representatives of the companies to allow for clarification of misunderstandings and for further reflection.

A.6.3 LONGITUDINAL CASE STUDY

As a consequence of an arising opportunity, one case study was turned into a longitudinal case study. This arose when it became clear that the HRM system was changing as the demand for projects increased, and the company became increasingly project-oriented. In this longitudinal case study, in addition to documentation analysis, formal single and group interviews with project managers, project team members, HR managers, Project Management Office managers and line managers were conducted. Several interviewees were interviewed multiple times in the course of the study to be better able to follow developments. In addition to these formal interviews, many informal conversations took place. I had been observing the developments of the company. Based on long-term research co-operation between the company and the Project Management Group of the WU Vienna, I was involved with the company on several different occasions as researcher. For example, I carried out an assessment of the competencies of project managers in one of the company's business units in 2000 (Huemann 2002), and a maturity assessment of several business units in 2004, and contributed to conceptualization of assessment centres for project managers. The company represents an example of an organization that was developing itself from a hierarchical, state-owned company to a project-oriented organization with the potential to professionally manage internal and external projects.

The case study covers the developments of the company between 1997 and 2010. For this research study, part of the data collection was conducted retrospectively, and part in real time (2006 and 2011). The findings were discussed with the interviewees in order to clarify understanding and interpretation. Although it was not the primary objective of the researcher, this long-term co-operation also allowed the company to reflect on and further develop its approach to HRM during the course of the study. Table A1.3 gives an overview of all case studies that were conducted.

A.6.4 DATA ANALYSIS

Rich descriptions of the different case study organizations were produced based on the interview records and transcripts of the field notes. Further differentiation criteria, such as the different roles, practices and project types, were identified and made explicit for the single case study organization. In the longitudinal case study, I identified different phases of the development and compared these phases with each other. After this within-case analysis, a cross-case analysis was conducted (Yin 2009) and the propositions and models were further developed.

Table A1.3 Overview on case studies

Case	Company	Projects	Interviewees	Data collection methods	Data collected	Locations
Case 1	Telecommunication company Wireline part	Small to large projects/ programmes Mostly internal Small external projects	PM office manager HRM manager Project manager Line manager Project team member PPG HRM Competence Centre manager	20 single interviews 5 group interviews Documentation analysis	2006, 2007, 2008, 2009, 2011	Austria
Case 2	IT consultancy Subsidiary of international company	Many small projects Mostly external projects	HR manager PMO manager Project manager Project team member	5 single interviews 2 group interviews Documentation analysis	2007, 2009	Austria
Case 3	Transportation systems International division of global company	Small to large projects Mostly external projects	Project manager HR manager PMO manager Project coach	10 single interviews 5 group interviews Documentation analysis	2008, 2009, 2010	Germany
Case 4	IT consultancy	Many small projects Mostly external projects	Management team Consultant Project manager HR manager	4 single interviews 2 group interviews Documentation analysis	2007	The Netherlands
Case 5	Division of a public sector organization involved in aerospace research and development	Medium size to very large projects/programmes Investment projects	Deputy project manager (Resources) Deputy project manager (Technical) Project manager Deputy programme manager Former project manager HR manager Project Academy manager	10 single interviews 5 group interviews Documentation analysis	2007, 2010, 2011	US

A.7 Further Research Methods

A.7.1 LITERATURE ANALYSIS

The literature analysis included HRM, general management, as well as project management literature. The purpose of the literature review was to find articles and further publications to describe the research objects. Firstly, I searched for literature to better clarify the basic constructs, such as HRM system, project and project-oriented organization. The literature review supported the development of the model shown in Chapter 6. More in depth literature research and analysis followed, as the research study evolved.

A.7.2 INTERVIEWS

In addition to the case studies, 40 interviews were conducted. The main purpose of these interviews, which were separate from the case studies, was to collect more evidence through examples to underpin and develop the propositions and the model of a project-oriented HRM system. The interviews were semi-structured, and the model and propositions always served as a guide. The interviews mostly focused on different aspects to get a better understanding of a topic, for instance the appraisal of project managers. The interviews were conducted with project managers, PMO managers, HR managers, project team members, line managers and were also based on purposeful sampling.

A.7.3 PRESENTATIONS

As I consider the research process as an iterative communication process, the engagement with the wider practice and research community in the course of the research study is of importance to ensure quality and viability of the research results. Engagement was organized by presentations for different audiences. Communication with further researchers was organized in research conferences, including annual meetings of the Academy of Management and the European Academy of Management, and bi-annual project management research conferences such as IRNOP and the PMI Research & Education conference. Communication with practitioners was organized in several workshops and practice conferences. Presentations were explicitly framed to communicate with the wider community and receive feedback on the research.

A.8 Ensuring Viability

> But if one denies that knowledge must in some way correspond to an objective world, what should it be
> related to and what could give it its value? (Von Glasersfeld 1995: 113)

In an instrumentalist approach, such as the systemic-constructivist approach outlined earlier in this chapter, I can neither claim that the models and propositions developed represent reality, nor that I can get closer and closer to the truth in the research process, despite it having been conducted with rigour (Kilduff et al. 2011). Thus, the measurement of the quality of the research results must be a different one.

It is suggested that research results can be measured regarding their potential for problem solving (Kilduff et al. 2011). Von Glasersfeld (1995) offers viability as quality criterion. With viability, he suggests that research results (models and propositions) fit reality, are useful, and provide value for problem solution.

The aim then is to develop useful models, viable models. In this case, the outcomes are the model and the description of a project-oriented HRM system for the project-oriented organization. The model and propositions are potentially useful as one possible, viable way for a HRM system to more adequately support the project-oriented organization and realize its HRM potential. While these models and propositions offered as research results have limits, they may be perceived as potentially applicable to practice, thus fitting reality. Last but not least, I aim to further develop theory on HRM in a specifically important temporary context, the project-oriented organization.

To ensure viability of the research results gained in the study, different measures were taken:

- The research process was designed as an exploratory and iterative communication process. It remained an open process and allowed reflection and integration of findings to build on prior studies and to further develop the propositions in the course of the study.
- A multi-method approach was applied. The methods included literature research, case studies and interviews, which allowed the comparison and integration of findings from different research methods.
- The case studies also followed a multi-source and multi-method approach, involving documentation analysis, group and individual interviews and presentations. The interviews were conducted with a wide range of company representatives in different roles to ensure the understanding of different perceptions and gain the widest range of views possible.
- The additional interviews taken with HR managers, project managers, PMO managers and other practitioners allowed for a further reflection of the propositions to ensure research results that fit reality.
- The research built on prior studies and exchange with these researchers was organized.
- Feedback from the wider scientific community was collected at academic conferences.
- Feedback from the practice community was collected in presentations at practice conferences and workshops that I conducted during the last years.
- Last but not least, I draw on my own (practical) experience and (participative) observations of projects and project-oriented organizations in my roles as researcher, educator and trainer, consultant and project manager of research projects.

Although the viability of the research was ensured, what remains to be questioned are the perspective taken and the limitation of the researcher as a knowledge creator.

References

Adams, W.M. 2006. The future of sustainability: Re-thinking environment and development in the twenty-first century. The World Conversation Union (IUCN).

Aitken, A. and Crawford, L. 2007. Coping with stress: Dispositional coping strategies of project managers. *International Journal of Project Management*, 25(7), 666–673.

Allen, T.J. and Katz, R. 1995. The project-oriented engineer: A dilemma for human resource management. *R&D Management*, 25(2), 129–140.

Alvesson, M. 2001. Knowledge work: Ambiguity, image and identity. *Human Relations*, 54(7), 863–886.

Andersen, E. 2008. *Rethinking Project Management – An Organisational Perspective*. London: FT Press.

Andersen, E.S. 2012. Illuminating the role of the project owner. *International Journal of Managing Projects in Business*, 5(1), 67–85.

Andersen, E.S. and Jessen, S.A. 2003. Project maturity in organisations. *International Journal of Project Management*, 21(6), 457–461.

Armstrong, M. 2007. *A Handbook of Human Resource Management Practice*. London and Philadelphia: Kogan Page.

Arthur, J.B. 1994. Effects of human resource systems on manufacturing performance and turnover. *Academy of Management Journal*, 37(3), 670–687.

Arthur, J.B. and Boyles, T. 2007. Validating the human resource system structure: A levels-based strategic HRM approach. *Human Resource Management Review*, 17(1), 77–92.

Artto, K.A. and Wikström, K. 2005. What is project business? *International Journal of Project Management*, 23(5), 343–353.

Asquin, A., Garel, G. and Picq, T. 2010. When project-based management causes distress at work. *International Journal of Project Management*, 28(2), 166–172.

Aubry, M., Hobbs, B. and Thuillier, D. 2007. A new framework for understanding organisational project management through the PMO. *International Journal of Project Management*, 25(4), 328–336.

Aubry, M., Hobbs, B., Müller, R. and Blomquist, T. 2010. Identifying forces driving PMO changes. *Project Management Journal*, 41(4), 30–45.

Bakker, R.M. 2010. Taking stock of temporary organizational forms: A systematic review and research agenda. *International Journal of Management Reviews*, 12(4), 466–486.

Barney, J.B. 1995. Looking inside for competitive advantage. *The Academy of Management Executive*, 9(4), 49–61.

Bateson, G. 1972. *Steps to an Ecology of Mind*. Chicago: University of Chicago Press.

Batt, R. 2002. Managing customer services: Human resource practices, quit rates, and sales growth. *Academy of Management Journal*, 45(3), 587–597.

Becker, B. and Gerhart, B. 1996. The impact of human resource management on organizational performance: Progress and prospects. *Academy of Management Journal*, 39(4), 779–779.

Beer, M., Spector, B., Lawrence, P.R., Mills, D.Q. and Walton, R.E. 1984. *Managing Human Assets: The Ground Breaking Harvard Business School Program*. New York: The Free Press.

Belout, A. 1998. Effects of human resource management on project effectiveness and success: Toward a new conceptual framework. *International Journal of Project Management*, 16(1), 21–26.

Belout, A. and G.C. 2004. Factors influencing project success: The impact of human resource management. *International Journal of Project Management*, 22(1), 1–11.

Bennis, W.G. 1966. Changing organizations. *The Journal of Applied Behavioral Science*, 2(3), 247–263.

Blackburn, S. 2002. The project manager and the project-network. *International Journal of Project Management*, 20(3), 199–204.

Bleicher, K. 1991. *Organisation: Strategien – Strukturen – Kulturen.* Wiesbaden: Gabler.

Blichfeldt, B.S. and Eskerod, P. 2008. Project portfolio management – There's more to it than what management enacts. *International Journal of Project Management,* 26(4), 357–365.

Blindenbach-Driessen, F. and Van Den Ende, J. 2006. Innovation in project-based firms: The context dependency of success factors. *Research Policy,* 35(4), 545–561.

Borum, F. and Christiansen, J. 1993. Actors and structure in IS projects: What makes implementation happen? *Scandinavian Journal of Management,* 9(1), 5–28.

Bowen, D.E. and Ostroff, C. 2004. Understanding HRM-firm performance linkages: The role of the 'strength' of the HRM system. *Academy of Management Review,* 29(2), 203–221.

Boxall, P. 1998. Achieving competitive advantage through human resource strategy: Towards a theory of industry dynamics. *Human Resource Management Review,* 8(3), 265.

Boxall, P. and Purcell, J. 2011. *Strategy and Human Resource Management.* Basingstoke: Palgrave Macmillan Ltd.

Boxall, P., Purcell, J. and Wright, P. 2010. *Human Resource Management: Scope, Analysis and Significance.* In Boxall, P., Purcell, J. and Wright, P. (eds), *The Oxford Handbook of Human Resource Management.* New York: Oxford University Press Inc.

Brandl, J., Ehnert, I. and Bos-Nehles, A. 2012. Organising HRM: the HRM department and line management roles in a comparative perspective. In Brewster, C.M.W. (ed.) *Handbook of Research on Comparative Human Resource Management.* Cheltenham: Edward Elgar Pub.

Bredin, K. and Soderlund, J. 2006. Perspectives on Human Resource Management: an explorative study of the consequences of projectification in four firms. *International Journal of Human Resources Development and Management,* 6(1), 92–113.

Bredin, K. and Söderlund, J. 2011. The HR quadriad: a framework for the analysis of HRM in project-based organizations. *The International Journal of Human Resource Management,* 22(10), 2202–2221.

Brewster, C. 2012. *Handbook of Research on Comparative Human Resource Management.* Cheltenham: Edward Elgar Pub.

Brewster, C., Larson, H.H. and Mayrhofer, W. 1997. Integration and assignment: a paradox in human resource management. *Journal of International Management,* 3(1), 1–23.

Brewster, C.J. and Mayrhofer, W. 2012. *Handbook of Research on Comparative Human Resource Management.* Cheltenham: Edward Elgar Pub.

Broderick, R. and Boudreau, J.W. 1992. Human resource management, information technology, and the competitive edge. *The Executive,* 6(2), 7–17.

Bryde, D. 2008. Perceptions of the impact of project sponsorship practices on project success. *International Journal of Project Management,* 26(8), 800–809.

Burns, T. and Stalker, G.M. 1961. *The Management of Innovation.* London: Tavistock.

Butler, J.E., Ferris, G.R. and Napier, N.K. 1991. *Strategy and Human Resource Management.* Cincinnati: South-Western.

Chandler, A.D. 1962. *Strategy and Structure: Chapters in the History of the American Industrial Enterprise.* Washington: Beard Books.

Charles A. O'Reilly, I. and Pfeffer, J. 2000. *Hidden Value: How Great Companies Achieve Extraordinary Results With Ordinary People.* US: Harvard Business School Publishing India Pvt. Limited.

Cheng, M.I., Dainty, A.R.J. and Moore, D.R. 2005. What makes a good project manager? *Human Resource Management Journal,* 15(1), 25–37.

Child, J. and Partridge, B. 1982. *Lost Managers: Supervisors in Industry and Society.* New York: Cambridge University Press.

Chuang, C.-H. and Liao, H. 2010. Strategic human resource management in service context: taking care of business by taking care of employees and customers. *Personnel Psychology,* 63(1), 153–196.

Cicmil, S., Hodgson, D., Lindgren, M. and Packendorff, J. 2009. Project management behind the facade. *Ephemera: Theory and Politics in Organization,* 9(2), 78–92.

CIPD, 2007. *Line Managers in Reward, Learning and Development.* London: CIPD.

Clark, I. and Colling, T. 2005. The management of human resources in project management-led organizations. *Personnel Review*, 34(2), 178–191.

Clegg, S.R. 1990. *Modern Organizations*. London: Sage.

Cleland, D.I. and Gareis, R. 2006. *Global Project Management Handbook*. New York: McGraw-Hill.

Cleland, D.I. and King, W.R. 1983. *Systems Analysis and Project Management*. New York: McGraw-Hill.

Collins, C.J. and Smith, K.G. 2006. Knowledge exchange and combination: The role of human resource practices in the performance of high-technology firms. *Academy of Management Journal*, 49(3), 544–560.

Combs, J., Liu, Y., Hall, A. and Ketchen, D. 2006. How much do high-performance work pratices matter? A meta-analysis of their effects on organizational performance. *Personnel Psychology*, 59(3), 501–528.

Cooke-Davies, T.J. 2000. Discovering the principles of project management: an interim report on the first five years of an investigation into the practices of project management in large projectised private-sector companies. In Crawford, L.H. and Clarke, C. (eds), *Paradoxes of Project Collaboration in the Global Economy: Interdependence, Complexity and Ambiguity: Proceedings of the IRNOP IV Conference, Sydney*, January 2000. Sydney: University of Technology.

Cooke-Davies, T.J. 2005. Measurement of organizational maturity: Questions for future research. In Slevin, D.P., Cleland, D.I. and Pinto, J.K. (eds), *Innovations: Project Management Research 2004*. Newtown Square: Project Management Institute.

Corley, K. and Gioia, D. 2011. Building theory about theory building: what constitutes a theoretical contribution? *The Academy of Management Review*, 36(1), 12–32.

Crawford, L. 2005. Senior management perceptions of project management competence. *International Journal of Project Management*, 23(1), 7–16.

Crawford, L., Cooke-Davies, T., Hobbs, B., Labuschagne, L., Remington, K. and Chen, P. 2008. Governance and support in the sponsoring of projects and programs. *Project Management Journal*, 39(S1), S43–S55.

Crawford, L. and Pollack, J. 2004. Hard and soft projects: a framework for analysis. *International Journal of Project Management*, 22(8), 645–653.

Creswell, J.W. 2007. *Qualitative Inquiry and Research Design: Choosing Among Five Approaches*. Thousand Oaks: Sage.

Davidson, J. 2000. Sustainable development: business as usual or a new way of living? *Environmental Ethics*, 22(1), 45–71.

Davies, A. and Hobday, M. 2005. *The Business of Projects: Managing Innovation in Complex Products and Systems*. New York: Cambridge University Press.

De Pablos, P.O. 2005. Strategic human resource management and organizational competitiveness: The importance of fit and flexibility. *International Journal of Human Resource Development and Management*, 5(1), 1–15.

DeFillippi, R.J. 2001. Introduction: project-based learning, reflective practices and learning outcomes. *Management Learning*, 32(1), 5–10.

Delery, J.E. and Doty, D.H. 1996. Modes of theorizing in strategic human resource management: Tests of universalistic, contingency, and configurational performance predictions. *The Academy of Management Journal*, 39(4), 802–835.

Delery, J.E. and Shaw, J.D. 2001. The strategic management of people in work organizations: Review, synthesis, and extension. *Research in Personnel and Human Resource Management*, 20, 165–197.

Deming, W.E. 1986. *Out of the Crisis*. Cambridge, MA: Massachusetts Institute of Technology.

Denison, D.R. 1990. *Corporate Culture and Organizational Effectiveness*. Toronto: Wiley.

Ehnert, I. 2009. *Sustainable Human Resource Management. A Conceptual and Exploratory Analysis from a Paradox Perspective*. Heidelberg: Physica Verlag.

El Sabaa, S. 2001. The skills and career path of an effective project manager. *International Journal of Project Management*, 19(1), 1–7.

Engwall, M. 2003. No project is an island: linking projects to history and context. *Research Policy*, 32(5), 789–808.

Engwall, M. and Jerbrant, A. 2003. The resource allocation syndrome: the prime challenge of multi-project management? *International Journal of Project Management*, 21(6), 403–409.

Eskerod, P. 1998. The human resource allocation process when organizing by projects. In Lundin, R.A. and Midler, C. (eds), *Projects as Arenas for Renewal and Learning Processes*. Boston: Kluwer Academic Publisher.

Fabi, B. and Pettersen, N. 1992. Human resource management practices in project management. *International Journal of Project Management*, 10(2), 81–88.

Fiedler, S. 1996. *Bewältigung von Projektkrisen auf der Grundlage eines systemisch-konstruktivistischen Management-Ansatzes*. Dissertation. Wirtschaftsuniversität Wien: Wien.

Foerster, H., von 1985. *Sicht und Einsicht: versuche zu einer operativen Erkenntnistheorie*. Braunschweig: Carl Auer Verlag.

Fombrun, C.J., Tichy, N.M. and Devanna, M.A. 1984. *Strategic Human Resource Management*. New York: Wiley.

Francis, H. and Keegan, A. 2006. The changing face of HRM: in search of balance. *Human Resource Management Journal*, 16(3), 231–334.

Freeman, R.E., Harrison, J.S., Wicks, A.C., Parmar, B.L. and De Colle, S. 2010. *Stakeholder Theory: The State of the Art*. Cambridge: Cambridge University Press.

Fuchs, P. 1999. *Intervention und Erfahrung*. Frankfurt am Main: Suhrkamp.

Gaddis, P. 1959. The project manager. *Harvard Business Review*, 37(3), 89–97.

Galbraith, J.R. 1971. Matrix organization designs How to combine functional and project forms. *Business Horizons*, 14(1), 29–40.

Galbraith, J.R. 1977. *Organization Design*. Reading, MA: Addison-Wesley.

Galbraith, J.R. 2001. Building organizations around the global customer. *Ivey Business Journal*, 66(1), 17–25.

Gällstedt, M. 2003. Working conditions in projects: perceptions of stress and motivation among project team members and project managers. *International Journal of Project Management*, 21(6), 449–455.

Gann, D.M. and Salter, A.J. 2000. Innovation in project-based, service-enhanced firms: the construction of complex products and systems. *Research Policy*, 29(7–8), 955–972.

Gareis, R. 1990. *Handbook of Management by Projects*. Wien: Manz.

Gareis, R. 2005. *Happy Projects!* Wien: Manz.

Gareis, R. and Huemann, M. 2007. Maturity models for the project-oriented company. In Turner, J.R. (ed.) *The Gower Handbook of Project Management*. Aldershot: Gower.

Gareis, R. and Huemann, M. 2010. Changes and Projects. *International Journal of Project Management*, 28(4), 311–412.

Gareis, R. and Stummer, M. 2008. *Processes and Projects*. Wien: Manz.

Gareis, R. and Titscher, S. 1992. *Projektarbeit und Personalwesen*. Stuttgart: Eduard Gaugler.

Gareis, R., Huemann, M. and Martinuzzi, A. with the assistance of Weninger, C. and Sedlacko, M. 2013. *Project Management and Sustainable Development Principles*. Newtown Square, PA: Project Management Institute.

Garrick, J. and Clegg, S. 2001. Stressed-out knowledge workers in performative times: A postmodern take on project-based learning. *Management Learning*, 32(1), 119–134.

Gedansky, L. 2002. Inspiring the direction of the profession. *Project Management Journal*, 33(1), 4.

Gelade, G.A. and Ivery, M. 2003. The impact of human resource management and work climate on organizational performance. *Personnel Psychology*, 56(2), 383–404.

Geraldi, J. and Lechler, T. 2012. Gantt charts revisited: A critical analysis of its roots and implications to the management of projects today. *International Journal of Managing Projects in Business*, 5(4), 578–594.

Geraldi, J.G. 2009. Reconciling order and chaos in multi-project firms. *International Journal of Managing Projects in Business*, 2(1), 149–158.

Godman R.A. and Godman, L.P. 1976. Some management issues in temporary systems: A study of professional development and manpower – The theatre case. *Administrative Science Quarterly*, 21(3), 494–501.

Gong, Y., Law, K.S. and Chang, S. 2009. Human resources management and firm performance: The differential role of managerial affective and continuance commitment. *Journal of Applied Psychology*, 94(1), 263–275.

Grabher, G. 2002. The project ecology of advertising: tasks, talents and teams. *Regional Studies*, 36(3), 245–262.

Grabher, G. 2004. Temporary architectures of learning: Knowledge governance in project ecologies. *Organization Studies*, 25(9), 1491–1514.

Guest, D.E. 1987. Human resource management and industrial relations. *Journal of Management Studies*, 24(5), 503–521.

Guest, D.E. 1997. Human resource management and performance: A review and research agenda. *International Journal of Human Resource Management*, 8(3), 263–276.

Guthrie, J.P. 2001. High-involvement work practices, turnover, and productivity: Evidence from New Zealand. *Academy of Management Journal*, 44(1), 180–190.

Hall, M., Holt, R. and Purchase, D. 2003. Project sponsors under New Public Management: lessons from the frontline. *International Journal of Project Management*, 21(7), 495–502.

Hammer, M. and Champy, J. 1993. *Reengineering the Corporation*. New York: Harper Collins Publishers.

Hauschildt, J. 2000. Realistic criteria for project manager selection and development. *Project Management Journal*, 31(3), 23.

Heitger, B. and Sutter, P. 1990. Project management in different corporate cultures: successfactors for internal projects. In Gareis, R. (ed.) *Handbook of Management by Projects*. Wien: Manz.

Helm, J. and Remington, K. 2005. Effective project sponsorship. *Project Management Journal*, 36(3), 51.

Hobday, M. 2000. The project-based organisation: an ideal form for managing complex products and systems? *Research Policy*, 29(7–8), 871–893.

Hodgson, D. 2002. Disciplining the professional: the case of project management. *Journal of management Studies*, 39(6), 803–821.

Hodgson, D. 2004. Project work: the legacy of bureaucratic control in the post-bureaucratic organization. *Organization*, 11(1), 81–100.

Hodgson, D. and Cicmil, S. 2006. *Making Projects Critical*. Basingstoke: Palgrave Macmillan.

Hodgson, D. and Muzio, D. 2011. Prospects for professionalism in project management. In Morris, P.W.G., Pinto, J.K. and Söderlund, J. (eds), *The Oxford Handbook of Project Management*. New York: Oxford University Press.

Hoegl, M. and Gemuenden, H.G. 2001. Teamwork quality and the success of innovative projects: A theoretical concept and empirical evidence. *Organization Science*, 435–449.

Hoegl, M. and Parboteeah, P. 2006. Autonomy and teamwork in innovative projects. *Human Resource Management*, 45(1), 67–79.

Hoegl, M. and Proserpio, L. 2004. Team member proximity and teamwork in innovative projects. *Research Policy*, 33(8), 1153–1165.

Hölzle, K. 2010. Designing and implementing a career path for project managers. *International Journal of Project Management*, 28(8), 779–786.

Hope-Hailey, V., Farndale, E. and Truss, C. 2005. The HRM department's role in organizational performance. *Human Resource Management Journal*, 15(3), 49–66.

Hovmark, S. and Nordqvist, S. 1996. Project organization: Change in the work atmosphere for engineers. *International Journal of Industrial Ergonomics*, 17(5), 389–398.

Huemann, M. 2002. *Individuelle Projektmanagment-Kompetenzen in projektorientierten Unternehmen*. Frankfurt am Main: Lang.

Huemann, M. 2005. Personnel management in the project-oriented company. In Gareis, R. (ed.) *Happy Projects!* Wien: Manz.

Huemann, M. 2010. Considering Human Resource Management when developing a project-oriented company: Case study of a telecommunication company. *International Journal of Project Management*, 28(4), 361–369.

Huemann, M. and Lauer, B. 2004. *The 'PM-personnel life cycle' in the Project-oriented Company – an integrated approach to high quality in PM-personnel management*. IPMA World Congress Budapest.

Huemann, M. and Turner, R.J. 2007. Human resource management in the project-oriented company: a review. *International Journal of Project Management*, 25(3), 315–323.

Huemann, M. and Turner, J.R. 2010. Human resource management in the project-oriented company: Aligning HRM in the line and on the project. In Mayer, T., Wald, A., Gleich, R. and Wagner, R. (eds) *Advanced Project Management: Leadership – Organization – Social Processes*. Nürnberg: GPM.

Huemann, M., Turner, J.R. and Keegan, A.E. 2004. Human resource management in the project-oriented organization: questions for future research. In Slevin, D.P., Cleland, D.I., Pinto, J.K. (eds), *Innovations: Project Management Research 2004*. Newtown Square: Project Management Institute.

Huselid, M.A. 1995. The impact of human resource management practices on turnover, productivity, and corporate financial performance. *The Academy of Management Journal*, 38(3), 635–672.

Hutchinson, S. and Purcell, J. 2003. *Bringing Policies to Life: The Vital Role of Front Line Managers in People Management*. London: Chartered Institute of Personnel and Development.

International Project Management Association, 1997. *Project Excellent Modell*. http://www.ipma.ch/awards/projexcellence/Pages/ProjectExcellenceModel.aspx.

International Project Management Association, I. 2006. *International Competency Baseline ver. 3.0*. Zürich: IPMA.

Janowicz-Panjaitan, M., Cambre, B. and Kenis, P. 2009. Introduction: Temporary organizations – a challenge and opportunity for thinking about organizations. In Kenis, P., Janowicz-Panjaitan, M. and Cambre, B. (eds), *Temporary Organizations: Prevalence, Logic and Effectivness*. Cheltenham, UK: Edward Elgar.

Jiang, K., Lepak, D.P., Hu, J. and Baer, J.C. 2012. How does human resource management influence organizational outcomes? a meta-analytic investigation of mediating mechanisms. *Academy of Management Journal*, 55(6), 1264.

Jones, C. and DeFillippi, R.J. 1996. Back to the future in film: combining industry and self-knowledge to meet the career challenges of the 21st century. *The Academy of Management Executive*, 10(4), 89–103.

Julian, S.D., Ofori-Dankwa, J.C. and Justis, R.T. 2008. Understanding strategic responses to interest group pressures. *Strategic Management Journal*, 29, 963–984.

Kasper, H. 1990. *Die Handhabung des Neuen in organisierten Sozialsystemen*. Berlin: Springer.

Keegan, A., Huemann, M. and Turner, J.R. 2012. Beyond the line: exploring the HRM responsibilities of line managers, project managers and the HRM department in four project-oriented companies in the Netherlands, Austria, the UK and the USA. *The International Journal of Human Resource Management*, 23(15), 3085–3104.

Keegan, A.E. and Turner, J.R. 2003. Managing human resources in the project-based organization. In Turner, J.R. (eds) *People in Project Management*. Aldershot: Gower.

Kepes, S. and Delery, J.E. 2006. Designing effective HRM systems: The issue of HRM strategy. In Burke, R.J. and Cooper, C.L. (eds) *The Human Resources Revolution: Why Putting People First Matters*. Amsterdam: Elsevier.

Kepes, S. and Delery, J.E. 2007. HRM systems and the problem of internal fit. In Boxall, P., Purcell, J. and Wright, P. (eds) *Oxford Handbook of Human Resource Management*. New York: Oxford University Press.

Kerzner, H. 2006. *Project Management: A Systems Approach to Planning, Scheduling, and Controlling*. Hoboken: Wiley & Sons.

Kerzner, H. 2009. *Project Management: A Systems Approach to Planning, Scheduling, and Controlling*. Hoboken: Wiley & Sons.

Kilduff, M., Mehra, A. and Dunn, M.B. 2011. From blue sky research to problem solving: a philosophy of science theory of new knowledge production. *The Academy of Management Review*, 36(2), 297–317.

Kirkpatrick, L., Davies, A. and Oliver, N. 1992. Decentralisation: Friend or foe of HRM. In Blyton O.T.P. (eds) *Reassessing Human Resource Management*. London: Sage.

Kloppenborg, T.J., Manolis, C. and Tesch, D. 2009. Successful project sponsor behaviors during project initiation: An empirical investigation. *Journal of Managerial Issues*, 21(1), 140–159.

Kossek, E.E., Young, W., Gash, D.C. and Nichol, V. 1994. Waiting for innovation in the human resources department: Godot implements a human resource information system. *Human Resource Management*, 33(1), 135–145.

Lampel, J. and Pushkar, P. Jha. 2007. Models of project orientation in multiproject organizations. In Morris, P. and Pinto, J. (eds) *The Wiley Guide to Project, Program, and Portfolio Management*. Hoboken: Wiley & Sons.

Lang, K. and Rattay, G. 2005. *Leben in Projekten: projektorientierte Karriere- und Laufbahnmodelle.* Wien: Linde.

Larsen, H.H. 2002. Oticon: Unorthodox project-based management and careers in a 'spaghetti organization'. *Human Resource Planning,* 25(4), 30–37.

Larsen, H.H. and Brewster, C. 2003. Line management responsibility for HRM: what is happening in Europe? *Employee Relations,* 25(3), 228–244.

Larson, E.W. and Gobeli, D.H. 1987. Matrix management: Contradictions and insights. *California Management Review,* 29(4), 126–126.

Lawrence, P.R. and Lorsch, J.W. 1967. Differentiation and integration in complex organizations. *Administrative Science Quarterly,* 1–47.

Legge, K. 1978. *Power, Innovation, and Problem-Solving in Personnel Management.* London: McGraw-Hill.

Legge, K. 2005. *Human Resource Management: Rhetorics and Realities.* Basingstoke, Hants: Palgrave Macmillan.

Lengnick-Hall, C.A. and Lengnick-Hall, M.L. 1988. Strategic human resources management: a review of the literature and a proposed typology. *The Academy of Management Review,* 12(3), 454–470.

Lengnick-Hall, M.L., Lengnick-Hall, C.A., Andrade, L.S. and Drake, B. 2009. Strategic human resource management: The evolution of the field. *Human Resource Management Review,* 19(2), 64–85.

Lepak, D. and Snell, S.A. 2010. Employment subsystems and the 'HR-architecture'. In Boxall, P., Purcell, J. and Wright, P. (eds) *The Oxford Handbook of Human Resource Management.* New York: Oxford University Press Inc.

Lepak, D.P. and Snell, S.A. 1999. The human resource architecture: toward a theory of human capital allocation and development. *The Academy of Management Review,* 24(1), 31–48.

Lindgren, M. and Packendorff, J. 2006. What's new in new forms of organizing? On the construction of gender in project-based work. *Journal of Management Studies,* 43(4), 841–866.

Lindkvist, L. 2004. Governing project-based firms: promoting market-like processes within hierarchies. *Journal of Management and Governance,* 8(1), 3–25.

Lindkvist, L., Söderlund, J. and Rell, F. 1998. Managing product development projects: On the significance of foundants and deadlines. *Organization Studies,* 19(6), 931–951.

Loosemore, M., Dainty, A. and Lingard, H. 2003. *Human Resource Management in Construction Projects: Strategic and Operational Approaches.* London: Taylor and Francis.

Love, P.E.D., Fong, P.S. and Irani, Z. ScienceDirect, 2005. *Management of Knowledge in Project Environments.* Oxford: Elsevier/Butterworth-Heinemann.

Luhmann, N. 1995. *Social Systems.* Stanford: Stanford University Press.

Luhmann, N. 2006. *Organisation und Entscheidung.* Wiesbaden: VS Verlag für Sozialwissenschaften.

Lundin, R. and Steinthórsson, R. 2003. Studying organizations as temporary. *Scandinavian Journal of Management,* 19(2), 233–250.

Lundin, R.A. and Söderholm, A. 1995. A theory of the temporary organization. *Scandinavian Journal of Management,* 11(4), 437–455.

MacDuffie, J.P. 1995. Human resource bundles and manufacturing performance: Organizational logic and flexible production systems in the world auto industry. *Industrial and Labor Relations Review,* 197–221.

Marquis, D.G. and Straight, D.M. 1965. *Organizational Factors in Project Performance.* Charleston: BiblioBazaar.

Marsden, P.V., Kalleberg, A.L. and Cook, C.R. 1996. Gender differences in organizational commitment: Influences of work positions and family roles. In Kalleberg, A.L., Knoke, D., Marsden, P.V. and Spaeth, J.L. (eds) *Organizations in America: Analyzing their Structures and Human Resource Practices.* Thousand Oaks: Sage.

Martens, P. 2006. Sustainability: science or fiction? *Sustainability: Science Practice and Policy,* 2(1), 36–41.

Martinsuo, M., Hensman, N., Artto, K., Kujala, J. and Jaafari, A. 2006. Project-based management as an organizational innovation: Drivers, changes, and benefits of adapting project-based management. *Project Management Journal,* 36(3), 87–97.

Maturana, H.R. and Varela, F.J. 1991. *Der Baum der Erkenntnis: Die biologischen Wurzeln des Menschlichen Erkennens.* München: Goldmann.

Maylor, H. 2001. Beyond the Gantt chart: Project management moving on. *European Management Journal*, 19(1), 92–100.

Mayrhofer, W. 1996. Personalentwicklung. *Personalmanagement, Führung, Organisation*, 2, 451–492.

Mayrhofer, W. and Meyer, M. 2002. 'No more shall we part?' Neue Selbständige und neue formen der Kopplung zwischen organisation und ihrem personal. *Zeitschrift für Personalforschung*, 16(4), 509–614.

Mayrhofer, W. and Steyrer, J. 2004. Systemtheoretische Ansätze des Personalmanagements. In E. Gaugler and W.O.W. Weber (eds) *Handwörterbuch des Personalwesens*. Stuttgart: Schäffer-Poeschel.

Mayrhofer, W., Brewster, C., Morley, M.J. and Ledolter, J. 2011. Hearing a different drummer? Convergence of human resource management in Europe – A longitudinal analysis. *Human Resource Management Review*, 21(1), 50–67.

McConville, T. 2006. Devolved HRM responsibilities, middle-managers and role dissonance. *Personnel Review*, 35(6), 637–653.

McGovern, P., Gratton, L., Hope-Hailey, V., Stiles, P. and Truss, C. 1997. Human resource management on the line? *Human Resource Management Journal*, 7(4), 12–29.

McGregor, D. 1960. *The Human Side Of Enterprise*. New York: McGraw Hill.

Meadowcroft, J. 2007. Who is in charge here? Governance for sustainable development in a complex world. *Journal of Environmental Policy and Planning*, 9(3), 299–314.

Meredith, J.R. and Mantel, S.J. 2006. *Project Management: A Managerial Approach*. New York: Wiley & Sons.

Midler, C. 1995. 'Projectification' of the firm: The Renault case. *Scandinavian Journal of Management*, 11(4), 363–375.

Miles, R.E. 1975. *Theories of Management: Implications for Organizational Behavior and Development*. New York: McGraw-Hill.

Mintzberg, H. 1979. *The Structuring of Organizations: A Synthesis of the Research*. New Jersey: Prentice-Hall.

Mintzberg, H. 1983. *Structure in Fives: Designing Effective Organizations*. New Jersey: Prentice-Hall.

Mintzberg, H. 1989. *Mintzberg on Management: Inside our Strange World of Organizations*. US: Free Press.

Mohrman, S.A. and Lawler, E.E. 1997. Transforming the HRM Function. *Human Resource Management*, 36(1), 157–162.

Morgan, D.L. 1997. *Focus Groups as Qualitative Research*. Thousand Oaks: Sage.

Morley, M.J., Gunnigle, P., O'Sullivan, M. and Collings, D.G. 2006. New directions in the roles and responsibilities of the HRM function. *Personnel Review*, 35(6), 609–617.

Morris, P.W.G. 1997. *The Management of Projects*. London: Telford.

Morris, P.W.G. and Pinto, J.K. 2004. *The Wiley Guide to Managing Projects*. Hoboken: Wiley & Sons.

Morris, P.W.G., Crawford, L., Hodgson, D., Shepherd, M.M. and Thomas, J. 2006. Exploring the role of formal bodies of knowledge in defining a profession – The case of project management. *International Journal of Project Management*, 24(8), 710–721.

Muzio, E., Fisher, D.J., Thomas, E.R. and Peters, V. 2007. Soft skills quantification (SSQ) for project manager competencies. *Project Management Journal*, 38(2), 30.

Müller, R. and Turner, R. 2010. Leadership competency profiles of successful project managers. *International Journal of Project Management*, 28(5), 437–448.

Müller-Camen, M., Jackson, S.E., Jabbour, C.J.C. and Renwick, D.W.S. 2011. Green Human Resource Management. *Zeitschrift für Personalforschung*, 25(2).

Office of Government Commerce, 2007. *Managing Successful Programmes*. London: The Stationery Office.

Office of Government Commerce, 2009. *Managing Successful Projects with PRINCE2*. London: Stationery Office.

Osterman, P. 1987. Choice of employment systems in internal labor markets. *Industrial Relations: A Journal of Economy and Society*, 26(1), 46–67.

Osterman, P. 1988. *Employment Future: Reorganization, Dislocation, and Public Policy*. New York: Oxford University Press.

Ouchi, W.G. 1980. Markets, bureaucracies, and clans. *Administrative Science Quarterly*, 129–141.

Paauwe, J. 2004. *HRM and Performance: Achieving Long-Term Viability*. Oxford: Oxford University Press.

Paauwe, J. 2009. HRM and performance: achievements, methodological issues and prospects. *Journal of Management Studies*, 46, 129–142.

Packendorff, J. 1995. Inquiring into the temporary organization: New directions for project management research. *Scandinavian Journal of Management*, 11(4), 319–333.

Packendorff, J. 2002. The temporary society and its enemies: projects from an individual perspective. In K. Sahlin-Andersson and A. Söderholm (eds), *Beyond Project Management: New Perspectives on the Temporary-Permanent Dilemma*. Malmö: Copenhagen Business School Press.

Pellegrinelli, S. 1997. Programme management: organising project-based change. *International Journal of Project Management*, 15(3), 141–149.

Pfeffer, J. 1994. Competitive advantage through people. *California Management Review*, 36(2), 9–9.

Pfeffer, J. 1998. *The Human Equation: Building Profits by Putting People First.* Boston, Massachusetts: Harvard Business School Press.

Pfeffer, J. and Baron, J.N. 1988. Taking the workers back out: Recent trends in the structuring of employment. In Staw, B.M. and Cummings, L.L. (eds) *Research in Organizational Behavior.* Amsterdam: JAI Press.

Pinto, M.B., Pinto, J.K. and Prescott, J.E. 1993. Antecedents and consequences of project team cross-functional cooperation. *Management Science*, 39(10), 1281–1297.

Pollack, J. 2007. The changing paradigms of project management. *International Journal of Project Management*, 25(3), 266–274.

Poole, M. and Jenkins, G. 1997. Responsibilities for human resource management practices in the modern enterprise: Evidence from Britain. *Personnel Review*, 26(5), 333–356.

Prencipe, A. and Tell, F. 2001. Inter-project learning: processes and outcomes of knowledge codification in project-based firms. *Research Policy*, 30(9), 1373–1394.

Project Management Institute, 2008. *A Guide to the Project Management Body of Knowledge.* Newtown Square, PA: Project Management Institute.

Project Management Institute, 2013. *A Guide to the Project Management Body of Knowledge: Pmbok Guide.* Newtown Square, PA: Project Management Institute.

Project Management Institute, 2013. *Project Management between 2010 and 2020.* Newtown Square, PA: Project Management Institute. http://www.pmi.org/~/media/PDF/Business-Solutions/PMIProject ManagementSkillsGapReport.ashx (redriven May 2015).

Ralston, P. 2010. *The Book of Not Knowing: Exploring the True Nature of Self, Mind, and Consciousness.* Berkeley: North Atlantic Books.

Rau, B.L. and Hyland, M.A.M. 2002. Role conflict and flexible work arrangements: the effects on applicant attraction. *Personnel Psychology*, 55(1), 111–136.

Reid, A. 2003. Managing teams: the reality of life. In Rodney, J.R. (eds) *People in Project Management.* Aldershot: Gower.

Riegler, A. 2012. Constructivism. In L'Abate, L. (eds) *Paradigms in Theory Construction.* New York: Springer Verlag.

Riordan, C.M., Vandenberg, R.J. and Richardson, H.A. 2005. Employee involvement climate and organizational effectiveness. *Human Resource Management*, 44(4), 471–488.

Robinson, J. 2004. Squaring the circle? Some thoughts on the idea of sustainable development. *Ecological Economics*, 48(4), 369–384.

Rousseau, D.M. 1995. *Psychological Contracts in Organizations: Understanding Written and Unwritten Agreements.* Thousand Oaks: Sage.

Rousseau, D.M. and Wade-Benzoni, K.A. 1994. Linking strategy and human resource practices: How employee and customer contracts are created. *Human Resource Management*, 33(3), 463–489.

Ruigrok, W., Pettigrew, A., Peck, S.I. and Whittington, R. 1999. Corporate restructuring and new forms of organizing: Evidence from Europe. *Management International Review*, 39(2), 41–64.

Sahlin-Andersson, K. and Söderholm, A. 2002. *Beyond Project Management: New Perspectives on the Temporary-Permanent Dilemma.* Malmö: Liber Ekonomie.

Sayles, L.R. and Chandler, M.K. 1971. *Managing Large Systems: Organizations for the Future.* New York: The Free Press.

Schein, E.H. 1978. *Career Dynamics: Matching Individual and Organizational Needs.* Reading, MA: Addison-Wesley.

Schelle, H. 1989. Zur Lehre vom Projektmanagement. In Reschke, H., Schelle, H. and Schnopp, R. (eds), *Handbuch Projektmanagement.* Köln: TÜV Rheinland.

Schuler, R.S. 1990. Repositioning the human resource function: transformation or demise? *The Executive,* 4(3), 49–60.

Schuler, R.S. and Jackson, S.E. 1987. Linking competitive strategies with human resource management practices. *The Academy of Management Executive,* 1(3), 207–219.

Senge, P., Kleiner, A., Roberts, C., Ross, R., Roth, G. and Smith, B. 1999. *The Dance of Change.* London: Nicholas Brealey Publishing.

Senge, P.M. 1994. *The Fifth Discipline Fieldbook: Strategies and Tools for Building a Learning Organization.* New York: Doubleday.

Shenhar, A. and Dvir, D. 2007. *Reinventing Project Management.* Boston: Harvard Business School Press.

Shenhar, A.J., Dvir, D., Levy, O. and Maltz, A.C. 2001. Project success: a multidimensional strategic concept. *Long Range Planning,* 34(6), 699–725.

Skilton, P.F. and Bravo, J. 2008. Do social capital and project type vary across career paths in project-based work? The case of Hollywood personal assistants. *International Journal of Career Management,* 13(5), 381–401.

Söderlund, J. 2004. On the broadening scope of the research on projects: a review and a model for analysis. *International Journal of Project Management,* 22(8), 655–667.

Söderlund, J. 2011. Pluralism in project management: Navigating the crossroads of specialization and fragmentation. *International Journal of Management Reviews,* 13(2), 153–176.

Söderlund, J. 2012. Project management, interdependencies, and time: Insights from Managing Large Systems by Sayles and Chandler. *International Journal of Managing Projects in Business,* 5(4), 617–633.

Söderlund, J. and Maylor, H. 2012. Project management scholarship: Relevance, impact and five integrative challenges for business and management schools. *International Journal of Project Management,* 30(6), 686–696.

Sparrow, P.R. and Hiltrop, J.-M. 1994. *European Human Resource Management in Transition.* New York: Prentice-Hall.

Starkweather, J.A. and Stevenson, D.H. 2011. PMP® certification as a core competency: Necessary but not sufficient. *Project Management Journal,* 42(1), 31–41.

Storey, J. 1992. *Developments in the Management of Human Resources.* Oxford: Blackwell.

Storey, J., Quintas, P., Taylor, P. and Fowle, W. 2002. Flexible employment contracts and their implications for product and process innovation. *International Journal of Human Resource Management,* 13(1), 1–18.

Sveiby, K.E. 1997. *The New Organizational Wealth: Managing and Measuring Knowledge-Based Assets.* San Francisco: Berrett-Koehler Pub.

Sydow, J., Lindkvist, L. and DeFillippi, R. 2004. Editorial: project organizations, embeddedness and repositories of knowledge. *Organization Studies,* 25(9), 1475–1489.

Tannenbaum, S.I. 1990. Human resource information systems: user group implications. *Journal of Systems Management,* 41(1), 27–37.

Thamhain, H.J. 2004. Linkages of project environment to performance: lessons for team leadership. *International Journal of Project Management,* 22(7), 533–544.

Thomas, J. and Mullaly, M. 2008. *Researching the Value of Project Management.* Newton Square: Project Management Institute.

Thomas, J.L. and Buckle-Henning, P. 2007. Dancing in the white spaces: Exploring gendered assumptions in successful project managers' discourse about their work. *International Journal of Project Management,* 25(6), 552–559.

Thomas, R., Marosszeky, M., Karim, K., Davis, S. and McGeorge, D. 2002. *The Importance of Project Culture in Achieving Quality Outcomes in Construction.* Presented at IGLC-10, Gramado: Brazil.

Truss, C., Mankin, D. and Kelliher, C. 2012. *Strategic Human Resource Management*. New York: Oxford University Press Inc.

Turner, J.R. 2009. *The Handbook of Project-Based Management: Leading Strategic Change in Organizations*. New York: McGraw-Hill.

Turner, J.R. and Keegan, A. 2001. Mechanisms of governance in the project-based organization: Roles of the broker and steward. *European Management Journal*, 19(3), 254–267.

Turner, J.R. and Müller, R. 2003. On the nature of the project as a temporary organization. *International Journal of Project Management*, 21(1), 1–8.

Turner, J.R. and Müller, R. 2006. *Choosing Appropriate Project Managers: Matching their Leadership Style to the Type of Project*. Newtown Square: Project Management Institute.

Turner, R., Huemann, M. and Keegan, A. 2008a. *Human Resource Management in the Project-Oriented Organization*. Newtown Square: Project Management Institute.

Turner, R., Huemann, M. and Keegan, A. 2008b. Human resource management in the projectoriented organisation: Employee wellbeing and ethical treatment. *International Journal of Project Management*, 26(5), 577–585.

Turner, R.J., Huemann, M., Anbari, F.T. and Bredillet, C.N. 2010. *Perspectives on Projects*. New York: Routledge.

Tyson, S. and Fell, A. 1986. *Evaluating the Personnel Function*. London: Hutchinson Radius.

Ulrich, D. 1997. *Human Resource Champions: The Next Agenda for Adding Value and Delivering Results*. Boston, MA: Harvard Business School Press.

Ulrich, D. and Brockbank, W. 2005. *The HR Value Proposition*. US: Perseus Books Group.

Unger, B.N., Gemünden, H.G. and Aubry, M. 2012. The three roles of a project portfolio management office: Their impact on portfolio management execution and success. *International Journal of Project Management*, 30(5), 608–620.

Van de Ven, A.H. 2007. *Engaged Scholarship: A Guide for Organizational and Social Research*. Oxford: Oxford University Press.

Von Foerster, H. 1984. *Observing Systems*. Seaside: Intersystems Publications.

Von Glasersfeld, E. 1995. *Radical Constructivism: A Way of Knowing and Learning*. London: The Falmer Press.

Walker, J.W. 1992. *Human Resource Strategy*. New York: McGraw-Hill.

Walton, R.E. 1985. From control to commitment in the workplace. *Harvard Business Review*, 63(2), 77–84.

Wheelwright, S.C. and Clark, K.B. 1992. Creating project plans to focus product development. *Harvard Business Review*, 70(2), 70–82.

Whitley, R. 2006. Project-based firms: new organizational form or variations on a theme? *Industrial and Corporate Change*, 15(1), 77–99.

Whittaker, S. and Marchington, M. 2003. Devolving HR responsibility to the line: Threat, opportunity or partnership? *Employee Relations*, 25(3), 245–261.

Whittington, R., Pettigrew, A., Peck, S., Fenton, E. and Conyon, M. 1999. Change and complementarities in the new competitive landscape: A European panel study. *Organization Science*, 10(5), 583–600.

Willke, H. 1987. *Systemtheorie: eine Einführung in die Grundprobleme*. Stuttgart: Fischer.

Willke, H. 2005. *Systemtheorie II: Interventionstheorie*. Ulm: Ebner and Spiegel.

Wilton, N. 2011. *An Introduction to Human Resource Management*. London: Sage.

Windeler, A. and Sydow, J. 2001. Project networks and changing industry practices collaborative content production in the German television industry. *Organization Studies*, 22(6), 1035–1060.

Wirth, I. 1996. How generic and how industry-specific is the project management profession? *International Journal of Project Management*, 14, 7–11.

Wittgenstein, L. 1933. *Tractatus Logico-Philosophicu*. London: Kegan Paul, Trench, Trubner & Co. Ltd.

Womack, J.P. and Jones, D.T. 1996. *Lean Thinking*. New York: Simon & Schuster.

Womack, J.P., Jones, D.T. and Roos, D. 1990. *The Machine that Changed the World*. New York: Macmillan.

Wood, S. 1999. Human resource management and performance. *International Journal of Management Reviews*, 1(4), 367–413.

Woodward, J., Dawson, S. and Wedderburn, D. 1965. *Industrial Organization: Theory and Practice*. London: Oxford University Press.

Wright, P.M. and Boswell, W.R. 2002. Desegregating HRM: A review and synthesis of micro and macro human resource management research. *Journal of Management*, 28(3), 247–276.

Wright, P.M. and McMahan, G.C. 1992. Theoretical perspectives for strategic human resource management. *Journal of Management*, 18(2), 295–320.

Wright, P.M., Dunford, B.B. and Snell, S.A. 2001a. Human resources and the resource based view of the firm. *Journal of Management*, 27(6), 701–721.

Wright, P.M., McMahan, G.C., Snell, S.A. and Gerhart, B. 2001c. Comparing line and HR executives' perceptions of HR effectiveness: services, roles, and contributions. *Human Resource Management*, 40(2), 111–123.

Wright, P.M., Gardner, T.M., Moynihan, L.M., Park, H.J., Gerhart, B. and Delery, J.E. 2001b. Measurement error in research on human resources and firm performance: Additional data and suggestions for future research. *Personnel Psychology*, 54(4), 875–901.

Yaghootkar, K. and Gil, N. 2012. The effects of schedule-driven project management in multi-project environments. *International Journal of Project Management*, 30(1), 127–140.

Yin, R.K. 2009. *Case Study Research: Design and Methods*, Thousand Oaks: Sage.

Yin, R.K. 2011. *Qualitative Research from Start to Finish*. New York: The Guildford Press.

Youker, R. 1977. Organization alternatives for project managers. *Management Review*, 66(11), 46–53.

Youndt, M.A., Subramaniam, M. and Snell, S.A. 2004. Intellectual capital profiles: an examination of investments and returns. *Journal of Management Studies*, 41(2), 335–361.

Zaugg, R.J. 2009. *Nachhaltiges Personalmanagement: Eine neue Perspektive und empirische Exploration des Human Resource Management*. Wiesbaden: Gabler Verlag.

Zika-Viktorsson, A., Sundström, P. and Engwall, M. 2006. Project overload: An exploratory study of work and management in multi-project settings. *International Journal of Project Management*, 24(5), 385–394.

Zwikael, O. and Unger-Aviram, E. 2010. HRM in project groups: The effect of project duration on team development effectiveness. *International Journal of Project Management*, 28(5), 413–421.

For Product Safety Concerns and Information please contact our EU
representative GPSR@taylorandfrancis.com
Taylor & Francis Verlag GmbH, Kaufingerstraße 24, 80331 München, Germany